THE RESOUNDING REVOLUTION

MUSIC IN AMERICAN LIFE

The Music in American Life series documents and celebrates the dynamic and multifaceted relationship between music and American culture. From its first publication in 1972 through its half-century mark and beyond, the series has embraced a wide variety of methodologies, from biography and memoir to history and musical analysis, and spans the full range of musical forms, from classical through all types of vernacular music. The series showcases the wealth of musical practice and expression that characterizes American music, as well as the rich diversity of its stylistic, regional, racial, ethnic, and gendered contexts. Characterized by a firm grounding in material culture, whether archival or ethnographic, and by work that honors the musical activities of ordinary people and their communities, Music in American Life continually redefines and expands the very definition of what constitutes music in American culture, whose voices are heard, and how music and musical practices are understood and valued.

For a list of books in the series, please see our website at www.press.uillinois.edu.

THE RESOUNDING REVOLUTION

Freedom Song after 1968

STEPHEN STACKS

Publication of this book was supported in part by grants from the AMS 75 PAYS Fund and General Fund of the American Musicological Society, supported in part by the National Endowment for the Humanities and the Andrew W. Mellon Foundation, and from the Judith McCulloh Endowment for American Music.

Manufactured in the United States of America
1 2 3 4 5 C P 5 4 3 2 1
♾ This book is printed on acid-free paper.

Library of Congress Cataloging-in-Publication Data
Names: Stacks, Stephen, author.
Title: The resounding revolution : freedom song after 1968 / Stephen Stacks.
Description: Urbana : University of Illinois Press, 2025. | Series: Music in American life | Includes bibliographical references and index.
Identifiers: LCCN 2024041053 (print) | LCCN 2024041054 (ebook) | ISBN 9780252046599 (hardcover) | ISBN 9780252088704 (paperback) | ISBN 9780252047909 (ebook)
Subjects: LCSH: African Americans—Music—History and criticism. | Black people—United States—Music—History and criticism. | Music—Political aspects—United States. | Civil rights movements—United States.
Classification: LCC ML3556 .S85 2025 (print) | LCC ML3556 (ebook) | DDC 780.89/96073—dc23/eng/20240909
LC record available at https://lccn.loc.gov/2024041053
LC ebook record available at https://lccn.loc.gov/2024041054

To my wife and our daughters—
I sing for freedom because of you.

Contents

THE RESOUNDING REVOLUTION

Introduction

Freedom Song after 1968

So now that he is safely dead,
We, with eased consciences will
Teach our children that he was a great man,
Knowing that the cause for which he
Lived is still a cause
And the dream for which he died is still a dream.
A dead man's dream.

Carl Wendell Hines Jr.

On April 4, 1968, the dynamite in the ghetto exploded.[1] News of Martin Luther King Jr.'s assassination ricocheted around a combustible country, igniting powder kegs of grief, righteous fury, and hopelessness from sea to shining sea. Some public figures, musicians among them, used their platforms to try to lower the temperature and maintain peace and order. Commentators often credit Robert F. Kennedy's speech in Indianapolis shortly after King was pronounced dead with preventing a riot in that city. The next night (April 5), James Brown was scheduled to play in Boston. Mayor Kevin White appeared on stage with Brown before the concert and appealed for peace and calm.[2] Brown called White a "swingin' cat," throwing his influence with the crowd behind the mayor's words. Mayor White's speech was a very early example of the leveraging of King's legacy to narrow "appropriate" responses to White violence and oppression. He said, "Martin Luther King loved this city and it's up to our generation to prove his faith in us. So all I ask you tonight is this: let us look at each other, here in the

Garden and back at home, and pledge that no matter what any other community might do, we in Boston will honor Dr. King with peace."

On April 7, Nina Simone took a very different tack. Rather than foreclosing on the people's grief and rage, she amplified those difficult emotions, giving them voice in a performance that articulated the uncertainty, the ambiguity, of the historical moment. The performance in question occurred at the Westbury Music Fair in New York. Halfway through the set, Simone and her band premiered "Why? (The King of Love Is Dead)," a song that bass player Gene Taylor penned in the hours after King's death.[3] The band had learned the song one day before their performance at Westbury, a fact belied by their remarkable performance. The song spoke to the state of a Black Freedom Movement in crisis—one of its most important leaders and a powerful voice for nonviolence had been murdered at a pivotal moment for the movement and country. One can hear Simone echoing the question King himself had asked—where do we go from here?—but leaving many more options on the table than he would have, violent revolution among them.[4] Rather than predicting the ultimate success of the movement, such as one finds in the optimistic freedom songs "We Shall Overcome," "I'm on My Way to Freedom Land," or "I'm Gonna Sit at the Welcome Table," Simone's performance of "Why?" cultivated a sincere uncertainty about the future direction of the struggle.[5]

As I listened to Simone in the wake of George Floyd's murder, I was struck by how effectively Simone channeled the sense of ambiguity about the future that often pervades freedom movements at some kind of crossroads. Simone introduces the song by softly saying, "We want to do a tune, written for today, for this hour . . . " underneath which she begins to vamp on the piano. The first sung phrase does not establish a strict pulse; it is only part of the way through the first verse that Simone's piano playing becomes more rhythmic and the pulse more regularized. This elision of the beginning is a frequent technique for introducing songs in the gospel tradition and adds to the performance's improvisatory, "Spirit-led" feeling.[6] At the end of the first two phrases, Simone collapses into a low, exhausted-sounding chest register, vocalizing the exhaustion many freedom fighters felt at this point in their struggle, as they faced continual, violent White backlash.[7]

The song's formal peculiarities heighten the uncertainty the lyrics convey. During the first and second stanzas I expected a strophic or perhaps a regular verse chorus form, but the song takes an irregular formal turn. At the end of the second verse, Simone quickly shifts off the resolution chord to a subdominant chord and then to a dominant chord, as if preparing to transition to a refrain. Instead, however, she begins yet another verse. Finally, at the conclusion of this third verse, she transitions into what sounds like a refrain at the lyric "He had seen the mountaintop . . . ." When the second half of the "refrain" returns to the chord progression of the verse, I began to see the song as some kind of extended and altered AABA form, with the second and third verses acting as a repeated AA to build tension (i.e., AA AA AA BA, etc.). The fourth verse then contains a third A (AAA instead of AA), and then each return of the BA refrain contains some kind of aberration.

The performance has an open, improvisatory feel, amplified by the introductory speech and spoken interlude, both of which are accompanied by unresolved piano chords. Simone frames the entire performance by remarking, "We had yesterday to learn it, so we'll see . . . ." This rhetorical uncertainty, in combination with the irregular form and the song's climactic question, "What will happen now that the king of love is dead?," create a powerful musical articulation of the ambiguity and disillusionment felt by Simone and others in the United States in the wake of King's death. When Simone sings the line "With his Bible in his hand" with increasing fortitude and then immediately lets out an affectionate but almost dismissive "hmm," she simultaneously voices admiration for King's idealism and casts doubt on its effectiveness. Simone's spoken monologue before the final iteration of the refrain clearly endorses self-defense over nonviolence and lays some of the blame for King's death at the feet of his aides for not protecting him.[8] Simone's singing and playing give voice to deep pain and ambiguity, deep investment and ambivalence, and also have the potential to elicit those paradoxical feelings in the listener.

Simone's performance was paradigmatic of a new kind of freedom song, containing within it the musical roots of the freedom struggle, but differentiating itself from the philosophy of the Southern, church-based movement (even while memorializing its most famous leader).[9] Tammy Kernodle has argued that Nina Simone's songs reveal a shift in that tradition but should nonetheless be included in discussions of the freedom song repertoire.[10] Kernodle describes Simone's music as representative of a "second generation of freedom songs that emerged in the mid-1960s and reflected the rhetorical and eventual philosophical transition of the movement from the nonviolent, interracial, church-based activism of Martin Luther King Jr. to the black nationalist, black power rhetoric of the Student Nonviolent Coordinating Committee (SNCC), the Black Panthers, and similar organizations."[11]

The four themes Kernodle draws out of "Mississippi Goddamn" are present in Simone's performance of "Why?": "1) explicit articulation of the anger and hatred that was bubbling under the surface in northern cities and younger segments of the freedom movement; 2) a growing sense of secularism; 3) a turn from the rhetoric of nonviolence; 4) the mythology of assimilation and politics of respectability." "Why?" contains within it the conflicted nature of the Black community's feelings about King and the movement in 1968, but points back to a more complex past as well. A simplistic narrative of the Civil Rights Movement papers over the internal struggle to discern the most effective (and for some, the most moral) way to stride toward freedom. Such ambivalence about the strategy and convictions of the Southern, Christian-led movement existed from the outset.[12] And yet, Simone's performance embraces Black church musical idioms and an affection for King, placing her squarely within the stream of freedom singers such as Fannie Lou Hamer and Bernice Johnson Reagon, and nuancing her critique.

Simone's ambivalence mirrored a larger negotiation happening in the movement. Although it had gained victories, the movement's direction was as hotly contested as ever. Leaders such as Stokely Carmichael, who were initially committed to nonviolence, began to question whether the losses they were absorbing were worth the gains that had been made. Even if his personal convictions did not allow him to consider the alternative, King himself had even begun to lose hope that the movement could sustain itself in the wake of so much resistance. Ralph Abernathy, one of King's closest associates, reported in the year after his death that King was considering resigning his leadership of the Poor People's Campaign to take a sabbath in order to stave off burnout and depression.[13]

The movement was also contending with a weakening of the coalition of Black organizations and institutions. While the National Association for the Advancement of Colored People (NAACP), Southern Christian Leadership Conference (SCLC), Student Nonviolent Coordinating Committee (SNCC), and other local and national organizations and institutions never had as unified a purpose as has been popularly depicted, they did find it more and more difficult to find common ground and maintain organizing momentum under the strain of the events of 1965 to 1968.[14] As Simone and her band performed "Why?" on April 7, several major U.S. cities—including Washington D.C., Chicago, and Baltimore—were on fire in the wake of massive uprisings after King's assassination.

For many looking back on the events of 1966 to 1968, King's assassination was the death blow for a movement in turmoil, and Simone's performance of "Why?" captured this intense moment of crisis. What if, however, we have overemphasized this narrative of rupture and decline in a way that obscures a more complicated, livelier, more relevant history?

Most overviews of the Civil Rights Movement begin in 1954 with the passage of *Brown v. Board of Education*, recount standard watershed moments connected primarily to King's activism, and conclude either in 1965 after the passage of the Civil and Voting Rights Acts, or in 1968 with the passage of the Fair Housing Act, the death of King, and the ascent of Black Power. There is a much more multifaceted picture to be considered by attending to the stories that do not fit into this oversimplified narrative, however. The centrality of an oft-misrepresented King—who has been "sanitized in order to evade and avoid his challenge"—within the dominant narrative of the movement does a disservice to the complex, nuanced, and thus, overlooked interweaving of various local movements that labored away from the spotlight to facilitate the victories that are attributed to the national movement with its towering (male) leaders.[15]

This short timeline also treats the events of 1954 through 1968 as if they emerged from a historical vacuum and as if no vestiges of the movement continued into the 1970s. It treats King and the coalition he worked with as far more monolithic than they were and dismisses the activism of less celebrated participants and ideologically divergent strands of the movement. It has also been used to suggest, somewhat ironically, that the movement both accomplished its goals and that it disintegrated in the late 1960s, thus placing the blame for the demise of the movement on the challenge brought by divergent strands of the movement coalition (Black Power, the Black Panther Party, etc.) rather than on the insidious combination of state-sponsored and vigilante White violence, the political adaptation of Jim Crow oppression, and the souring of the U.S media and public to the movement's activities.[16]

With a few notable exceptions, the history of freedom song has been similarly simplistic, taking its cues from—and often contributing to—these dominant and oversimplified narratives of the movement it accompanied. One especially understudied area of this history is the place of freedom song in U.S. society after 1968, the year the dominant narrative claims the Civil Rights Movement ended. At the heart of this book's inquiry are questions about how the complexity of what we hear in the years since 1968 reflects a truth about freedom singing's capaciousness from the outset. What might we learn, about the present and the past, if we open our ears to the history of freedom song after 1968? What other types of musicmaking should we be considering as expansions of freedom song? How might these expansions call into question conventional understandings of the Civil Rights Movement? Might we begin to hear a more complex and nuanced history than our dominant narratives have allowed, a history with the power to affect our present?

Freedom Song as a Site of Contestation

Much of the scholarship about freedom song has focused on its roots in the Black American church and its mobilization of those cultural resources to index the righteousness and inevitability of the cause. Ron Eyerman and Andrew Jamison argue that "the music of the black community contained a transcendental or emancipatory potential that could be mobilized in the struggle for integration."[17] In the words of SNCC activist Mary King, "the repertoire of 'freedom songs' had an unparalleled ability to evoke the moral power of the movement's goals, to arouse the spirit, comfort the afflicted, instill courage and commitment, and to unite disparate strangers into a 'band of brothers and sisters' and a 'circle of trust.'"[18] T. V. Reed argues that the act of singing is inherently nonviolent, thereby transmitting effectively the movement's ideology, saying, "Singing (along with prayer) became a perfect way both to keep a mass from becoming a mob, and to convey to opponents that one was witnessing an organized event, not a mob action. Songs conveyed messages of quiet defiance, not rage, and clarified the values, stakes, and issues of the action . . . . By their very posture and activity, the singing activists conveyed their nonviolent intentions."[19]

As early as 1964, however, Malcolm X had begun to use freedom singing as a proxy in order to critique nonviolence as a strategy. On April 3, 1964, Malcolm gave his well-known "The Ballot or the Bullet" speech, in which he argued that Black people needed "new allies" and to "expand the civil rights struggle to a higher level," to the world court where they were no longer subjected solely to the fickle justice of "Uncle Sam."[20] The speech was an ultimatum: either things start changing and Black people get the freedom and just treatment they deserve in the United States, or violent revolution was coming. As part of this approach to forcing the hand of White power in the United States, Malcolm called for abandoning previous strategies that, in his estimation, had not led Black Americans any closer to freedom. He said, "Black people are fed up with the dillydallying, pussyfooting, compromising approach that we've been using toward getting our freedom. We want freedom now, but we're not going to get it saying 'We Shall Overcome.' We've got to fight until we overcome."[21]

Five days later in a speech entitled "The Black Revolution," Malcolm again referenced "We Shall Overcome" several times as he highlighted the lack of progress that had been made toward freedom for Black Americans. The first reference is not overtly hostile, but it is dismissive. He says:

> Our people, 22 million African-Americans are fed up with America's hypocritical democracy. Who are ready, willing and justified to do the same thing today to bring about independence for our people that your forefathers did to bring about independence for your people. And I say your people, because I certainly couldn't include myself among those for whom independence was fought in 1776. How in the world can a negro talk about the Declaration of Independence and he's still singing "We Shall Overcome?"[22]

As the speech continued, Malcolm's critique became more caustic:

> Revolution is never based on begging somebody for an integrated cup of coffee. Revolutions are never fought by turning the other cheek. Revolutions are never based upon love-your-enemy and pray-for-those-who-despitefully-use-you. And revolutions are never waged singing "We Shall Overcome." Revolutions are based on bloodshed.[23]

Throughout the speech, Malcolm deftly uses "We Shall Overcome" as a stand-in for freedom song and for nonviolent resistance more broadly, calling attention to the inadequacy of previous approaches to Black liberation, in his view.

> He [the Black man] doesn't see any progress that he has made since the Civil War. He sees not one iota of progress because, number one, if the Civil War had freed him, he wouldn't need civil-rights legislation today. If the Emancipation Proclamation, issued by that great shining liberal called Lincoln, had freed him, he wouldn't be singing "We Shall Overcome" today.[24]

Malcolm paints a picture of a long Black Freedom Movement, beginning before the Civil War and continuing unabated through the judicial decisions and legislative pushes of the 1950s and 60s. He rejects the weight given to *Brown v. Board of Education* and instead argues that none of the milestones to which his contemporaries typically point has had a real and lasting impact on the Black American experience.

Malcolm's goal was to demonstrate the ineffectiveness of nonviolent resistance and to inspire Black Americans to take what he saw as the necessary next step toward revolution. In order to achieve this, he deployed a rhetorical strategy that implied the passivity of nonviolence by equating it with freedom singing. Every time he mentioned singing in his speeches, he layered indexical meaning on freedom singing itself.[25] If singing and nonviolence were synonymous, and nonviolence was passive, and passive was bad, then singing was bad.

Within Malcolm's critique are shades of a gendered understanding of effective and noneffective struggle. In "The Ballot or the Bullet," he laid the blame for the lack of progress toward freedom at the feet of so-called handkerchief heads who have been "dillydallying and pussyfooting and compromising."[26] He also famously connected this understanding of Black masculinity with nonviolence and freedom singing in his introduction of Fannie Lou Hamer in 1964:

> When I listen to Mrs. Hamer, a black woman—could be my mother, my sister, my daughter—describe what they had done to her in Mississippi, I ask myself how in the world can we ever expect to be respected as men when we will allow something like that to be done to our women, and we do nothing about it? . . . No, we don't deserve to be recognized and respected as men as long as our women can be brutalized in the manner that this woman described, and nothing being done about it, but we sit around singing "We Shall Overcome."[27]

Malcolm's performance of Black masculinity, contrary to popular understanding, was not extraordinary but "typical of the generation of southern blacks who launched the civil rights movement in the 1950s."[28] Peter Ling describes how King was constantly aware of and curating for himself a Black masculinity that included his Christian nonviolence over and against this more traditional, heteronormative notion of the role of the Black man in the home and the community. As Ling states, "More commonly, black men delighted in the athleticism, financial success and physical power of Joe Louis and Jackie Robinson. It was too easy to confuse nonviolence, sometimes misleadingly referred to as passive resistance, with a pacifism that seemed to require an 'unmanly' repudiation of the right to self-defense."[29] The preponderance of women who excelled as songleaders in the movement—figures such as Fannie Lou Hamer, Betty Maye Fykes, and Bernice Johnson Reagon—reinforced this gendered perception of singing. Men did function in this role as well, but women in the Black church particularly gravitated toward songleading; it was one of the roles in patriarchal church life in which they were allowed to function, and which they rose to fill.[30]

Of the songs that were prevalent at the time, Malcolm X's favorite target was "We Shall Overcome" in part because it was the most recognizable anthem of the nonviolent resistance. Malcolm also disliked its vague timetable and what he perceived to be its unrealistic idealism with regard to interracial cooperation and harmony. In *The Autobiography of Malcolm X*, he scathingly critiqued the March on Washington, once again using "We Shall Overcome" as his foil:

> Yes, I was there. I observed that circus. Who ever heard of angry revolutionists all harmonizing "We Shall Overcome . . . Suum Day . . . " while tripping and swaying along arm-in-arm with the very people they were supposed to be angrily revolting against? Who ever heard of angry revolutionists swinging their bare feet together with their oppressor in lily-pad park pools, with gospels and guitars and "I Have a Dream" speeches? And the black masses in America were—and still are—having a nightmare.[31]

Malcolm was not the only figure who resisted freedom singing, conflated it with nonviolence, and accused it of a masculinity deficit. Activist Julius Lester, a songleader himself earlier in the movement, wrote in 1966:

> America has had chance after chance to show that it really meant "that men are endowed with certain inalienable rights." . . . Now it is over. The days of singing freedom songs and the days of combating bullets and billy clubs with Love. We Shall Overcome sounds old, outdated, and can enter the pantheon of the greats along with the IWW songs and the union songs. As one SNCC veteran put it after the Mississippi March, "Man, the people are too busy getting ready to fight to bother with singing anymore."[32]

The increasing accent on Black nationalism and tendency toward separatism also inflected the shift away from singing as the primary signifier of Black protest. The "Black and White together" rhetoric of many freedom songs—"We Shall Overcome" being the "worst offender"—emphasized interracial cooperation and a concern for the oppressor that more militant Black activists were tired of entertaining. These activists had developed a healthy fear of White colonization of their movement and were suspicious of cooperation with Whites that did not address the unjust power differential in interactions between White and Black.

In the struggles of the late 1950s and early 60s freedom singing indexed the righteousness of the cause and mobilized that feeling for internal and external momentum. But commentators picked up on that same indexing framed negatively by more militant activists in their attempts to contest the strategy of the Freedom Movement and used the sentiment to associate it solely with the "good 1960s" in the post-1968 moment. Once it became synonymous with nonviolence and unmanliness, freedom song could not easily shake this association.

Jon Michael Spencer sums up the narrative of freedom song's decline:

> What the historical record of song indicates is that the height of the civil rights movement corresponds with the height of singing as a means of expression (ca. 1960–1964), and that the move toward black nationalism was registered in the lyric and ultimate decline of singing as a mode of protest. From "We Shall Overcome" to "We Shall Overrun," SCLC to the Black Muslims, nonviolence to violence, singing to silence—the history of the movement is documented in the music, with appended footnotes perpetuated in the oral tradition.[33]

Spencer is not the only one to forward this declension narrative. In the Preface to their 2007 edition of *Sing for Freedom*, Guy and Candie Carawan argue, "This [the 1965 Selma March] would be the last great march with a hopeful spirit of black and white together. Soon the cry for black power would be heard and the singing would give way to chanting and an angrier mood."[34] Rhetorical theorist Elizabeth Ellis Miller also writes that

> the genre of the freedom song, important as it was for a time, did not persist as the key social action for activists throughout the Civil Rights Movement. As the 1960s wore on and the goals and strategies associated with nonviolence came to be questioned by large groups of activists, the need for the freedom song genre dissipated. As many looked to exchange spiritual nonviolence for Black Power, freedom songs became less valuable as strategies of activism and for organizing large groups.[35]

The death certificate issued by these sources, however, is premature. While traditional freedom song did become a proxy for negotiation within the Freedom Movement, and while singing in the style of the Southern, Christian-led movement fell out of fashion for some, we will see throughout this book that freedom singers did not go silent after Black Power and Black nationalism became more prominent. The dichotomy that exists in the dominant narrative between those who sang and those who rejected singing is not an accurate depiction of a movement that perpetually contested the best path forward. On the contrary, after 1968 the music of artist-activists such as Nina Simone expands our conception of freedom song; figures such as Bernice Johnson Reagon compose and perform new freedom songs as a method for curating complex and nuanced political identities; protestors continue freedom singing in the vein of the protests of 1950s and 60s; and filmmakers and record producers use freedom song to tell the history of and memorialize the movement as they remember it. By perpetuating the idea that freedom singing went silent in 1968, the historiography of freedom song perpetuates myths about the movement that obscure the political and cultural importance of freedom singing after 1968, and limit understanding of the capaciousness of the tradition during the 1950s and 60s.[36]

Although Malcolm X was the arch critic of freedom singing inasmuch as it represented an approach to revolution with which he disagreed, even he can be found gesturing toward a more complex understanding of the tradition. In the same address with Fannie Lou Hamer quoted above, Malcolm begins by saying, "I couldn't help but be very impressed at the outset when the Freedom Singers were singing the song 'Oginga Odinga' because Oginga Odinga is one of the foremost freedom fighters on the African continent . . . . Oginga Odinga is not passive. He's not meek. He's not humble. He's not nonviolent. But he's free."[37]

Despite the finality of Spencer's assessment above, he also seems to leave open the possibility of freedom song as an ongoing site of contestation with regard to the memory and meaning of the movement. He says, "Notwithstanding, singing as a symbol did not stop being a symbol when the singing ceased. In fact, its symbolism was confirmed by means of the militant signification of *silence* heard loud at length in the rhetoric of the Black Muslims. Singing would remain a symbol as long as tension persisted between the philosophies of nonviolence and violence."[38] While I am questioning the idea that the movement went silent, Spencer's point about the tension between differing philosophies animating the ongoing negotiation of the meaning of singing is well taken. In addition to the continuation and evolution of freedom singing as a practice, freedom song as a historicized repertoire is frequently used in the ideological struggles to control the meaning of the Black Freedom Movement today.

When a freedom song is sung and heard after 1968, it acts as a miniature public sphere, a site within which ongoing meanings and ideologies of the Black Freedom Movement are created, debated, and contested through sound.[39] In the same way Eric Lott speaks of minstrelsy as a "site of conflictual intensity," freedom song is a domain where conflicting memories, ideologies, and visions of the future come together, sometimes dissonantly and sometimes harmoniously.[40] A rethinking of the legacy and memory of the movement and its music in U.S. culture will not only shed light on where we can find freedom singing as living praxis, but also how instances of freedom singing after 1968 fortify or contest the consensus memory of the movement.

Chapter Summaries

The chapters that follow unpack, via various contexts and case studies, the myriad ways freedom song thrives in U.S. society and consciousness, and the ways it continues to exert powerful and widespread influence on our understanding of the Civil Rights Movement and our interpretation of contemporary social movements.

Chapter 1, "Memory, History, and Freedom Song," reviews the history of the Civil Rights Movement as it exists in U.S. consensus memory and describe how freedom song became inseparably tethered to the nonviolent, Southern movement. This tethering narrowly defines the musical characteristics of freedom song as a genre and confines our understanding of the impact of freedom song (with a few notable exceptions) to the period between 1954 and 1968, hindering our analysis of the way freedom singing functions after that period. It then introduces the historiographical intervention of the Long Civil Rights Movement and argues for its fruitfulness within musicological study of freedom song. Lastly, it theorizes what we will call the 1968 lens—a prevalent interpretive framework that stems from a misremembering of the Civil Rights Movement—and argue that many in the United States continue to rely on the 1968 lens to understand current events. The theme of the 1968 lens will return throughout the book, as it has continuously obscured our ability to understand contemporary instances of freedom singing and the struggles that singing has accompanied since 1968. "Following the music," so to speak, calls attention to acts of misremembering the Civil Rights Movement and its music and thereby sheds light on both the pre- and post-history of freedom song in U.S. culture and the state of the larger Black Freedom Movement itself.

Chapter 2, "From Freedom Song to Freedom Singing," takes cues from the inconsistencies, discrepancies, and missed opportunities that arise when traditional genre-based norms are applied to instances of freedom song, and constructs a new framework for understanding how freedom singing generates meaning and enables action in the post-1968 United States. The chapter leverages the concept of musicking in order to decouple freedom song from the boundaries of a circumscribed repertoire and the idea of the songs as objects. By doing so, a more fruitful way emerges to approach the study of freedom song—one that shifts the focus of analysis to the act of *freedom singing* as the primary bearer of meaning.

Chapters 3, 4, and 5 then move on to focus on three contexts in which freedom singing plays an active role in post-1968 U.S. society. Chapter 3, "Bernice Johnson Reagon, Freedom Singing, and Musical Coalition Politics," argues that the performance of freedom song provided Bernice Johnson Reagon (and by extension other performers) fertile ground for the curation of her own political identity and her relationship to the ongoing legacy of the Civil Rights Movement. This chapter analyzes three periods of Reagon's performing career between 1966 and 2003: her time with the Harambee Singers, her collaboration with Anne Romaine on the Southern Folk Cultural Revival Project, and her leadership of Sweet Honey in the Rock. In her freedom singing during these three performing contexts, Reagon curated a political identity that rejected the oversimplified ideological poles on which the 1968 lens relies, and instead advocated for a robust musical coalition politics, charting a new path for continued engagement with the Freedom Movement.

Chapter 4, "Warren County, Environmental Justice, and Freedom Singing in Protest," analyzes how freedom singing functions in protest movements in the post-1968 United States, taking the 1979–82 environmental justice movement in Warren County, North Carolina, as the primary case study. Through ethnographic and ecomusicological lenses, it describes how protestors in Warren County expanded the tradition of freedom singing to include environmental concerns. It draws on analysis of memory and nostalgia to argue that there are two types of nostalgia active in the Warren County protests that are typical of freedom singing protest movements after 1968: a productive nostalgia and a counterproductive nostalgia. The degree to which a protest movement draws on one or the other clarifies when and how that movement is undergirding or undercutting the 1968 lens. Because the Warren County movement is held up as a multiracial movement, this chapter also includes critical analysis of White participation in Black freedom struggles.

Chapter 5, "Documentary Media, Freedom Song, and the Construction of Sonic Blackness," analyzes how documenters of the movement have used freedom singing to advance their understandings of the movement's history. It begins by describing and critiquing a strain of primitivism at work in the early documentation of freedom song by figures such as Alan Lomax and Guy and Candie Carawan. This primitivist lens not only limited the ability of these documenters to understand the music culture they were observing, but it also has had wide-ranging ramifications for how music scholars and the U.S. public continue to (mis)understand the Civil Rights Movement. The chapter then moves to a discussion of Henry Hampton's multipart television documentary *Eyes on the Prize*—a counterexample of an effective documentary that uses freedom singing to depict the movement in all its complexity.

Lastly, the Conclusion and Afterword bring the book's content back into the present, exploring the personal and societal resonances of the preceding material. The Conclusion reasserts the fact that both freedom singing and silence continue to be meaningful and to play a vital role in political struggles in the United States. The Afterword discusses the author's positionality as it relates to the study of freedom song.

One final note on the structure of the chapters: each chapter begins with one or more contemporary vignette(s).[41] This book is not an exhaustive history of the use of freedom song in U.S. culture after 1968—it would be impossible to address every relevant instance of freedom singing in fifty years—but rather, an exploration of the general contours of the freedom song soundscape via in-depth examples throughout that time period. The contemporary vignettes that begin each chapter serve to support one of the book's overriding theses: that freedom singing is alive, well, and full of meaning in contemporary U.S. political praxis. The contemporary vignettes return at the conclusion of each chapter to demonstrate how the arguments developed from the historical case studies apply.

The contemporary vignettes are also meant to exemplify a certain type of close listening and storytelling that is attentive to the complexities and negotiations of the types of freedom singing U.S. Americans might encounter in their daily lives. The vignettes serve as the counter-memories from which the argument of each chapter is built. In keeping with George Lipsitz's argument that counter-memory starts with "the local, the immediate, and the personal" and then "builds outwards towards a total story," each chapter follows that pattern, circumscribing the historical case studies with the narrative and the personal.[42] In this way the vignettes highlight a politics of the personal and should not be distanced from the positionality of the author. I narrate the vignettes from my own subject position and acknowledge that what I draw out of them is directly connected to my experience and identity, and that the idiosyncrasies to which I attune my ear within the vignettes have also been shaped by my research.[43] Wherever possible I have included links to videos of the vignettes so that readers can experience them for themselves, and enter into this book's arguments on memory, storytelling, and musicmaking.

Along similar lines, the disparate audiences I hope to address with this book will likely experience the historical claims I make differently. For the average White American, the claims of this book will be revisionary and sometimes alternative. This book will hopefully correct faulty historical memory and suggest some fundamentally different histories altogether. For Black Americans and the activist community that has persisted in struggle since 1968, the claims of this book will be restorative. The trajectory of my argument will hopefully remind this public of the beautiful complexity of the movement and its sounds, enriching the memories from which they draw in their daily freedom work. For academics, the claims are largely compensatory—I am arguing for the inclusion of underemphasized aspects of freedom singing and civil rights history into our disciplines and historiographies to participate in the ever-expanding and evolving understanding of our history and our present. It is also my hope that this book will provide a toolkit for interrogating the ongoing praxis of freedom singing, providing correctives when necessary, and insisting on the "hopeful possibilities" of a different future conditioned by the renovation of the dominant narrative of the Civil Rights Movement.[44] As Lipsitz contends, "we may never succeed in creating a truly total story inclusive of the plurality of experiences on our planet, but the pursuit of such totality is essential."[45]

* * *

Ralph Abernathy's autobiography contains a story about King's death: On April 4, 1968, the shot that killed King rang out at the Lorraine Motel in Memphis. Andrew Young, who was beneath King in the parking lot, and Abernathy, who was inside the room at the time, ran to the balcony where King was standing. When Young saw how bad King's injury was, he turned to Abernathy and shouted, "O God! Ralph. It is over!" Abernathy responded, "Don't you say that! He'll be alright."[46] While Young's statement, "it is over," was likely just referencing King's life, the "it" is ambiguous; Young's exclamation and Abernathy's response could be read as a conflation of King's life with the very Freedom Movement itself. Is it all over or will he be all right?

This exchange reflects the fundamental tension of King's death in the hearts and minds of those involved in the movement. It was traumatic to be sure—a tremendous loss for the movement, for U.S. society, and for Black people around the world. But was the movement so synonymous with King, so bound up with his activity, that killing him also killed the movement? Although the dominant narrative suggests this, neither King nor the Black Freedom Movement itself were ever so monotoned in philosophy or practice. Nor was the movement's music. Just as the roots of freedom song are located long before 1954 and its branches extend long past 1968, so does the movement extend chronologically and ideologically into areas not contained by the dominant narrative. Freedom song—broadly conceived—and its contested meanings clue us in to this alternate history that goes "beyond amnesia," as Vincent Harding puts it.[47] If, instead of focusing on freedom song as a historical repertoire in active use from the 1950s through around 1968, we widen our gaze, we will discover an ever-evolving body of music and a way of musicking that challenges our assumptions about the very Freedom Movement itself.

Freedom song did not disappear after 1968, and the fact that it became a contested music, a site to challenge the memory of the movement's earlier years and the meaning and evolution of the movement in the present, reveals that it always was such complex and fertile ground. Studying the use of freedom song after 1968 contributes to the broader historical conversation about the Long Civil Rights Movement and the troubling before and after 1968 binary that the dominant narrative imposes. By attending to freedom song after 1968, we discover that the narrative of declension is far too simplistic; the movement adapted, evolved, continued, but did not die suddenly or even decline—certainly not given the enduring place of the movement as an omnipresent referent and site of meaning-making in U.S. cultural life. In the same way that King and his legacy have been coopted and subsumed by the U.S. imperial project, so occasionally have the sounds of the freedom singing that once shook the foundations of White supremacy in America to their core. As Jacques Attali argued of popular music and rock, freedom songs "have been recuperated, colonized, [and] sanitized" by the pervasiveness of the American project.[48] But just as American exceptionalism's stranglehold on King's memory has begun to loosen in popular understanding, so too can the sounds of freedom singing be reclaimed as the complex sites of negotiation that they are.

This reconsideration has important implications not just for the academic disciplines of musicology and history, but also for contemporary U.S. politics. The way collectives within the United States remember the movement, in song or otherwise, "may call forth not only remembrance of the American and southern past but also social action in the global present."[49] Emphasizing the connections rather than the distinctions between branches of the movement and the music that accompanied them can enable a substantive theoretical grasp of Black political rhetoric and activity, such that freedom singing can resonate across constructed temporal divides.

We are still living in the world that was created after 1968, a world that often does ideological violence to the history of the Black freedom struggle in order to enforce a status quo built upon a consensus memory constructed in the decades that followed. "The history of music," as David Garcia says, channeling James Baldwin, is "always constituting the ground of our present."[50] By paying closer attention to one facet of music history in the United States, that of the freedom song, this book challenges the consensus memory and raises counter-memories of the Civil Rights Movement into the collective consciousness of the United States, thereby freeing the interpretation of the political present from the 1968 lens and opening up "hopeful possibilities" for the future.[51]

1

Memory, History, and Freedom Song

Perhaps all sound memories turn into romances. And the more quickly new sounds are hurled at us the more we are thrust back into the wells of memory, attractively fictionalizing the sounds of the past, smoothing them out into peaceful fantasies.

—R. Murray Schafer

On May 25, 2020, two months after Breonna Taylor was murdered in her home by police in Louisville, Kentucky, and three months after Ahmaud Arbery was murdered by White residents of a South Georgia neighborhood, George Floyd was murdered in police custody in Minneapolis, Minnesota. Cities across the United States erupted into protests that took various forms—some chaotic, some organized and controlled. In the days that followed Floyd's death, outrage gave way to looting and burning in many U.S. cities, including Minneapolis. President Donald Trump poured fuel on the fire, tweeting inflammatory statements about protestors, including "when the looting starts, the shooting starts."[1] On June 3, at a planned protest near Lafayette Square in Washington, D.C., thousands of demonstrators sang Bill Withers's "Lean on Me," led by street performer Kenny Sway.[2] Protestors held their cell phones and lighters aloft in the traditional concertgoer's acknowledgment of a moving ballad performance. The protestors were quite sedate, many sitting, others standing and swaying, most singing along to the song of support for others in their hour of need. The crowd broke out into applause as Sway sang the final note up an octave in a clear, dulcet falsetto.

In the days and weeks after the uprisings prompted by George Floyd's death, commentators spilled much ink. One of the most revealing responses came from Robert F. Darden, a journalism and public relations professor at Baylor University, who has also written a two-volume history of Black music and is the founder of Baylor's Black Gospel Music Restoration Project. In the *Dallas Morning News*, Darden wrote, "In the years to come, historians and social scientists will argue over exactly when the 2020 protests about George Floyd transformed from demonstrations into a movement, the moment when sporadic violence and looting by a few individuals gave way to a universal call for justice and equity. I believe it occurred when the righteous anger became augmented with singing."[3]

On January 8, 2023, five Memphis police officers brutally beat Tyre Nichols during a traffic stop.[4] After his arrest, he complained of shortness of breath. He was transferred to the hospital and died on January 10. The Memphis Police Department released bodycam footage on January 27, after which protests broke out across the country. Benjamin Crump, the lawyer for Nichols's family, compared the videos to the footage of the police beating of Rodney King in 1991, which eventually led to massive rioting in Los Angeles when the police officers were acquitted of charges. The Rev. Al Sharpton gave the eulogy at Nichols's funeral service on February 1. Sharpton began his eulogy by recounting that early that morning, he and his daughter had visited the Lorraine Motel where Martin Luther King Jr. was assassinated.[5] "Here we are 55 years later," he said, "looking at the balcony where Martin Luther King shed his blood for Black city workers. The reason this is so personal to me," he continued, "is that five Black men, who wouldn't have a job in the police department, in the city where Dr. King lost his life, not far from that balcony, you beat a brother to death." Sharpton then addressed the former officers and the police department directly for several minutes, saying, "There's nothing more offensive to those of us who fight to open doors, that you walk through those open doors, and act like the folks we had to fight to get you through them doors," and then later, "I believe if that man had been White, you wouldn't have beat him like that. We're not asking for nothing special, we're asking to be treated equal. And just like they marched and boycotted and went to jail for nine years, from the 55 Montgomery Bus Boycott to the 64 Civil Rights Act, we're going to pay the same dues to get this George Floyd Justice in Policing Act." Invoking King's famous "I've Been to the Mountaintop" speech, he admonished them further: "He [King] expected you to bring us to the mountaintop." At the very end of the service, Darrel Petties sang Sam Cooke's song "A Change

Is Gonna Come," as Nichols's family prepared to recess out of the church. Pettie opted to update the vocal style of the song, eschewed Cooke's smooth tone for a grittier, run-heavy, sanctified gospel-inflected sound. Directly following "A Change Is Gonna Come," the family was escorted out and the service was closed in prayer.

This chapter is all about how the Civil Rights Movement is remembered. Singing often accompanies memory work, and its own meaning-making power interacts with the process of reinforcing or resisting the memory of the movement. The preceding contemporary vignettes raise questions related to music and memory: How is the memory of the Civil Rights Movement being mobilized? *What* and *whose* memory of the Civil Rights Movement are the participants and commentators relying on here? How does music enhance or complicate this memory work? These questions lie at the heart of the exploration below. We explore how the memory of the Civil Rights Movement is produced, altered, and biased in U.S. culture, after which we return to the contemporary vignettes to discover how the intervening concepts make freedom singing after 1968 more legible.

Remembering the Movement

Throughout the book terms and concepts from memory studies are employed to describe the ways people in the United States recall the Civil Rights Movement, and how those memories impact their stances in the present. While scholarly interest in memory multiplied exponentially over the course of the twentieth century, the exact meaning of memory-related terminology and the connection of memory to other concepts such as "history" and "narrative" are often obscure. Conventionally, history is thought of as an objective narrative of the past deduced from evidence and is, thus, contrasted with memory, which is traditionally defined as the (often unreliable) recollections of the individual. This understanding of memory persisted until the second half of the twentieth century and perpetuated many colonialist, racist, and sexist assumptions about what types of people think historically and what types of knowledge are considered relevant for historical inquiry.

Scholars such as Pierre Nora and Yosef Yerushalmi brought about a paradigm shift by reconsidering memory and its relationship to history and historiography.[6] While both Nora and Yerushalmi maintain the idea that history and memory are oppositional in nature, they began to advocate for the study of memory as vital for identity formation and as a potential antidote to the ills of history-making that excludes and totalizes. More recently, the idea that memory and history are fundamentally oppositional has fallen out of favor. In much scholarship of the late twentieth century, the "distinction between history and memory" is "a matter of power rather than that of epistemological privilege."[7] In this formulation, history and memory are "entangled rather than oppositional."[8] Renee Romano and Leigh Raiford put it simply: memory is the "process by which people recall, lay claim to, understand, and represent the past," and "whether individual, collective, or official, memories of the past are not static."[9] In this sense, it is very similar to the production of history, where narratives about the past are constructed and continually revised from sources in order to make sense of the past and present. Even in the most objectivist approach to history, biases are always inherent in the selection and interpretation of those sources and within the master narratives they are often made to fit.[10]

There are four terms regarding the sociality of memory that need to be clarified as we move forward: collective memory, cultural memory, consensus memory, and counter-memory. *Collective memory* was first theorized by Maurice Halbwachs, who insisted that although it is individuals who remember, they always do it together; memory cannot be separated from its sociality.[11] Similarly, sociologist Iwona Irwin-Zarecka defines collective memory as "a set of ideas, images, and feelings about the past" that are "best located not in the minds of individuals but in the resources they share."[12] This definition maintains the ritual and intellectual components of Halbwachs's understanding but, importantly, subsumes the ways in which memory is transmitted through material objects as well. In the case of the Civil Rights Movement, such "shared resources" are ubiquitous and multivalent, and they will be discussed below in detail. Irwin-Zarecka argues for the importance of examining the dynamics of collective memory because "a collective memory is intricately related, though in variable ways, to the sense of collective identity individuals come to acquire. And second, it is imbued with moral imperatives—the obligations to one's kin, notions of justice, indeed the lessons of right and wrong—that form the basic parts of the normative order. On both counts, collective memory is a significant orienting force."[13] In the case of the collective memory produced and reproduced in U.S. culture about the Civil Rights Movement, this orienting force is one with wide-ranging political, social, and cultural repercussions. David Blight makes a similar point about collective memory, defining it as a "set of practices and ideas embedded in a culture, which people learn to decode and convert into their identities."[14] Ideas about the Civil Rights Movement, some accurate and some inaccurate, are embedded in our culture, and learning to make the decoding and conversion process obvious is of vital importance.

Along the same lines, Marita Sturken theorizes the term *cultural memory* as follows:

> [T]he process of cultural memory is bound up in complex political stakes and meanings. It both defines a culture and is the means by which its divisions and conflicting agendas are revealed. To define a memory as cultural is, in effect, to enter into a debate about what that memory means. This process does not efface the individual but rather involves the interaction of individuals in the creation of cultural meaning. Cultural memory is a field of cultural negotiation through which different stories vie for a place in history.[15]

Sturken goes on to argue that cultural memory is "essential in [the] construction" of history even while being distinct from it. Sturken prefers cultural memory to the more ubiquitous collective memory for her study because of the "self-consciousness with which notions of culture are attached to these objects of memory."[16] She further clarifies that although "cultural memory may constitute opposition" it is "not automatically the scene of cultural resistance." Cultural memory is more specific than collective memory because of the emphasis it puts on products of mass culture, and the ways it interrogates the interaction of collective memory and historical narrative in the public sphere.

Consensus memory comes from Renee Romano and Leigh Raiford's *The Civil Rights Movement in American Memory* as a way to describe the overriding dominant narrative of the Civil Rights Movement that is policed, repeated, and frequently recalled in U.S. cultural life.[17] Consensus memory is related to what is known as "consensus history" only in the sense that the processes are similar; both consensus memory surrounding the Civil Rights Movement and what has been critiqued as the consensus school of U.S. history achieve their narratives about the past by deemphasizing complexity and contradiction in favor of a master narrative that is useful for present political ends. Consensus memory is a compelling term to describe the ways in which the dominant narrative of the Civil Rights Movement is consistently reinforced and ostensibly agreed upon, even as memories that contradict and nuance it are legion. As we will see, however, consensus memory is vital to a certain understanding of American identity. David Thelen argues that "people develop a shared identity by identifying, exploring, and *agreeing* on memories" and it is this agreement that challenges to consensus memory call into question.[18]

Lastly, the term *counter-memory* is essential to understanding how freedom singing after 1968 interacts with the dominant narrative of the Civil Rights Movement. Counter-memory was first theorized by Michel Foucault as an "important factor in the struggle" to contest the disciplinary power of nationalist historiography.[19] Its usage here, however, is more in line with George Lipsitz, who argued, "Counter-memory looks to the past for the hidden histories excluded from dominant narratives. Unlike myths that seek to detach events and actions from the fabric of any larger history, counter-memory forces revision of existing histories by supplying new perspectives about the past."[20] Lipsitz emphasizes the revisionist capacity of counter-memory. Rather than counter-memory being a mode of discourse that stands entirely outside of the totalizing effects of historical narrative, Lipsitz argues that it is vital for counter-memory to speak back against those narratives, challenging and hopefully renovating them. He contends, "Storytelling that leaves history to the oppressor cannot challenge the hegemony of dominant discourse. But storytelling that combines subjectivity and objectivity, that employs the insights and passions of myth and folklore in the service of revising history, can be a powerful tool of contestation."[21] Counter-memory is central to the conception of the contemporary vignettes that begin each chapter.[22] Counter-memory enables a more precise way to describe how some acts of remembering contest dominant narratives and, conversely, how other acts of remembering support the status quo of those dominant narratives.

Myriad forms of cultural production and public discourse work together to shape the collective memory of the Civil Rights Movement in U.S. culture—heritage tours, museum exhibits, textbooks, literature, political speeches, commemorative events, various media productions, consumer products, art, etc. Of particular concern in this book is the way music in general, and a broad conception of freedom song in particular, helps to craft cultural memory, including the creative tension that occurs when private memory impinges on public memory and vice versa.

Currently, one of the most widely used shared resources for gathering information and maintaining ostensibly common knowledge is the online encyclopedia Wikipedia. When read as a primary source, Wikipedia is a telling repository of popular (if sometimes unreliable) knowledge on any given subject. The Wikipedia page for the Civil Rights Movement is no exception. Wikipedia has both a prose history of the Civil Rights Movement and, embedded in this page, a hyperlink to a timeline that succinctly captures the abridged narrative of the "classical phase" of the movement.[23] The "Timeline of the African-American Civil Rights Movement" begins in

1954 and ends in 1968, and the primary page on the history of the movement is titled "African-American Civil Rights Movement (1954–1968)."

Both of these pages reinforce the consensus memory that the movement began *ex nihilo* in 1954, and the narrative of rupture and decline, which argues that the movement proceeded until 1968 following the passage of the Civil Rights, Voting Rights, and Fair Housing Acts, internal disagreements about tactics of the movement, and ultimately King's assassination.[24] Interestingly enough, Wikipedia also has pages titled "African-American Civil Rights Movement (1865–1896)" and "African-American Civil Rights Movement (1896–1954)," a fact that seems to acknowledge the deep historical roots of the classical phase. However, the site reinforces the normative understanding by redirecting anyone who simply types "Civil Rights Movement" to the 1954–68 page. The page for history after 1968 is titled "Post-civil rights era in African American history." While editors have added recent entries on (a few of) the police and vigilante killings that catalyzed the Black Lives Matter movement in the 2010s, as well as the impact of the COVID-19 pandemic on Black American life in the 2020s, the page emphasizes the election of Barack Obama as the first Black president and the subsequent election of Kamala Harris as the first Black woman vice president, which makes its own overly conclusive and simplistic declaration on the state of racial justice in the United States.

It makes sense that Wikipedia would reinforce the consensus memory of the Civil Rights Movement based on who contributes to Wikipedia and what the stated values of the Wikipedia community are. Wikipedia's contributors/editors are volunteers, and a 2012 survey of the editors revealed that the vast majority (91%) of them are male.[25] Most of the editors are between the ages of 35 and 44, have an undergraduate degree or higher, and live in the United States or Europe.[26] Although in theory anyone can edit Wikipedia, this demographic picture represents the normative arbiter of what knowledge and which histories have historically been recorded and preserved. In addition, Wikipedia places a heavy emphasis on consensus building and collaboration. As Dariusz Jemielniak reports, "Wikipedia rules suggest that editors seek agreement. These rules are interesting from the point of view of organization studies, as they are unique and oriented to consensus building."[27] Joseph Michael Reagle also confirms that "[c]onsensus is Wikipedia's fundamental model for editorial decision making."[28] In effect, the history of the Civil Rights Movement preserved on Wikipedia represents a consensus of the Wikipedia editors, who in turn represent the demographic that has curated public knowledge on many topics in addition to the Civil Rights Movement.

Brittanica.com, another online encyclopedia, features an article on the Civil Rights Movement by historian Clayborne Carson.[29] While Carson's article features an extensive discussion of the historical precursors to the movement of the 1950s and 60s, it also interprets the events of 1965–68 as a result of backlash to Black militancy rather than discussing the long history of White backlash to the push for Black freedom and the ever-present contestation over tactics within the movement:

> The Selma-to-Montgomery march in March 1965 would be the last sustained Southern protest campaign that was able to secure widespread support among whites outside the region. The passage of voting rights legislation, the upsurge in Northern urban racial violence, and white resentment of black militancy lessened the effectiveness and popularity of nonviolent protests as a means of advancing African American interests.[30]

Contrary to Carson's portrait of a distinct Southern, church-based movement and a secular, Northern militant movement, Jenny Walker argues, "the historiography of the Movement still turns largely around a media-inspired, but historically flawed contrast between a southern, church-based nonviolent civil rights movement and a secular, violent black power era centered on the cities of the North."[31] This narrative is due to, in part, the media's tendency to "ignore, downplay, or depoliticize incidents of black violence and inflammatory rhetoric in civil rights protests" and to "disassociate such phenomena from the mainstream civil rights movement."[32]

As Walker suggests, media outlets and journalists at the time were largely responsible for generating this interpretation. While they were eager to capture the story of the century and broadcast it into U.S. households via the new medium of choice, the television, they abruptly soured on the movement with the rise of Black Power and the uprisings of 1965–68, "training a hostile eye on those developments, ignoring the southern campaign's evolving goals, obscuring interregional connections and similarities, and creating a narrative breach between what people think of as 'the movement' and the popular struggles of the late 1960s and 1970s."[33]

Just as the mainstream press was largely responsible for generating this faulty narrative, historians have been largely responsible for reproducing it. Walker goes on to argue:

> All too often, less sensitive historians evoke a new breed of black power militants whose threat to society, while exaggerated in the press, was nevertheless predicated upon a very real—and a very new—repertoire of violent gestures, language, and action that would have been anathema in the

> nonviolent era. What, perhaps, is underemphasized in the historiography is the degree to which this symbolic, rhetorical, and actual violence was not a new departure in the black freedom struggle at all, but an extension of some decidedly violent aspects of the supposedly "nonviolent" era.[34]

History textbooks and other material for public school education frequently reinforce this oversimplified master narrative of the Civil Rights Movement, a problem that James Loewen illuminated with regard to textbook treatment of many aspects of U.S. history.[35] The vast majority of these texts treat the Civil Rights Movement in its most simplistic form, beginning with *Brown v. Board of Education*, focusing on King's activism, and ending with the passage of legislation and a negative interpretation of the rise of Black Power. Daniel Boorstin and Mather Kelley's *A History of the United States*, which was one of the top five selling textbooks in the United States in the twentieth century, describes Black Power as an inherently "angry" ideology seeking to "get even," and describes its effects like this: "By the fall of 1966 the civil rights movement was divided and in disarray. White backlash grew stronger. For the first time in recent years, a civil rights measure failed to pass Congress. The summer of 1967 saw the worst rioting in United States history. Blacks went on the rampage, destroying their own neighborhoods."[36] *American History: A Survey* argues that the most notable political manifestation of Black Power was its creation of "a deep schism within the civil-rights movement."[37]

George Tindall and David Shi's *America: A Narrative History*, now in its eighth edition, frames the Civil Rights Movement through the lens of the accomplishments of the president who was in power first, and King's activism second.[38] The authors mention SNCC only twice, once during their section on sit-ins and freedom rides, and once as they narrate the ascendency of Black Power.[39] Tindall and Shi do train a more sympathetic eye on urban rioting in the mid-1960s than Boorstin and Kelley, arguing that the violence may have been an attempt by Blacks to "destroy what they could not stomach and what civil rights legislation *seemed* unable to change [emphasis added]." They also note two positive impacts Black Power had on the movement, "despite its hyperbole, violence, and small number of adherents." In the end, however, they dismiss Black Power and Black nationalism and reinforce the idea that the radical politics of groups such as the Black Panthers were a bridge too far, placing the blame for a fragmented coalition and a lack of national traction at their own feet. They make no mention of the campaign of surveillance, harassment, and violence the FBI waged against groups such as the Black

Panthers when remarking that the Panthers "terrified the public, but eventually fragmented in spasms of violence."[40] Tindall and Shi conclude their chapter on the civil rights years by commenting about 1968: "So at the end of a turbulent year near the end of a traumatic decade, a nation on the verge of violent chaos looked to Richard Nixon to provide what he had promised in the campaign: 'peace with honor' in Vietnam and a middle ground on which a majority of Americans, silent or otherwise, could come together."[41]

Public monuments, museums, and heritage tours are also important sites for the construction and maintenance of collective memory of the Civil Rights Movement. According to Owen Dwyer, there are "significant elisions and exclusions in the cultural landscape's treatment of the civil rights era," including a coalescence around the mainstream narrative that forces "women's, working-class, and local histories to the margins in order to focus on charismatic leaders and dramatic events" and a focus on the "most violent, brutish expressions [of racism]" that "overlooks the more insidious and pervasive elements that constitute contemporary white privilege and patriarchy."[42] As Dwyer argues, these public sites frequently contain within them contradictions—hinting at a more complex past than they sometimes clearly call to mind. For instance, the Southern Poverty Law Center's Civil Rights Memorial in Montgomery, Alabama, which was designed by Maya Lin, features a wall with an inscription of Martin Luther King Jr.'s quotation of the biblical prophet Amos: "until justice rolls down like water, and righteousness like a mighty stream." Below this sits a round granite table with dates, major events of the movement, and the names of martyrs encircling it. The events begin with the *Brown v. Board of Education* decision in 1954, feature the primary events of the Southern campaign, and end with the assassination of Martin Luther King Jr. in 1968, mirroring the abridged narrative. Dedicated in 1989, it was the first memorial to be constructed to honor the martyrs of the movement.

The monument makes a small gesture toward a more complex story—Lin placed a space between 1968 and 1954 intended to indicate that the movement began before 1954 and continued after 1968.[43] However, this minute signal is overwhelmed by the monument's reinforcement of the traditional movement narrative and its highlighting of key movement figures.[44] In a similar way, freedom song itself participates in the construction of public and cultural memory of the Civil Rights Movement. The meanings generated in this process are certainly not settled or static; the singing of freedom song opens up space for the ongoing negotiation of what the Civil Rights Movement means in contemporary U.S. culture.

Freedom Song and the Long Civil Rights Movement

In recent decades, a cadre of scholars has been working to deconstruct the dominant narrative of the Civil Rights Movement and add nuance to U.S. consensus memory. Jacquelyn Dowd Hall's influential article "The Long Civil Rights Movement and the Political Uses of the Past" crystallized this impulse and narrated the ways in which neoconservatives in the 1970s were able to reinvent themselves by appropriating the meaning of the Civil Rights Movement, using it to bolster their political clout and reverse the gains for which the movement itself fought. She writes:

> By confining the civil rights struggle to the South, to bowdlerized heroes, to a single halcyon decade, and to limited, noneconomic objectives, the master narrative simultaneously elevates and diminishes the movement. It ensures the status of the classical phase as a triumphal moment in a larger American progress narrative, yet it undermines its *gravitas*. It prevents one of the most remarkable mass movements in American history from speaking effectively to the challenges of our time.[45]

In a similar way, freedom song has often been coopted in support of the dominant consensus narrative, which has the effect of both elevating and diminishing its importance. Its role in the successes of the 1950s and early 60s is elevated to near mythic status. We know from the words of activists at the time that singing was vital for their activities; however, one would think freedom song was the sole reason the movement succeeded (inasmuch as it did), to say nothing of the decades of diligent organizing work that undergirded the public protests of the classical phase. At the same time, freedom song is diminished. It is circumscribed as a historical phenomenon, its meanings are confined to a brief period, and its continuing prominence in U.S. culture is overlooked.

The work of historian Peniel Joseph effectively deconstructs the periodization of the Civil Rights Movement into a good and bad 1960s and, thereby, exposes the scapegoating of Black Power that is prevalent in the consensus memory of 1965 to 1968. Joseph argues:

> The Civil Rights Movement is generally accepted as comprising the years 1954–1965. These years contour the beginning of the demise of legal segregation and the acquisition of black voting rights. The sit-ins, protests, marches, beatings, and boycotts that highlight this period represent the *heroic period* of the Civil Rights Movement in both public memory and historical

> scholarship. However, such a characterization removes from the spotlight important civil rights-era political organizations and figures (some of whom simultaneously participated in more conventional civil rights struggles) that went beyond the call for civil rights to advocate radical systemic social and political change. Furthermore, such a description creates a situation in which the Black Power Movement can be conveniently blamed for the demise of the Civil Rights Movement, rather than being viewed as an alternative to the ineffectiveness of civil rights demands in critical areas of American life.
>
> From this perspective, Black Power simultaneously triggered the demise of civil rights and the New Left's apocalyptic descent into destructive "revolutionary" violence. 1968, the year of Tet, May Day revolts, the assassinations of King and Bobby Kennedy, and the election of Richard Nixon have all become signposts (interpreted after the fact) for the end of a more hopeful era. Such narratives of declension diminish continuities between postwar black freedom struggles and late 1960s- and 1970s-era black radicalism . . . . Cumulatively, this scholarship posits a good 1960s, filled with hope and optimism reflected in SNCC's early interracialism and SDS's youthful idealism, and personified in Martin Luther King Jr., with a bad 1960s, characterized by the omnipresent Black Panthers, urban rioting, and black separatism.[46]

Joseph moves the conversation from the limitations of the consensus memory of the Civil Rights Movement to a more expansive Black Freedom Movement. The Black Freedom Movement has always been animated by various modes of cultural production, most obviously by music. This book adds another layer to the conversation: perhaps in our haste to align freedom song exclusively with the classical Civil Rights Movement, we have boxed in its meaning and prevented ourselves from understanding its full and continued importance to the broader Black Freedom Movement. If we question the simplistic and dichotomous memory of the 1960s, we will discover a more complex understanding of freedom singing as an ever-present, contested site of struggle and meaning for a movement that did not die in 1968, but continues.

There is a legitimate concern that, in its haste to expand the boundaries of the movement, Long Civil Rights Movement scholarship has rendered the historical particularities of the movement's idiosyncratic periods and ideologies illegible.[47] If "everything is everything," then particular historical analysis, along with its attendant application to the present, may be lost. The insightful critique by Sundiata Keita Cha-Jua and Clarence Lang of Dowd Hall et al. is a helpful warning—for Long Movement scholarship to do what it intends (which is to preserve the importance of the history of

Black Liberation and to clearly understand its broad effects on the present), it must take care not to blur definitions into oblivion. While taking this critique to heart, the research on freedom song in this book bolsters the Long Movement thesis that overemphasizing distinctions between various branches of the larger Black Freedom Movement has done more damage than exploring continuities. To apply this directly to freedom song, we should not lose our understanding of the particularities of classical freedom song as detailed by the excellent scholarship reviewed in the following chapter. Completely erasing the genre distinctions of what constitutes a "freedom song" should not be the goal. Shifting our frame of analysis, however, may allow us to see the continuities (and the discontinuities) more clearly, thus strengthening rather than weakening the application of the history to the present.[48]

Freedom singing is active remembering, a site for constructing and negotiating the memory of the classical movement as it pertains to present struggles, memory that reinforces narratives that impact the present. In this way, we can conceive of freedom singing as what Raphael Samuel might call a "theater of memory" or what Pierre Nora would deem a *lieu de memoire* or "site of memory."[49] Shana Redmond describes a similar idea in her discussion of Black anthems, saying that the politics that are embodied by the performance of Black anthems in the post–Civil Rights era are "successful in part due to their significations of the past."[50] Freedom singing opens up a space for the production of collective memory surrounding the movement. One of the animating questions of this book is if scholars, practitioners, and the U.S. public alert ourselves to freedom singing that remembers the more porous and expansive Long Civil Rights Movement rather than the oversimplified version in U.S. consensus memory, how might that change both the historiography of freedom song for the movement's classical phase as well as the period after 1968?

Encouragingly, the Long Civil Rights Movement impulse has begun to take root in the types of shared resources that serve as the reservoir for U.S. cultural memory. In the fiftieth anniversary week of Martin Luther King Jr.'s death, many online think pieces, radio and television segments, and other public information forums picked up on the theme of King's sanitized legacy.[51] If music studies can more thoroughly incorporate the Long Civil Rights Movement into its interpretive frameworks as well, it can begin to better understand freedom singing. The purpose of this expansion is not simply to enlarge the category of "freedom song," but to develop a new and more accurate understanding of the Black Freedom Movement as it was articulated before 1968 and as it continued after 1968. This broader and more accurate reading of freedom song and the movement will facilitate a deconstruction of the dominant way U.S. Americans continue to understand instances of Black revolt—an understanding that perpetually stalls momentum toward freedom.

The 1968 Lens

As it stands, an interpretive framework built upon the foundation of our flawed consensus memory frequently neutralizes freedom song and the Black protest it accompanies. This interpretive framework, which I will call the *1968 lens*, operates in U.S. culture largely unacknowledged and unchallenged. The 1968 lens is a prevalent interpretive framework that reads instances of Black uprising through a sanitized and limited memory of the Civil Rights Movement. This interpretive process often leads to a mobilization of this oversimplified past to delegitimize current efforts for freedom. This is the kind of activity Marita Sturken would deem "strategic forgetting," or the ways in which cultures and the states that are formed within them often engage in active "forgetting of painful events that may be too dangerous to keep in active memory."[52] In the case of the Civil Rights Movement in U.S. culture, this strategic forgetting takes place paradoxically through acts of remembering, where the memory being recalled is stripped of its complexity and historical contingency. It is more akin to what Toni Morrison called "disremembering."[53] Morrison's evocative writing about memory offers us terminology to grapple with the effect of the past on the present, especially in relation to story and personal narrative. For the characters in Morrison's novel *Beloved*, to "disremember" someone or something is to intentionally forget in such a way that the impact of that person or event on the present is ignored. A similar dynamic is at play in U.S. collective memory as we intentionally forget the complexity of the Black Freedom Movement for an oversimplified and mythologized version of events and then proceed to ignore the ways such acts of disremembering impact contemporary politics.

Sanitizing and domesticating the memory of the movement is a way of "making remembering safe" for predominantly White Americans who never fully reckoned with the movement's demands.[54] The 1968 lens is activated as an escape hatch when a counter-memory strays dangerously close to deconstructing the dominant narrative and enabling a different present. With the 1968 lens firmly in place, only collective actions that perfectly recall the sterilized memory of civil rights activism led by King—down to the songs themselves—are acceptable (i.e., safe); any perceived deviation is immediately associated with the post-1968 "breakdown" and deemed unacceptable, violent, and deviant. Any negative outcomes are then blamed not on the systemic causes but on the uprising's failure to live up to this flawed memory. This filtering serves to insulate White power from the advances of people of color seeking liberation. As James Baldwin said, "The real reason that nonviolence is considered to be a virtue in Negroes is that white men do not want their lives, their self-image, or their property threatened."[55]

At the same time, because protests that effectively recall the aesthetic of a sanitized King's activism are deemed safe, those who are committed to radical change sometimes ignore, downplay, or denigrate the resources of freedom song, further accentuating the dichotomy that has worked to the advantage of the status quo. To challenge the 1968 lens would both be to question the mythic status of our "bowdlerized [Civil Rights] heroes" but also to open the door for a remembering that suggests a more revolutionary trajectory, which is why the dominant narrative of the Civil Rights Movement and its soundtrack is so vigilantly maintained. Another aspect of the 1968 lens is that, similar to the declension narrative that blames Black Power for backlash in the late 1960s, contemporary instances of backlash are read as a reaction to protestor violence, rather than a continuation of the initial violence against Black people and resistance to their liberation.

The process of applying the 1968 lens begins with the ongoing maintenance of the sanitized memory of the Civil Rights Movement, always with an eye to the political usefulness of the "good" and "bad" 1960s as articulated above. Then an event occurs, recalling and stimulating the racial anxiety that stems from the events of 1965 to 1968. Commentators proceed to view and interpret the event through the 1968 lens, often mobilizing this mythic memory to praise "agreeable" aspects of the protest or revolt, and critique and suppress "deviant" aspects. One can see this process at work in major instances of Black uprising since 1968, such as the Rodney King riots of 1992 and the organizing of the Black Lives Matter movement in Ferguson after the police killing of Michael Brown in 2014.

Let's turn briefly to a recent example of the 1968 lens at work: the "Unite the Right" rally in Charlottesville, Virginia, and its aftermath. On the Friday evening of August 11, 2017, White supremacists descended on Charlottesville, Virginia. They marched through the center of the University of Virginia's campus carrying torches and chanting Nazi slogans ahead of a planned demonstration on Saturday. On the other side of town, clergy and activists gathered for an interfaith mass meeting in preparation for their counterprotest. Before their mass meeting was over, torch-bearing White supremacists had surrounded the church, already threatening the counter-protestors by holding them hostage. In the morning, the two groups met again at Emancipation Park—the White supremacists carrying firearms and continuing their chanting while the counter-protestors marched, linked arms, and alternated between silent defiance and the singing of freedom songs. After police dispersed the rally, White supremacists attacked counter-protestors, killing one woman and injuring several others, despite the counter-protestors' efforts to recall the nonviolent activism of the Civil Rights Movement.

In the aftermath, one can see the 1968 lens at work shaping the interpretation of the event. First, before any other framing of the event had taken place, President Donald Trump tweeted out a call for "unity" that is undergirded by "acceptable" and "unacceptable" forms of protest shaped by the 1968 lens. In the aftermath, many media pundits and Trump himself coalesced around the narrative that both sides were at fault for the escalation and violence because of the presence of some self-identified antifascist protestors who defended the others.[56] Responding to criticism of his response, Trump doubled down on his position and said, "I think there is blame on both sides. You had a group on one side that was bad. You had a group on the other side that was also very violent."[57] Evidence of the 1968 lens could be seen throughout media coverage via various outlets. In a remarkable segment on Fox News reflecting on the violence in Charlottesville, Martin Luther King Jr.'s niece Alveda King asserted that King would have supported Trump's call to unity and nonviolence.[58] In an article for *Time Magazine*, David Kaiser explicitly drew the comparison between Charlottesville and protests in 1968, saying, "Though 50 years have passed the pattern that emerged in 1968–70 could be the template for what we are about to witness . . . . Just as in the past, protests and counterprotests can escalate each other. The experience of the late 1960s does not hold out much hope for how this cycle might end."[59]

Musicians entered the fray as well. John Legend—who has participated in multiple projects featuring freedom singing, including the documentary *Soundtrack for a Revolution* (discussed in chapter 5) and an album of protest songs with The Roots entitled *Wake Up!*—tweeted, "We have Nazi sympathizers and white nationalists in the White House. Condemn them too. They should not be receiving taxpayer money." In response to a tweet by Speaker of the House Paul Ryan condemning the violence in

Charlottesville, Legend tweeted, "Impeach the white supremacist in the White House or STFU [shut the fuck up]." A month later, Dave Matthews Band hosted "A Concert for Charlottesville," featuring Justin Timberlake, Pharrell Williams, The Roots, Ariana Grande, and others. The concert did not include any overt statements but did feature some subtle political digs, including Timberlake's performance of Sam Cooke's "A Change Is Gonna Come" and Pharrell Williams's reference to kneeling as an appropriate response to the U.S. flag, a reference to Colin Kaepernick's NFL national anthem protest. The streaming service Spotify removed several artists deemed to be supportive of White supremacy from its platform in response to Charlottesville.[60]

Four of the clergy who were present in Charlottesville penned a response to all this, arguing that this "both sides" narrative springs from "sanitized images of the Rev. Dr. Martin Luther King Jr. and the Civil Rights Movement" that have led to "paralyzingly unrealistic standards when it comes to what protest should look like."[61] They said:

> Thanks to the sanitized images of the Rev. Dr. Martin Luther King Jr. and the civil rights movement that dominate our nation's classrooms and our national discourse, many Americans imagine that protests organized by the Southern Christian Leadership Conference, the Student Nonviolent Coordinating Committee and countless local organizations fighting for justice did not fall victim to violent outbreaks. That's a myth. In spite of extensive training in nonviolent protest and civil disobedience, individuals and factions within the larger movement engaged in violent skirmishes, and many insisted on their right to physically defend themselves even while they proclaimed nonviolence as an ideal (examples include leaders of the SNCC and the Deacons for Defense and Justice in Mississippi).
>
> The reality—which is underdiscussed but essential to an understanding of our current situation—is that the civil rights work of Dr. King and other leaders was loudly opposed by overt racists and quietly sabotaged by cautious moderates. We believe that current moderates sincerely want to condemn racism and to see an end to its effects. The problem is that this desire is outweighed by the comfort of their current circumstances and a perception of themselves as above some of the messy implications of fighting for liberation.
>
> The civil rights movement was messy, disorderly, confrontational and yes, sometimes violent. Those standing on the sidelines of the current racial-justice movement, waiting for a pristine or flawless exercise of righteous protest, will have a long wait.

This piece highlights a flawed consensus memory of the Civil Rights Movement and indicts it for hindering present efforts for freedom. The both sides narrative was insinuated not just by rightwing pundits but also by most mainstream media outlets, which were eager to be "objective" and "evenhanded" in their coverage by avoiding the charge that they "supported violence." Here, the 1968 lens obscured the fact that White supremacists marched through a college town in the United States in 2017, making no attempt to disguise their identities, and physically attacked people, killing one. Instead, the 1968 lens ginned up national anxiety rooted in an incomplete and faulty narrative of the 1960s, and prevented a broad-based and unequivocal repudiation of White supremacy. Throughout the book, we will see more instances of the 1968 lens at work in interpretation of freedom singing and its contexts. Deconstructing this interpretive process is vital not only for accurate and meaningful analysis of freedom singing after 1968, but also to prevent further stonewalling of present movements for freedom in the United States and beyond.

Returning to the Contemporary Vignettes

Now that the 1968 lens and the consensus memory it maintains have been laid out, as well as the counter-memory that the Long Civil Rights Movement provides, let's return to the contemporary vignettes from the beginning of this chapter and look closely at the ways they mobilize the memory of the movement.

In addition to arguing that the moment the protests over George Floyd's murder turned from "sporadic violence" into a movement was when they began singing traditional freedom songs, Robert Darden also recounts that when he finally heard the protestors begin to call on the songs of the Civil Rights Movement he "knew that everything would—eventually—work out."[62] Amid quotations from John Lewis, Harry Belafonte, and Prathia Hall, Darden waxes poetic about the "transformational power" of traditional freedom songs and their ability to "transcend time" and provide a "fountain overflowing with love and encouragement." In a telling aside directed at police, Darden argues that "to those who stand and watch over these demonstrations, you don't have to worry about the singers. It's the folks who aren't singing that you need to keep an eye on."

Even an expert on the music of the Civil Rights Movement such as Darden is susceptible to the 1968 lens. Darden is drawing from the consensus memory of a sanitized movement, and using freedom songs as his marker for when contemporary movements begin to live up to that memory. Just as Jon Michael Spencer equated Black silence with Black rage in his narration of the late 1960s, so also do Darden and other anxious observers view current events through the 1968 lens. Darden goes so far as to warn the police that the nonsingers should be surveilled with suspicion—a suggestion that is not only counterproductive but dangerous for the activists on the frontlines of the Black Lives Matter movement struggling against police brutality.

At Tyre Nichols's funeral, the Rev. Al Sharpton mobilized a similarly mythic memory of King and the movement, which he used to judge the five Black police officers who attacked Nichols, finding them wanting. In the sense that Sharpton is connecting the movement of today against police brutality with the long Black Freedom struggle, this framing is productive.[63] And yet, Sharpton's analysis, as he presented it in this eulogy, seems to lack a thorough critique of a system that produces police officers who enforce White supremacy regardless of their own race. Rather than question the entire institution of U.S. policing, Sharpton's proposed solution was for Congress to pass the George Floyd Justice in Policing Act, a reform bill that had stalled in the Republican-controlled Senate the year before. Not only did Sharpton not systematically critique U.S. policing, he implied support for policing in general by saying, "Many of us are concerned about public safety, but you don't stop criminals by becoming criminals yourselves. You don't stop thugs by becoming thugs yourselves. You don't stop gangs by becoming a gang yourself." The use of the word "thugs" is particularly troubling in this case because it validates the stereotypes and derogatory language that police departments have used to justify the very types of task forces that killed Nichols. When "A Change Is Gonna Come" was sung at the conclusion of the funeral, the meaning of the performance in relationship to the Black Freedom Movement was obscured. Exactly what change is being advocated here? Is it change that is stuck in the time period from which the song itself comes, or is it change that is listening to the updated demands of the present movement? In both of these cases, the consensus memory of the Civil Rights Movement and its bowdlerized heroes presents complications for ongoing Black Freedom struggles, and in both, singing plays a central, if convoluted, relationship to that mobilization of memory.

2

From Freedom Song to Freedom Singing

> The younger people may not sing "This little light of mine." They do sing a freedom song. If you listen to their songs, they are very, very clear about using their songs to echo the world they look at. I don't know where it will go, where it will end. They don't have to sing what I sing but I have to tell them how I did what I did and they can make some use of it. A freedom song is a freedom song. The only requirement within the African tradition is that it must express your need to change your situation.
>
> —Bernice Johnson Reagon

On June 24, 2014, congressional leaders marked the fiftieth anniversary of the passage of the Civil Rights Act of 1964 in the Capitol Rotunda by presenting Martin Luther King Jr.'s children with a Congressional Gold Medal in his honor. The event was punctuated by a performance of "We Shall Overcome" in which these congressional leaders crossed arms and held hands while they sang.[1] The performance was very formal; it featured a full choral arrangement of the song sung by the U.S. Army Chorus, was accompanied by piano, and included an elaborate choral tag to which the crowd responded with polite applause. Video of the performance appears even stiffer because of the awkward body language of the members of Congress present. Conspicuously, Republicans Mitch McConnell and John Boehner are not singing and appear uncomfortable with the ritualized holding of hands that accompanies it. The most enthusiastic participant is Nancy

Pelosi, who later remarked that she "thought it was the best thing" and that it "brought so many good things together about our country."[2] In the same interview, Pelosi pointed to the evocative symbolism of the location with busts of Dr. King and Abraham Lincoln in view during the performance.

Before the performance of "We Shall Overcome," several of the members of Congress made speeches that attempted to marshal the symbolic power of the moment for specific and conflicting political ends. Civil Rights Movement participant and Democratic Congressman John Lewis mentioned the recent Supreme Court decision that struck down provisions of the Voting Rights Act of 1965, legislation for which people in the movement struggled and died, and argued for legislation that would restore those provisions. Republican Senate Minority Leader Mitch McConnell praised the bipartisan work of Republican senators from 1964 and imagined a Senate that could "be that place again," a veiled critique of Democrats in the Senate who, despite a Republican majority in the House, had been making it difficult to legislate a Republican agenda since 2012 by using their narrow majority in the Senate to stymie Republican efforts.[3] Although many would consider this a clear instance of freedom song without a second thought, it is important to look beyond the mere sounding of a canonical freedom song to deeper questions. Is this performance connected to the Black Freedom Movement? If so, in what ways, and how do those ways impact how we hear and interpret the singing? If not, how can we alter our understanding of freedom song to account for performances such as this? If one deemphasizes the song being sung and focuses on the act of the singing itself, how does that change one's interpretation of this sound event? Perhaps the situation is even more complex than an either/or will accommodate. We might pause to consider how to interpret and analyze a song's meanings when everyone singing and receiving it understands it differently.

Three weeks later in Staten Island, NYPD officers approached and harassed Eric Garner, whom they suspected of selling individual cigarettes without tax stamps. Officer Daniel Pantaleo put Garner in an illegal chokehold and restrained him in a prone position, while he cried out "I can't breathe!" eleven times. Garner was pronounced dead at the hospital one hour later. His death was ruled a homicide by the New York Medical Examiner's Office; the medical examiner determined the cause to be breathing difficulty due to compression of the neck and chest, with asthma, heart disease, and obesity listed as contributing factors.[4] Despite that determination, a grand jury elected not to indict Pantaleo on December 3, 2014.[5] Widespread protests and demonstrations followed, with Garner's last words

"I can't breathe!" crystallizing as a new rallying cry for the Black Lives Matter movement against police brutality.

The Peace Poets, who in their words are a "mix of a rap crew and a humanitarian initiative, a blend of a rising artistic army of music makers who are making freedom songs contagious," composed a song called "I Can't Breathe" in response to Garner's death.[6] The lyrics of the short refrain are:

> I still hear my brother crying "I can't breathe"
> Now I'm in the struggle singing "I can't leave"
> We're calling out the violence of these racist police
> And we ain't gonna stop 'til our people are free!

The Peace Poets joined with the activist campaign Communities United for Police Reform to block the Manhattan Bridge while singing "I Can't Breathe."[7] In a case of social media activism, actor Samuel L. Jackson recorded himself on December 13 singing the song and challenged "all you celebrities who poured ice water on your head [a reference to the recently viral 'ice bucket challenge' in support of ALS awareness]" to record themselves singing the song in solidarity with the movement against police violence. In Jackson's video, he updates the lyrics:

> I can hear my neighbor crying "I can't breathe"
> Now I'm in the struggle and I can't leave
> Calling out the violence of the racist police
> We ain't gonna stop 'til people are free

The song quickly became prominent in protests and Jackson's #icantbreathechallenge spread widely on social media. This instance showcases a newly composed freedom song functioning in the traditional space of protest, but also sounding through social media. The Peace Poets explicitly consider their work a part of the freedom song tradition. How do traditional understandings of freedom song map onto both the composition and use of new freedom songs? What work can freedom song do via social media in circumstances such as this, and how does it differ from traditional conceptions of freedom song's role?

On July 13, 2015, after being arrested violently at a traffic stop, Sandra Bland was found hanged in a holding cell in Waller County, Texas, under suspicious circumstances. The FBI investigated and determined that, though there was no foul play, the police department had violated proper procedure at a number of points in the process of detaining and holding Bland. The video of Bland's arrest and the news of her death sparked protests and continued organizing from groups such as Black Lives Matter fighting for an end to police brutality and for increased accountability. Exactly one month later, hip hop artist Janelle Monáe, with her musical collective Wondaland, released the protest anthem "Hell You Talmbout" and began appearing with Bland's mother Geneva Reed-Veal to lead protestors in singing.[8] The song is visceral and catchy; it combines a driving percussive rhythm, the chanting of the names of victims of police brutality such as Sandra Bland, and the full-throated singing of a simple and singable refrain. The song ties into the freedom singing tradition further by heavily utilizing call and response—after each name is chanted a collective responds "say her name!" or "say his name!," a phrase that has become a rallying cry for the movement against police violence. By traditional genre definitions, can this be analyzed effectively as a freedom song? It contains mostly chanting, it began its life as a studio recording, it does not contain any references to Christian spirituality, and yet it is deeply connected to the larger Black Freedom Movement and functions perfectly within the freedom singing tradition.

On July 5, 2016, Alton Sterling was shot and killed by Baton Rouge, Louisiana, police while selling CDs outside a convenient store. The next day, Philando Castile was shot dead in his car by a St. Paul, Minnesota, police officer after being pulled over for a broken taillight. On July 7, Black Lives Matter rallies were held throughout the country. At many of the rallies, including one in downtown Los Angeles, protestors used an adapted version of Kendrick Lamar's 2015 track "Alright" as a protest chant.[9] Most adaptations of the song feature the repeating of the refrain "we gon' be alright" with vocal interjections by a song/chant leader that spur the next repetition. This example raises the question of whether a chant such as this one can be considered a part of the freedom song tradition. It is arguably not "song" by any technical definition. And yet, we do have a form of vocal musicking connected to the Black Freedom Movement being used at a protest. Does limiting our view to songs that sound similar to the songs of the classical phase of the movement prevent us from hearing where the freedom song tradition is still active and how that singing is articulating a connection to the history of the Freedom Movement? "Alright" and the other examples above seem to trouble the preexisting water in a way that calls for new pathways of freedom song analysis.

* * *

These four contemporary vignettes highlight the quagmire that can result from applying restrictive analytical frameworks when discerning the meanings of freedom song. The complexity of the meanings generated by these instances raises several questions: What has the term "freedom song" meant, and what are its most prominent meanings now? What types of musicking can and should be considered within the stream of freedom song in order to capture a fuller picture of the myriad ways the Black Freedom struggle is transmitted in U.S. culture?[10] How can we better account for the full musical, social, political, and cultural context of freedom song after 1968? Would freeing our understanding of freedom song from the bounds of repertoire aid us in analyzing the breadth and depth of its activity?

This chapter argues that the shift from understanding freedom song as a repertoire to analyzing it as an activity will greatly aid in evaluating its importance after 1968. It first reviews definitions of freedom song in the literature with an eye toward how these definitions often preclude analysis of freedom singing in its fullness. It then adapts Christopher Small's concept of musicking, infusing it with other ethnomusicological work and literature on improvisation, to theorize "freedom singing" as a fruitful analytical framework that allows for more thorough and flexible analyses to occur. The chapter concludes by returning to the contemporary vignettes, considering them in light of this new analytical framework, and proposing a working definition of freedom singing for the remainder of the book.

Defining Freedom Song

Before proceeding, we must define the terms of analysis and review how the literature has approached freedom song. Once the ground on which we stand is established, we then can expand how students of freedom song have understood it to date. The most pressing question to answer is: what is freedom song? Although musicological engagement with the Black Freedom Movement has been sporadic, several foundational studies have offered answers to this question. Bernice Johnson Reagon was the first to devote significant scholarly effort to the songs of the Civil Rights Movement. Her role as a member of the Student Nonviolent Coordinating Committee (SNCC) and the SNCC Freedom Singers during the 1960s, in combination with her scholarly reputation, gives significant weight to her interpretations of the music of the movement. Reagon's dissertation established the methodological terms of future freedom song scholarship by putting forth a taxonomical method for classifying songs employed in the movement, by arguing for the formational role of African American congregational singing in the freedom singing of the Civil Rights era, and by defining the freedom songs as oral history source material worthy of rigorous scholarly attention.[11] Reagon's work as a whole is some of the most sustained engagement with the protest music of the Civil Rights Movement.[12] In an influential article entitled "African Diaspora Women: The Making of Cultural Workers," Reagon further theorizes that the African American women leaders of the movement did "cultural work," and emphasized African American spiritual praxis as the framework through which she has studied and interpreted the singing of the movement.[13] Alongside Reagon's foundational work, practitioners, folklorists, musicologists, and scholars from related academic fields of study have added to the historiography of freedom song.[14]

Along with these foundational studies of the songs used by the protestors in demonstrations and mass movements during the 1950s and 60s, recent scholarship has begun to expand the notion of the freedom song. In a subtle way, music scholarship has made the same move as historical scholarship on the Civil Rights Movement in shifting its focus from the heavily church-influenced, rural Southern movement, to the more urban, secular, youth-centric Northern movement. This shift was signaled by the expansion of the genre of freedom song to include more than the group participation songs widely associated with the movement. In her groundbreaking article on Nina Simone, Tammy Kernodle weaves Simone's music from the late 1960s into the narrative of freedom song.[15] Other authors such as Ingrid Monson, Scott Saul, Brian Ward, and Pete Guralnik have continued expanding the scope of music and musicians considered relevant to the Black Freedom Movement to include the contributions of jazz and rhythm and blues artists (among others).[16]

The vast majority of this literature on freedom song implicitly assumes that it is, first and foremost, a genre—often while assuming a definition of said genre without explicitly articulating it. "Freedom song" does not, however, receive its own entry in the Oxford Dictionary of Music (formerly Grove) and is not mentioned by name in Oxford's article on protest music.[17] In the Encyclopedia of African American Music it is defined under the cumbersome, more restrictive, and rarely used moniker "Civil Rights Movement music." In her 1975 dissertation, Bernice Johnson Reagon does offer a broad definition of freedom song as "a body of songs sung in jails, meetings, rallies, on marches, and in informal settings, that utilized all forms of Black music from all segments of the Black community, and were linked by a common message: involvement in the Civil Rights Movement."[18] This description is narrow enough to provide some definition to what she is considering freedom song and expansive enough not to exclude any music used during the primary years of the movement. Despite the breadth of this foundational definition, however, most scholars have defined freedom song by the small canon of songs that have survived in popular memory.

This canon developed not because movement participants gradually forgot the nuances of their experiences and the breadth of the musicmaking in which they were involved (although this certainly happened), but as a result of the direct interventions of people doing canon-forming work. The most significant of these people initially were Guy and Candie Carawan, who not only shaped the canon by composing songs themselves, but also collected, compiled, and taught songs to movement participants.[19] They were often responsible for introducing songs that were specific to certain localities to broader movement culture, as has been well documented in the case of "We Shall Overcome."[20] The Carawans were specifically interested in the preservation and importance of roots/folk music to the struggle, which can be seen in their writings and recordings.[21]

In an attempt to describe the music within this canon, many of the foundational writings on freedom song have developed taxonomies for categorizing different types of freedom songs. Bernice Johnson Reagon argues that "the songs created during the Civil Rights Movement can be placed in two general categories: group participation songs and topical songs. Different methods of performance and creation characterize each type."[22] Reagon defines group participation songs as "those most widely recognized" songs that "were easily sung by masses of people as they participated in various group activities of the Movement." She goes on to say that "the musical structure, historical base, and function of this body of song has its roots in Black culture." Serge Denisoff and Thomas Turino establish similar dichotomies between what they label magnetic protest song versus rhetorical protest song and participatory versus presentational performance, respectively.[23]

One of the major flaws in these taxonomical systems is that they set up a dichotomy between the participatory and the performative, a tension that tends to privilege the participatory over the performative as a more "authentic" and grassroots expression of the Black Freedom struggle. Many of the early documenters of freedom song such as Guy Carawan were deeply invested in preserving and elevating Black folk traditions (what Carawan sometimes referred to as "genuine Negro music") rather than Black popular styles as the heart and soul of the movement.[24] Ron Eyerman and Andrew Jamison transmit some of this bias by locating the efficacy of freedom songs as sources for collective identity formation in the fact that "their melodies were simple but emotive, geared to being sung collectively. They invited participation, simple repetitive choruses, and rhyming couplets, with an emotional and political content."[25] This evaluation has broad implications for what has and has not been considered within the stream of freedom song to this day. Moreover, the emphasis U.S. culture has placed on its consensus memory of the good 1960s as epitomized by the Southern, church-based movement led by King has further tilted what is considered the core of the freedom song repertoire toward this folk repertoire and away from the diverse interactions of other musicians with the freedom singing tradition.

Viewing freedom song as a genre creates the need to define the boundaries of the genre. In the case of freedom song this is even thornier a proposition than is typical. If the songs as a defined repertoire are the primary object of research, what do you do with the singing of the Christian hymn "Onward Christian Soldiers" at a mass meeting? If the text or performance is not altered in any way from normative practice, is it still a freedom song or is it simply a hymn? Where do you draw the line between popular music and freedom song when it flows in and out of the tradition so freely? What are the criteria for inclusion of new compositions into the genre?

Even those scholars such as Kernodle and Ward who are working to expand freedom song to include a broader array of musics still tend to work from the premise that freedom song is a genre whose boundaries need to be widened. As genres and subgenres have proliferated since the 1960s, maintaining a firm grasp on where participants, practitioners, and scholars draw these boundaries has become increasingly untenable. Music scholarship has largely ignored the ways in which many forms of musicmaking interact with the Black Freedom Movement because viewing freedom song through the lens of genre has limited the conversation. But a different approach is in order. For the remainder of the chapter we turn to understanding freedom song as a *practice*, not as a *thing*. We must move from freedom songs to *freedom singing* in order to better understand the way this tradition functions in the years after 1968. The light that the post-1968 years shed on the way freedom singing functions will also have implications for the study of freedom singing in the classical phase of the movement. We now turn to the work of Christopher Small to begin to establish this new framework for analyzing freedom singing in the post-1968 United States.

Musicking/Freedom Singing

Toward the beginning of his book *Musicking: The Meanings of Performing and Listening*, Christopher Small quips, "[T]here is no such thing as music."[26] Small goes on to clarify, "Music is not a thing at all but an activity, something that people do." He argues that the Western world has fallen short in its investigations into the meaning of music because it has reified music as an abstraction and gone about trying to understand that abstraction, while often ignoring the activity of musicmaking itself. While this problem is often more prevalent in the traditional musicological inquiry with which Small is familiar than it is in the field of ethnomusicology, a similar reification process has affected freedom song's historiography. In the same way that "music is not a thing but an activity," freedom song should not be considered an abstract collection of songs, frozen in time, but an activity—a living practice.

Scholars, participants, and other commentators have grappled with how to explain the power of freedom song and its pivotal role in the freedom struggle that erupted in the 1950s. While focusing on the songs themselves and the ways in which songleaders manipulated them *as objects*, these commentators have left a bevy of musical meaning unexplored, musical meaning that can help us understand how and why this way of musicmaking has maintained its influence since 1968. For these reasons, the term *freedom singing* as theorized here more accurately describes the source of meaning and power at stake in these instances. Freedom singing as a framework will also provide much-needed analytical flexibility, accounting, in a suppler way, for how different musical sources flow in and out.

This proposed analytical shift also helps overturn the effects of the 1968 lens as discussed in chapter 1. Rather than myopically focusing on instances of freedom song that conform to the misleading consensus memory of the Civil Rights Movement, freedom singing broadens what types of musicking (and what types of activists and activism) we consider relevant to the complex dynamics at work when people make music in conversation with the Black Freedom Movement, whether that be during the 1950s and 60s or after 1968. This shift should also lead to a renovation of the narrative of rupture and decline that surrounds the events of the 1960s and a nuancing of the before/after 1968 dichotomy.

In Small's context (the world of Western classical music), the emphasis on "the work" as the sole conveyor of meaning and the disassociation of the listener as participant in the production of that meaning is absolute. In the freedom singing tradition, we must contend with a different valuation: freedom singing in a more performative vein (versus a participatory or congregational vein) has been viewed with suspicion, primarily because it typically draws from more popular traditions and does not allow for the kind of folk participation that was held up as more authentic by early commentators on the music of the movement.[27] Even though the participatory has been elevated above the performative in freedom singing, the emphasis and location of meaning has remained with the songs as abstractions rather than the act of freedom singing. Shifting to freedom singing will free the field up to recover the importance of performer-driven freedom singing, and to investigate the ways that participation in this part of the tradition goes well beyond the performer.

Small further argues that once one shifts one's focus to the activity rather than the object, the meanings of music can be found in the relationships being articulated by the musicking:

> If we think about music primarily as action rather than as thing and about the action as concerned with relationships, then we see that whatever meaning a musical work has lies in the relationships that are brought into existence when the piece is performed. These relationships are of two kinds: those between the sounds that are made . . . and those between the participants in the performance.[28]

The relationships that are brought into existence through musicking articulate the value system of the group participating in the musicking. In this way, the rituals of musical performance serve to define individuals in relation to the group, define relations between groups, and define relationships that the individuals in the group aspire to create. In the case of freedom singing, one further relationship is articulated in musical performance—the relationship between the contemporary struggle for freedom and the Freedom Movement out of which freedom singing arose. Small argues for musicking's ability to articulate such ever-evolving relationships by saying: "The gestural language of a musical performance never means one and only one set of relationships but is open to reinterpretation over and over again as listeners create new contexts for their reception and their ritual use."[29]

Freedom singing has continued to articulate relationships unabated since 1968—relationships between individuals, between groups of individuals, between people and the ongoing movement, and between people and the cultural memory of the movement's classical phase. Freedom singing brings a world into being where relationships between individuals, relationships between races, relationships between people and their government, relationships between people and their environment, and relationships between people and their past are ideally defined. It is precisely the complexity of the relationships that people are articulating in the act of freedom singing that produce the power of their singing to buoy spirits, demand change, and even generate pushback. One of the primary questions of this book is: as we begin to pay attention to the breadth of the freedom singing tradition after 1968, what new relationships do we find being articulated between actors, between groups of people, and between the present and the past being articulated?

There is another outcome of conceiving of music as an object that applies to this work on freedom song: valuing the written text over the performed music leads to a problematic privileging of the "composer" as the arbiter of all meaning.[30] In the same way the composer becomes the ultimate authority in European art music, the song collector/transcriber becomes the authority on freedom song rather than the freedom singers doing the singing and articulating the meaningful relationships. This is an effect that is beyond the control of—and immune to the good intentions of—a figure such as Guy Carawan, who by most accounts was a great ally of the Black Freedom Movement but whose work has had a kind of sedimentation effect on freedom singing as a living tradition.[31]

Small was writing against the idea that symphony concerts are only (or primarily) articulating relationships with the past—with mythic composers long dead, with works frozen in time, with a style of music heard long ago. Freedom singing is rarely done for the purpose of "contemplation of the works" themselves. Instead, freedom songs as works are often viewed as utilitarian; they exist and are made to sound not as aesthetic objects but as fuel for whatever movement they are being mobilized to assist. Some interpreters have gone beyond this hyperfunctional understanding, but not to the degree necessary to capture the meaningfulness of freedom singing after 1968. We have often assumed freedom song carries the same meanings it carried in the 1950s and 60s, without fully interrogating the relationships to the past enacted in the singing. At the same time, traditional interpretations of freedom singing have not fully appreciated the evolving relationships being articulated in the continuing persistence of freedom singing in U.S. culture.

Small also discusses the role musicking plays in rituals that relate contemporary relationships to the myths of a culture:

> Myths are stories of how the relationships of our world, or a part of it, came to be as they are. They deal with exemplary acts of creation and destruction, carried out by exemplary heroes or villains, on a scale that ranges from the cosmic to the intimate and domestic, and those acts provide us with models and paradigms of human experience and behavior and lay the foundation for all social and cultural institutions. We can put it another way and say that the relationships established in the mythical time ("once upon a time" which is to say, out of historical time altogether) by the mythical characters give us models for how we should relate to ourselves, to one another, and to the rest of the animate and inanimate world.[32]

Small goes on to argue that "myth . . . is always concerned with contemporary relationships. Whether it is historically true is beside the point; its value lies not in its truth to any actual past whose reality we can establish or disprove but in its present usefulness as guide to values and to conduct."[33] Freedom singing after 1968 always participates in this liaison between myth and contemporary relationships. The myth of the sanitized Civil Rights Movement is invigorated or undercut by instances of freedom singing in U.S. culture after 1968. Uncovering the intricacies of freedom singing's connection to this myth and what statements it is making about contemporary relationships is a primary goal of this book's analytical technique.

It is not as if "freedom singing" is completely absent from the literature on the music of the Civil Rights Movement. On the contrary, several commentators have pointed to the experience of singing freedom songs as the location of their scholarly interest rather than the repertoire itself.[34] Despite this, however, discussions of freedom singing continue to center around the songs and the repertoire rather than around the act of singing.[35] The approach to music-cultural analysis described here is not entirely new to ethnomusicology or Black music research either.[36] Several studies within the ethnomusicological literature on Black music also inform "freedom singing" as a framework. Guthrie Ramsey's monograph *Race Music* develops an understanding of Black music as a signifying practice or discourse through which audiences generate and perceive meaning.[37] Ramsey's analyses center the interaction of music and cultural ritual in a way that complements Small's concept of musicking nicely. Ramsey also discusses spaces where African Americans create identity through music, such as the church, the cinema, house parties, the social dance, etc., as "community theaters" or "sites of cultural memory." Similarly, we can conceive of freedom singing as a site or practice in which identity is formed, relationships are articulated, and the consensus memory and future direction of the movement are contested by the articulation of counter-memories.

Benjamin Tausig has advocated for a shift similar to the one proposed here for protest music as a whole.[38] He argues that interpreters have missed much of the music accompanying dissent by focusing too narrowly on "protest music" and its generic conventions. Instead, he proposes "vernaculars of sonic dissent" "as an analytic that might aid in the recognition of the diverse ways that political dissent is made audible."[39] A parallel argument can be made about freedom song—that in order to hear, appreciate, and analyze the ways in which freedom singing continues to be meaningful after 1968, we must be attuned to what actual and varied sounds are accompanying the dissent of the ongoing Black Freedom Movement in the United States rather than searching solely for the familiar sounds of traditional freedom songs.

Andrew Mark has built on Small's concept of musicking from an ecomusicological standpoint, arguing that musicking on Hornby Island demonstrates the fruitfulness of the concept for understanding how community solidarity is built in the midst of social and environmental problems.[40] Mark says:

> Musicking, when observed as a social phenomenon, fosters particular social habits. When abstracted from genre and perhaps even place, the habits of musical coordination even appear potentially universal. Ensembles usually require participants to confront group decision making, consensus, organization, ego-management, leadership, visioning, fundraising, event planning, space management, power dynamics, neighborly volume negotiation, time management, media outreach, and—most important for ever-shifting environmental problems—creative response.[41]

These social habits that are practiced in the act of musicking begin to reveal the potential of an analysis of freedom singing that would take them into account. Instead of asking whether or not something "is a freedom song," would it not be more interesting to ask, what does this example of people musicking in relation to the Black Freedom Movement say about their group decision-making praxis, about how they view consensus between people of difference or between the government and its citizens, about their vision of a future that liberates all? The notion of how freedom singing articulates and develops solidarity between community members and between people and the environment will also be especially crucial in chapter 4, where we explore freedom singing during the beginning of the environmental justice movement with ecomusicological inquiry as a primary methodology.

Once one's attention is shifted from the songs as objects to the act of freedom singing, thoroughly understanding the intricacies of the practice, what social habits are being articulated and cultivated, and what memories are brought into play and why becomes necessary for complete analysis. Improvisation plays a central role in the praxis of freedom singing, and the social relationships and meanings that can be developed through improvisation are vital to understanding why freedom singing remains a living tradition in U.S. culture. We turn now to improvisation as an additional source of illumination on the practice of freedom singing.

Freedom Singing and Improvisation

When describing the role of the song "Amen" in the Nashville movement, Bernice Johnson Reagon said, "[T]he power of this traditional song came from the richness of Afro-American harmonic techniques and improvisation in choral singing."[42] Reagon has also argued that the freedom songs are "learned in the singing, unrehearsed."[43] T. V. Reed relates the introduction of new songs or new changes into the new freedom song repertoire to the "improvisations in jazz in which 'inspiration' is built on hours and hours of careful preparation." Ingrid Monson argues that "at the moment of performance, jazz improvisation quite simply has nothing in common with a text (or its musical equivalent, the score) for it is music composed through face-to-face interaction."[44] In a 1974 interview, freedom singer Jamila Jones said, "[W]e would make up songs. All the songs I remember gave us strength to go on. It was kind of spontaneous; if somebody was beating us over the head with a billy club we would start singing about the billy club, or either the person's name would come out in a song."[45] While the freedom song literature has established the importance of improvisation, it has overwhelmingly focused on how improvisational practices manipulate the freedom songs as texts, objects, or sound material. This emphasis on the song repertoire leaves unexplored the meanings generated in the context of improvisational freedom singing when the interpreter centers the practice rather than the repertoire.

In the Introduction to *The Fierce Urgency of Now*, Daniel Fischlin, Ajay Heble, and George Lipsitz ask the question, "What if, in fact, improvisation as a musical practice filters into other cultural practices, virally spreading its aesthetic and ethical challenges in as yet misunderstood or unstudied ways?"[46] They go on to argue that there is a "link between the performative symbolics of improvisational music and embodied rights struggles, both framed as a function of the performance of community."[47] In this sense, improvisation as a central component of freedom singing is both an organic use of a practice that is in harmony with the stated ambitions of the participants, but is also efficacious in furthering the sought ideals, perhaps in more powerful ways than we have realized. Peter Townsend makes a similar argument in relation to the collective improvisation of free jazz of the 1960s, calling it "not only a procedure, but an ideal."[48] "The listener, like the player," Townsend goes on to say about Ornette Coleman's *Free Jazz*, "is more conscious of interplay between the instruments, and of the need for responsiveness to this network of relationships within the group. This kind of collective work imposes its own etiquette, even its own ethics, which are different from the prevailing norms of jazz musicianship."[49] Townsend also notes that Charles Hersch hears *Free Jazz* as the musical analogue of Martin Luther King Jr.'s beloved or redemptive community, where the community, through equal and just relationships, overcomes the dichotomy between group and individual.[50]

The improvisatory practices of freedom singing index and generate a similar ethic. Freedom singing is the musical performance of community, a community where the difference and equality of members are simultaneously embraced, where members respond to each other creatively and with deference to each other's autonomy, where the diversity of the community's cultural resources are celebrated and drawn upon to cast a vision for the future. The musical practice of improvisation in freedom singing enables such relationships to emerge in the context of the Black American struggle for freedom and equality. In this sense, to borrow terms from theological inquiry, freedom singing is both *teleological* and *apocalyptic*—it both envisions the end goal of the creation and sustenance of this type of community, and it embodies and practices that future goal in the present.

Although many commentaries seem hyperbolic in their discussion of the power of freedom singing to effect change, there may be a power they have yet to fully claim. Angela Davis has argued that

> art may encourage a critical attitude and urge its audience to challenge social conditions, but it cannot establish the terrain of protest by itself. In the absence of a popular mass movement, it can only encourage a critical attitude. When the blues "name" the problems the [Black] community wants to overcome, they help create the emotional conditions for protest, but do not and could not, of themselves, constitute social protest.[51]

Davis does not give enough attention to what is happening in the act of musicking, however. If, as Panagiotis Kanellopoulos has said, "improvisation creates a 'public space' where freedom may appear,"[52] then the power of freedom singing is not just in the ideas it puts forward or the feelings it generates but in the actualization of the thing to which it aspires—people relating to one another in freedom.

Carefully considering improvisation also illuminates the relationship with the memory of the movement that freedom singing establishes. Fischlin, Heble, and Lipsitz argue that "[i]mprovisation is both deeply historical (diachronous) and profoundly here and now (synchronous) in its symbolics, both a remembrance of past freedoms and of human potentialities set to erupt in the present moment."[53] Because the foundation of improvisation is shared structures and resources drawn from the wells of cultural experience, it is always connected to history, no matter how innovative the sounds are. At the same time, improvisation is a practice that emphasizes the contemporaneous. Being well versed in the past and fully present in the fleeting here and now are necessary prerequisites for good improvisational praxis. In the case of freedom singing, the historical referent is always the long Black Freedom struggle. In the post-1968 world, the events of 1954–68 loom largest in U.S. collective memory. This means that if we can think outside of the box of freedom song as a repertoire, we can investigate how even the most far-flung sounds people make in the movement for Black freedom are related to, and find their meaning in, the pre-1968 Civil Rights Movement. Focusing on the practice rather than the repertoire is the key to liberating ourselves from the limitations in the current conversation.

Returning to the Contemporary Vignettes

How does this new theorization for understanding the freedom singing tradition work in practice? What sound practices can we highlight in order to explore the meanings being generated in freedom singing? What different meanings are generated when we attend to the act of singing more than the songs as objects and discern how contemporary practice is connected to memories of the movement? To answer these questions, we turn back to the contemporary vignettes that began the chapter.

Vignette one featured a performance of "We Shall Overcome" in the Capitol Rotunda at a fiftieth anniversary commemoration of the passage of the Voting Rights Act. The most conspicuous participants were Republican Speaker of the House John Boehner and Senate Minority Leader Mitch McConnell, alongside Democratic House Minority Leader Nancy Pelosi, Senate Majority Leader Harry Reid, and Congressman John Lewis. Lewis was present to speak from his experience as an active organizer in the Civil Rights Movement that secured the passage of the Voting Rights Act in 1965. McConnell and Boehner appear to be very uncomfortable with the performance; it is clear that McConnell is not singing and Boehner only joins in hesitantly on a phrase or two. John Lewis is singing with a determined expression on his face after speaking about the gutting of the Voting Rights Act for which he marched and bled in the street in the 1960s. Nancy Pelosi is singing with a smile on her face. Harry Reid appears as uncomfortable and deadpan as McConnell and Boehner as he holds hands with them.

As an example of freedom singing, this performance is fraught. The competing attempts to frame the political moment that preceded the singing make clear that the participants are not in agreement on who "we" is and what "overcome" means. Not only this, but Lewis and McConnell are each struggling to marshal the memory of the Civil Rights Movement in their favor. McConnell is impugning Democrats for not cooperating with his agenda and attempting to use a memory of the passage of civil rights legislation that imagines it as a bipartisan effort of people of good will, who simply came together to do what was right. Of course, this is far from an accurate memory of the way the Voting Rights Act was passed. McConnell seems to view the present moment as a point on an inevitable continuum of progress, where things have gotten better and will continue to get better regardless of how civil rights legislation from fifty years prior fares during his tenure. Lewis has a more complicated view of the present; he understands that the gains made during the 1960s were made through massive organizing efforts, intense political pressure, and the willingness on the part of freedom fighters to sacrifice blood, sweat, and even their lives. Based on her comments after the ceremony, Pelosi seems not to have noticed the inherent contradictions of this act of singing. Her brand of optimistic White American liberalism allows for an oversimplification of the problems and the road to the solutions. What does it mean to participate in freedom singing in such a context?

As mentioned above, students of music, politics, and race can (and should) allow for the openness of interpretation that accompanies any act of musicking to exist here as well. It is certain that McConnell, Lewis, Pelosi, and every other individual in the room will make different individual meanings for themselves in the act of freedom singing. If one were viewing this performance from a repertoire-based approach to freedom song, one might discuss the long-reaching impact of "We Shall Overcome" and its prominent place in the canon of freedom songs. One might even go so far as to argue that performances like this signal that "We Shall Overcome" has become more than a freedom song—it is now a "great American" song with the potential to unify Americans around our values and our history of progress.[54]

Contrary to the way it was often sung during the classical phase of the movement, this performance of "We Shall Overcome" is prefixed, allowing for no improvisational possibility in the act of singing. There is no life or creative tension that is opened up by the singing; this is evident in the body language and lack of vigor with which the visible members of Congress participate. The civilians present follow the lead of the U.S. Army Chorus, a representation of U.S. imperialism and military might. Not only does this contradict the political philosophy of many movement participants who opposed state violence and U.S. imperial escapades around the world, but singing an arrangement that ascends through two key changes before an elaborate choral finish creates a triumphalism that, to this author's ear, is at odds with the competing frameworks proffered by Lewis and McConnell beforehand.[55] There is no sense that this singing is bringing these competing sides closer together in a relationship of reconciliation or compelling those present toward an as of yet unattained future; on the contrary, the singing creates a finality that relegates the circumstances of the passage of the Voting Rights Act to blurry memory and blesses the present indiscriminately.

This example of freedom singing is complex in that there are various competing individual interpretations colliding with a collective ritual that props up damaging myths about the Civil Rights Movement, oversimplifying and appropriating its challenge, and papering over with a false unity the actions taken by the very body doing the singing to reverse the gains made by the pre-1968 movement. Focusing solely on the fact that a freedom song was sung would cause one to miss the relational work being done in the act of singing. Ultimately, the relationships articulated by this moment of freedom singing are alienating. The participants are alienated from each other, and the cultural memory being enacted is alienated from the movement it purports to memorialize.

Under the conventional narrative of the Civil Rights Movement, it would be difficult to place or interpret the featured song of vignette two, "I Can't Breathe" by the Peace Poets, as a part of the freedom singing tradition. If freedom singing was silenced as Black Power arose in the late 1960s, then students of this repertory would consider that such newly composed songs for contemporary movements should either be considered passé or severed from the pre-1968 movement. The Peace Poets, however, consider their work to be in the freedom singing vein and the use of "I Can't Breathe" in the Black Lives Matter (BLM) movement does perform connective work between BLM and other incarnations of the Black Freedom Movement that have preceded it.

In their press kit, the Peace Poets say that they "have made an indelible mark on the social movements of our times by supporting the reemergence of the art of collective singing in action."[56] Although one of the conceits of this book is that the "disappearance" or "silence" of freedom song after 1968 has been overemphasized, the fact that the Peace Poets see their work as restoring the place of collective singing within social movements articulates an important connection to the pre-1968 movement. The Peace Poets also shared the stage with Sweet Honey in the Rock, among others, at the February 2017 relaunch of the Poor People's Campaign in New York City, clearly placing themselves within the tradition of King, but also calling into question the separation between contemporary movements such as BLM and the larger Black Freedom Movement of the 1960s. The singing of "I Can't Breathe" while blocking the Manhattan Bridge articulates a similar synthesis. The collective action of occupying a major thoroughfare in New York City while singing about the "violence of the racist police" troubles the dichotomy often enforced between the Southern singing movement of the 1950s and the Northern "silent," "angry" movement of the late 1960s and beyond. If one's analytical categories do not have space to include the Peace Poets, however, this synthesis may be missed or, at best, underemphasized.

The Peace Poets argue that the goal of their music is to "beautify" social justice movements and make them "more inspiring, effective, and sustainable."[57] They also explicitly tie their freedom singing to the type of relationships to which Christopher Small points in his work: "[The Peace Poets] create spaces of dignity, respect and healing. They connect people to each other, to history, to purpose and to the truth of our intertwined destiny."[58] The ways they see their musicmaking functioning within freedom movements sound remarkably similar to the ways participants and songleaders of the 1950s and 60s understood the work of their freedom singing. But in this case, these ideas work themselves out not just in singing together in the same physical space, but through the uniquely twenty-first-century medium of a social network platform.

What can we say about the relationships being established and/or articulated in the singing if the people singing are only singing together virtually? The best performances I have heard of "I Can't Breathe" are #icantbreathechallenge performances recorded by individuals or small groups of musicians and uploaded to YouTube or Facebook. The most striking aspect of these recordings is that many of them feature significant improvisation on the musical and lyrical material provided by the Peace Poets. These online freedom singers did everything from adding verses to the simple refrain to mixing Samuel L. Jackson's version on a turntable, to improvising entirely new melodies and words in alternative styles such as jazz or hip hop. These improvisations emphasize the individual creativity of each participant, providing a way for them to engage with the collective freedom singing by adding a musical representation of themselves to the online chorus.

The examples of this song being sung by a group at a protest, on the other hand, are generally weak; the singing lacks conviction, it deteriorates quickly, and does not seem to engender the sense of connection that activists point to as the most important goal of freedom singing. This type of connection was established, however, by the many recordings of "I Can't Breathe" that were uploaded to YouTube, Facebook, and other online platforms.[59] Person after person framed their performance by stating that they felt compelled to join in by adding their voice to the virtual collective. This type of participation does create a sense of solidarity for those submitting their version of "I Can't Breathe" online and increases their commitment to "the struggle," even if that struggle remains vague. This type of freedom singing provides a soundtrack for the increase in social media activism that has marked current efforts for social and economic justice. The question becomes: can a collective emerge from this collection of individuals that is powerful enough and committed enough to each other to drive a sustained, organized effort for change?

Vignettes three and four also raise concerns of categorization unless you consider freedom song as a process and not a genre. Freedom singing as a framework allows for the inclusion of Janelle Monáe's "Hell You Talmbout" and Kendrick Lamar's "Alright" in their production, performance, and appropriation as examples of musicking for and with the Black Freedom struggle. Bringing these examples into the fold of freedom singing deconstructs the false binary between the songs of the 1950s and 60s Civil Rights Movement and the hip hop and chant of today. As explored in the Introduction, commentators often associate singing with the "good 1960s," whereas the so-called less melodic forms of Black musicking such as hip hop become associated with the "angry" and "aggressive" late 1970s and beyond. Understanding the chanting of "we gon' be alright" as a part of the freedom singing stream allows for a similar kind of synthesis as singing while shutting down the Manhattan Bridge. These instances of musicking and the political actions they accompany are a continuation of the political action of Martin Luther King Jr., Rosa Parks, Ella Baker, Malcolm X, and Fannie Lou Hamer.

Toward a Definition of Freedom Singing

This chapter concludes with a working definition of freedom singing, which is used for the remainder of the book. Even as analysis of freedom song is unburdened from the boundaries that plague it, defining the term risks reinstating undue limitations. At the same time, without any definition we risk building on a concept that is too amorphous to bear the critical work asked of it. This definition of freedom singing attempts to leave enough flexibility such that it does not become too restrictive.

Freedom singing is *vocal musicking that interacts with the Black Freedom Movement, whether lyrically, melodically, or contextually.* Baked into this definition through the term musicking is the shift from a focus on the study of songs as objects or as a canonized repertoire to a focus on the act of making music in connection to the Black Freedom Movement, enabling the analysis to consider the myriad ways in which performers engage in and make meaning from this experience. In this definition "vocal musicking" is broadly defined as the practice of organizing sound produced by the human voice. Chant is intentionally incorporated into this model. This is important particularly for the study of freedom singing after 1968 when styles of musicking such as rap that draw more heavily on rhythmic vocal utterances rise to prominence. The term Black Freedom Movement (as opposed to Civil Rights Movement) is used to imply the more expansive understanding not bound by the short timeline of the classical phase of the Civil Rights Movement discussed in the Introduction.

This new definition is not meant to suggest that scholarship that focuses on the study of freedom songs as a genre is not valuable. Rather, in order to recover a fuller picture of the movement and to understand how the practice of freedom singing continues to be meaningful after 1968, students of freedom singing must add this approach to our toolkit. Studying freedom singing will still involve some of the types of analysis that are foundational to the study of freedom song. In order to study the act of freedom singing, one will still need to be able to trace a song's evolution through history. The studying of freedom singing builds upon the study of freedom songs rather than replacing it.

In addition, while it does not fall under the umbrella of this definition, nonvocal musicking within the Black Freedom Movement is both prominent and important. Instrumental musicking, particularly the music of jazz artists, was vital to the classical phase of the movement, and has continued to be integral after 1968. Instrumental music is simply beyond the scope of this book. However, the framework developed here should prove fruitful for scholarship on instrumental musicking within the Black Freedom Movement as well.

In moving from freedom songs to freedom singing, from genre to act, the practice of freedom singing after 1968 becomes more variegated and complex than traditional understandings of freedom song as a genre would have allowed. Equipped with this focus on freedom singing, the remainder of the book examines the practice in various contexts as an active and rich site of meaning-making in U.S. life, a site where meanings are both generated and contested in light of the actors' own political lives, the struggle to create a more just common life, and the memory of collective political struggles in the United States.

3

Bernice Johnson Reagon, Freedom Singing, and Musical Coalition Politics

While under emergency financial management in April 2014, the majority Black city of Flint, Michigan, switched its water source from Lake Huron to the Flint River. Unlike the water from Lake Huron, the less expensive water from the Flint River had not been treated with corrosion inhibitors. Lead leached into the water as it made its way through Flint's outdated plumbing lines. Over the course of 2015, doctors and public health officials discovered that around 12,000 children had lead poisoning and dozens of adults had cases of Legionnaires' disease likely linked to elevated lead levels. Governor Rick Snyder declared a state of emergency in January of 2016; later in the month, President Barack Obama declared a federal state of emergency as well. Public figures and activists—including pop superstar Beyoncé—reacted strongly to the Flint water crisis, and wasted no time connecting the poverty and demographic makeup of Flint to the crisis and the government's response.

On February 6, 2016, Beyoncé released the music video for her single "Formation," featuring a post-Katrina New Orleans where a Black child confronts, through dance, a line of police officers in riot gear.[1] The words "stop shooting us" appear in graffiti on a wall connecting the song's repeated rhythmic call to "get in formation" with the ongoing protests against police killings of Black men and women. The following day, Beyoncé and a crew of Black women dressed in Black Panther–inspired garb performed "Formation" at the halftime show of the Super Bowl, taking her political statement to arguably the largest stage in U.S. popular culture.[2] Beyoncé's outfit featured a gold X across her chest and the dancers even formed an X on the field during the routine, which many interpreted as an allusion to civil rights leader Malcolm X.[3] The references to Black Consciousness were made even more conspicuous by the context: Beyoncé's performance was staged as an interruption of the headliner Coldplay's set and of the Super Bowl's nationalistic-leaning program, which since September 11, 2001, has featured increasingly ostentatious, ritualized, and unquestioning support of the military and law enforcement. On the same evening as the Super Bowl performance, Beyoncé announced her Formation World Tour, and stated that a portion of the tour's proceeds would go to her charity organization in order to help victims of the Flint water crisis.

Although many affirmed her consciousness-raising music, activists and commentators were split on Beyoncé's motives and her commitment to the cause. Some positively connected her mode of performance with Black identity and activism. About Beyoncé's Super Bowl performance and the release of the "Formation" video, *New York Times* pop music critic Jon Caramanica said, "This is high-level, visually-striking, Black Lives Matter-era allegory. The halftime show is usually a locus of entertainment, but Beyoncé has just rewritten it—overridden it, to be honest—as a moment of political ascent."[4] In a review of the performance for the *Washington Post*, pop music critic Chris Richards wrote, "For an artist cranking up the politics this far into her fame, she might deserve an entire chapter in the great book of celebrity miracles. Yes, Beyoncé is still a one-percenter, but she doesn't seem disconnected, or even fake-connected. Her halftime gig reminded us of this."[5]

Caramanica's and Richards's effusive praise downplays the commercial aspects of Beyoncé's performance in favor of its political impact. Indeed, by their strong backlash, many conservative pundits confirmed the political power of Beyoncé's performance as well. Former New York City mayor turned conservative commentator Rudy Giuliani said of the performance: "I thought it was really outrageous that she used it as a platform to attack police officers who are the people who protect her and protect us, and keep us alive."[6]

It was not solely conservative pundits who were critical of Beyoncé's performance. Others drew attention to what they analyzed as Beyoncé's problematic commercialization of Black activism. Dianca London wrote her response in *Death and Taxes* magazine:

> Yes, "Formation" and its viral Super Bowl Sunday performance is inherently a black narrative, yet its mode of presentation is rooted in the same corrupt system that has led us to this historical moment we stand in now. Activism and consumerism are one and the same. Its impact is temporary and perhaps "ineffective" in the long run due to being crafted by a capitalist we so lovingly call Bey. The impact of her latest single and the visually arresting symbolism of her performance is undeniable, yet it is alarming how we as a community unabashedly endorse without question or pause the soft politics of pop icons. It's problematic to consume without caution, even if we see a reflection of ourselves, our mothers or sisters in their narratives.[7]

Well-known Black feminist thinker bell hooks penned a critique of *Lemonade*, the visual album from which "Formation" came, calling it "capitalist money making at its best." hooks's problem with "Formation" and *Lemonade*, however, was less rooted in its commodification of Black culture and more in its maintenance of patriarchy and its suggestion that violence is empowering. She argues that although the intention of *Lemonade* is to "challenge the ongoing present-day devaluation and dehumanization of the black female body," much of it "stays within a conventional stereotypical framework, where the black woman is always the victim."[8] hooks goes on to say that "contrary to misguided notions of gender equality, women do not and will not seize power and create selflove and self-esteem through violent acts. Female violence is no more liberatory than male violence."[9]

Those critical of Beyoncé from the left were suspicious of the lateness of Beyoncé's political conversion, whether or not she is able to overcome modes of racist and patriarchal representation, and the overt integration of capitalist endeavor with the radical politics of a group like the Black Panthers. In short, while conservatives questioned the political nature of the Beyoncé's performance in and of itself, some progressives questioned whether she was the right messenger.

Contrast Beyoncé's mode of political engagement with that of Rhiannon Giddens. Giddens was the frontwoman for the Carolina Chocolate Drops, a Black string band known for elevating African American contributions to the old-time string band tradition. Giddens often speaks about how many of the traditional songs she sings deal with racism implicitly rather than explicitly, and her work often has at its core the issue of racial and economic justice. After the passage of North Carolina House Bill 2 (HB2), which usurped municipal power and eliminated discrimination protections for LGBTQ individuals passed earlier by cities in the state, Giddens attended a protest rally at College Park Baptist Church in Greensboro, North Carolina.

At the rally Giddens led the gathered protestors in a rendition of two traditional freedom songs: "Ain't Gonna Let Nobody Turn Me Around" and "Woke Up This Morning with My Mind Stayed on Freedom." She dressed casually in a sweatshirt and jeans and drew no commercial attention prior to, or after, her participation. It is clear from video of the event that Giddens is not only familiar with the songs themselves, but is also an accomplished songleader, conversant in the cues and mores of freedom singing from the Civil Rights era.[10] She can be seen giving subtle hand gestures to the other singers indicating when to repeat and when to move to the next line. She also improvised new lyrics to "Ain't Gonna Let Nobody" pertinent to the situation: instead of "keep on walking," Giddens sang "keep on voting" and repeated the line several times for emphasis, generating an enthusiastic response from the audience.

All of this indicates a fluency with the freedom song tradition that, to my knowledge, Beyoncé has not demonstrated. Giddens is also from North Carolina and is connected to the activist community in the state. Four years before her involvement in the HB2 protest, she participated in the fight against Amendment 1, which outlawed same-sex marriage in North Carolina until the U.S. Supreme Court ruled laws banning marriage for same-sex couples unconstitutional in 2015. Her engagement is sustained and inconspicuous when compared to Beyoncé's. The persona she inhabited at the HB2 protest communicates the same perception of authenticity she cultivates in her commercial musicmaking.

Even so, her motives for participating in acts of political dissidence while also maintaining a performing career were questioned. In an interview for *Indy Week*, Giddens spoke about her decision not to cancel her shows in North Carolina after the passage of HB2, even while many artists did (including most famously, Bruce Springsteen):

> There was a lady who was like, "You can't say that you're fighting a battle while you're putting on a show that you're getting paid to do." I could also cancel, and then all of my guys don't get paid, and the crew doesn't get paid, and the theater doesn't get paid. So, yeah, I'm continuing with my shows, but I'm saying something about it, and I'm saying something in my shows about it. I've spoken to people in rallies about it.[11]

Giddens viewed her choice to be present in her home state of North Carolina and speak out as a more effective way to protest the passage of HB2, given the prominence of her voice and the ways in which it functioned in the public square. Giddens went on to frame all her commercial performances as politically engaged as well:

> People were coming, new to my page, maybe because I posted it, and they just think I sing songs for a living. Every show, I talk about slavery. I talk about oppression. I talk about stereotypes. I talk about hidden corners of history that need to be aired. Every show I do is fighting a fight. I know what my job is, and I'm going to do my job. And if I can convince one person in my audience who hasn't read the bill and maybe didn't think it was that bad of a thing to read it, great.
>
> I've written songs of protest. I've put them out there. I have a limited platform, but I'm going to do what I can with it, while not betraying what I'm already doing, which is already fairly heavy . . . . Is it Freedom Riding? No, I never said it was. I just do what I can. I feel like if we all do what we can, then we can get somewhere, whether that's with Bruce Springsteen canceling and making headlines, or whatever.[12]

Although Giddens means to downplay the impact of her performance by referencing freedom riding, in effect this reference solidifies the connection between what she is doing musically and the Black Freedom Movement. If the comparison were not being drawn, she would not feel the need to position herself and her musicmaking within a hierarchy of movement participation. This type of deference and humility to those who have gone before actually reinforces her understanding of the tradition, thereby reinforcing her musicmaking as a part of that tradition.

* * *

The juxtaposition of these two contemporary vignettes highlights several questions: How do performers use freedom singing to articulate their political identities and their relationship to the Freedom Movement? What types of freedom singing do different audiences receive as normative or "authentically" performed? Who, in the eyes of these various audiences, has the right to perform freedom song? What role can/does commercialism play in protest music more broadly and in freedom singing more specifically? How close does your connection with a social movement need to be for your musical participation to be meaningful?

While the performing career of Bernice Johnson Reagon is the focus of the remainder of the chapter, it began with Beyoncé and Rhiannon Giddens as a way to suggest that Reagon's freedom singing in the wake of the

Civil Rights Movement has great relevance for how we might arrive at a broader and more nuanced understanding of freedom singing in the present. As one of the most prominent songleaders during the movement and the most prolific scholar-performer of movement music after it, Reagon is responsible for both establishing lasting paradigms as well as expanding notions of what it means to perform freedom song that still resonate.

As a contested site of meaning-making, performances that include freedom singing are a rich venue for discovering how musicians, listeners, and commentators negotiate their own political, cultural, and commercial identities in relationship to this music and the larger Black Freedom Movement. Bernice Johnson Reagon is an apt case study with which to explore these issues because her career negotiates and blurs the boundary between the more commercial mode of freedom song performance Beyoncé inhabited in the above example and the less commercial mode Rhiannon Giddens illustrated. Giving the performances of Bernice Johnson Reagon a close reading shows how one of the most important interpreters of freedom song negotiated her emerging political identity through her music by insisting on a unique positionality with regard to other political and musical actors. In turn, what we learn from Bernice Johnson Reagon as a model and a precursor will allow us to approach the questions raised by the comparison between Beyoncé and Rhiannon Giddens with fresh ears. Reagon's career as a performer lays a pivotal foundation for understanding both Giddens and Beyoncé within the stream of freedom singing.

This chapter explores three periods of Reagon's performing career as efforts to articulate an emerging political identity. It begins with her work in the SNCC Freedom Singers and the Harambee Singers between 1961 and 1969, focusing on how she used performance in the Harambee Singers to begin to establish a political persona distinct from the one she inhabited during the movement that she would continue to hone throughout her career. We then move to a much less often discussed period of her work—her collaboration with Anne Romaine in the Southern Folk Cultural Revival Project (SFCRP) from 1966 to 1981. The chapter concludes with an analysis of Sweet Honey in the Rock's performance style while Reagon performed with the group and oversaw its direction. Moving from the Harambee Singers to the SFCRP, Reagon made musical attempts to cultivate the moments of collision and cooperation on which the praxis of coalition politics relies. In her sometimes contentious but always fruitful relationship with Anne Romaine, Reagon was able to further refine her individual identity in relation to the Freedom Movement, performance being one of the key tools she used for articulation of this identity. Sweet Honey in the Rock then represents the most mature articulation of Reagon's political thought and identity in performance. In the performances of Sweet Honey, one can see aspects of all of Reagon's previous work come to fruition, demonstrating a complex approach to freedom singing that met the challenges of a different time with expanded tools.

By viewing her performative work through the lens of coalition politics, Reagon curated an evolving political identity distinct from her previous movement activity but also implicitly critical of those in other strands of the Black Freedom Movement who argued for—and remained committed to—a radical separatism that nurtured blackness but often failed to engage potential partners. Much of Reagon's performative work is also an unexplored example of applied ethnomusicology. Throughout her performing career, Reagon's musical activity and academic theorizing flowed into and out of one another, leading to musical and cultural interventions in the South in the wake of the Civil Rights Movement that defined her own place in the struggle and demonstrated how freedom singing could be used vibrantly and purposefully beyond the context of the classical Civil Rights Movement protest.

Bernice Johnson Reagon and Freedom Singing in Performance

The guiding assumption of this chapter is that one constructs and maintains a political identity through musical performance. As Diana Taylor has said, "Performances operate as vital acts of transfer, transmitting social knowledge, memory, and a sense of identity through reiterated actions."[13] Taylor's work on performance and politics plays a role in how this chapter analyzes the effects of Reagon's performance, whether it is implicitly or explicitly political, as well as how Reagon communicates collective memory through performance. In this regard, Tia DeNora's work on music and identity is integral to this understanding as well. DeNora argues that while "identity has been recast conceptually as a product of social 'work'" in scholarship of the later twentieth century, "equally significant [to the construction of identity] is a form of introjection," which "involves the social and cultural activity of remembering."[14] DeNora adds that, in this process, music is a vital "part of the retinue of devices for memory retrieval (which is simultaneously memory construction)." Not only is music a site for memory in the reflective, backward-looking sense, DeNora continues, but it is also a "device for the generation of future identity and action structures, a mediator of future existence."[15] The connection between Black women musicians and memory is further quarried by Daphne Brooks, who argues that Black women musicians are "archivists, excavators and agitators who use sound and musicality as ways to galvanize and disturb historical memory in the public sphere."[16] It is valuable to hear Bernice Johnson Reagon's performances that center freedom singing as interventions that disturb historical memory in the public sphere.[17]

Judith Butler's theory of performativity has also been influential in this book's consideration of Reagon. While Butler's work focuses on gender, her understanding of the work of performativity itself is flexible and valuable in this context. Butler argues that gender is constructed by repeated performance of gendered acts, and that the gendered self does not completely precede or follow this construction but emerges within it.[18] Her concepts of what can be constructed through performativity can be expanded to include other political identities, specifically focusing on how those identities are clarified through musicking. In other words, Reagon articulates a political identity closely tied to the Freedom Movement through performance of freedom song. In keeping with Butler's understanding of gender, we can also understand that Reagon's political identity is not created by her performance of freedom song, nor does it precede it, but it emerges within the act of performing, and continues to emerge in repeated performance.

Moya Lloyd also offers incisive critiques of Butler's theory, particularly her concern with Butler's neglect of the space and context in which performance happens. In discussing Butler's tendency toward individuation, Lloyd says:

> What is occluded, as a consequence, is the space within which performance occurs, the others involved in or implicated by the production, and how they receive and interpret what they see [or hear]. The possibility for continual resignification immanent to performativity hides the fact that not all resignifications are pertinent or efficacious politically; indeed they are highly contingent. Only some performances in some contexts can impel categorical rethinking.[19]

Lloyd points us toward reception, audience, and context as vitally important to the effect and political consequences of performance. Along these lines, the chapter's analysis of freedom song performance also draws from Stanley Fish's reader-response theory, particularly the concept of the interpretive community.[20] There are many interpretive communities at work influencing the meanings of freedom song performances. To avoid investing the songs themselves or the performers with all the meaning-making potential, one must look to how interpretive communities bring their authority to bear on any instance of freedom singing. This analytical shift fits more comfortably with Bernice Johnson Reagon's own understanding of freedom song as "free" to be altered and invested with meaning by the communities that sing them.[21]

To fully capture all the intricacies at work in a performance, the chapter also draws on Christopher Small's *musicking* theory as detailed in chapter 2. Thinking of *freedom singing* instead of freedom songs invests the meaning in the act rather than in an abstract, static object or repertoire. This allows for much more flexible understandings of what is happening in a performance and the evolution of the music and its interpretation. This framework also allows an expansion of what counts as "freedom song" while directing our attention toward the musicmaking rather than the historicized song in some ideal form. Without this shift in focus, one would be left to search through Reagon's catalogue of performances after 1968 for the few instances in which she performed a traditional freedom song from the classical phase of the Civil Rights Movement.

The efficacy of this analytical frame is borne out when one notes the importance Reagon herself places on live performance and participation. She says:

> The premiere Sweet Honey experience is created *live* with and in our audiences, as well as within members of the group. We use the technologies of this century to extend that experience and to provide an expanded context. We have consciously decided to try to move this ensemble and her vision intact through this societal maze of that system—touring, creating new songs, recordings, television, films—always looking for new, expanding collaborations with others traveling similar paths. We have worked to maintain an integrity with our goal to offer a different standard for our time. It has been a constant struggle . . . . Our recordings were never the same as a live performance, but they serve as scores, a way for our audiences to find songs and lyrics they have heard us sing.[22]

Lastly, Thomas Turino's distinction between participatory and presentational performance is useful in this analysis.[23] Freedom singing tends to blur the dichotomy that Turino's taxonomy establishes. It is in the tension of this boundary blurring that much of the interest of freedom song performance can be found. The research questions posed above—what types of freedom singing are received as "authentically" performed, who has the right to perform freedom song according to the audience, what role can/does the commercial play in protest music—center around the intersection of the participatory and the presentational.

Freedom singing in performance then (1) is capable of transmitting social knowledge, memory, and identity; (2) is *performative* and constructs political identity; (3) is always embedded in a context, which includes the immediate setting and interpretive community but also always includes the memory of the Black Freedom Movement; (4) should be considered holistically in the musicking sense, focusing not solely on the "works" but on the entire act and process of freedom singing; and (5) can be participatory and/or presentational, with the boundary between these categories containing particularly fertile ground for analysis.

Musical performance, often in churches or in the concert hall, was always a part of the political toolkit of activists involved in the Civil Rights Movement. Music surrounded the activity of the Black community, including church gatherings and mass meetings. Musical performance was also an integral part of the protest traditions from which the Civil Rights Movement drew much of its tactical inspiration, including most notably the labor struggles of the early twentieth century. Beginning with the Montgomery movement and crystallizing in the Nashville and Albany movements, musical performance became a powerful tool for activists and participants in their freedom struggle. At the same time, throughout the years of the classical Civil Rights Movement, popular artists commented on, influenced, and participated in the movement with their recorded and live performances.[24] Taking our cues from the musicians and participants themselves, we can consider formal performance as a distinct context from protest and music during worship. Although these designations frequently overlap in the freedom singing tradition, participants often point to the commercial and presentational aspects of performance as characteristics that distinguish it from singing a freedom song during a march or singing "Wade in the Water" during a church service. However, let's pay special attention to when the boundaries erected between these contexts are transgressed.

Bernice Johnson Reagon and Musical Coalition Politics

In 1981, Bernice Johnson Reagon gave a talk at the West Coast Women's Music Festival that was later published under the title "Coalition Politics:

Turning the Century."[25] In the piece she argued that the way forward for activists was not the constructive and nurturing atmosphere of work with only like-identifying people (nationalism), but the uncomfortable and stretching atmosphere of coalition work, where activists cooperated while still emphasizing difference. It was an idea far ahead of its time—a time in which the popular (White) American imagination forwarded a colorblind ethic that effectively erased difference instead of pressing into it.[26]

Reagon's talk was a critique of feminists who hoped women's festivals and feminist gatherings would be a safe, homogenous place. Reagon believed that, in spaces like the West Coast Women's Music Festival, "woman" and "feminist" had always been categories full of differing identities sublimated to fulfill the illusion of comfort for the normative few. Her words on the topic are frank:

> We've pretty much come to the end of a time when you can have a space that is "yours only"—just for the people you want to be there. Even when we have our "women-only" festivals, there is no such thing. The fault is not necessarily with the organizers of the gathering. To a large extent it's because we have just finished with that kind of isolating. There is no hiding place. There is nowhere you can go and only be with people who are like you. It's over. Give it up.[27]

She goes on to offer a critique of nationalism as well:

> Of course the problem is that there ain't nobody in there but folk like you, which by implication means you wouldn't know what to do if you were running it with all of the other people who are out there in the world. Now that's nationalism. I mean it's nurturing, but it is also nationalism. At a certain stage nationalism is crucial to a people if you are going to ever impact as a group in your own interest. Nationalism at another point becomes reactionary because it is totally inadequate for surviving in the world with many peoples.[28]

Her view of this changing landscape was not negative or apocalyptic, however. Reagon understood how deeply the Black Freedom and feminist movements had formed her identity. She also understood, however, that the only way to organize effectively in the present crisis was to put the idiosyncratic concerns of each group into conversation, as challenging and even dangerous as the work would be.

This insistence on the crucial role of coalition work puts Reagon in continuity with prominent Black male thinkers of the Civil Rights Movement.

In "From Protest to Politics," Bayard Rustin argued, "We need allies. The future of the Negro struggle depends on whether the contradictions of this society can be resolved by a coalition of progressive forces which become the *effective* political majority in the United States . . . . The task of molding a political movement out of the March on Washington coalition is not simple, but no alternatives have been advanced. We need to choose our allies on the basis of common political objectives."[29] King articulated a similar sentiment in *Where Do We Go from Here?*, saying:

> What is most needed is a coalition of Negroes and liberal whites that will work to make both major parties truly responsive to the needs of the poor . . . . The ability of Negroes to enter alliances is a mark of our growing strength, not of our weakness. In entering alliances, the Negro is not relying on white leadership or ideology; he is taking his place as an equal partner in a common endeavor. His organized strength and his new independence pave the way for alliances. Far from losing independence in an alliance, he is using it for constructive and multiplied gains.[30]

Although Reagon's coalition politics embrace identity expression more forcefully than this, Rustin and King did argue for the political necessity and moral importance of building allies between groups of differing racial, ethnic, class, and gender backgrounds. Because of their respectability politics, however, Rustin's and King's insistence on cooperation with White allies was meeting resistance among younger activists by the mid-1960s. In this sense, Reagon's coalition politics were more in line with a figure such as Fred Hampton, whose "Rainbow Coalition" brought together White, Brown, and Black people to fight police brutality without requiring members to defer to the cultural expectations of a dominant group.[31]

In addition to continuing the legacy of the Civil Rights Movement's male intellectual leaders, Reagon's encouragement of coalition politics locates her at the forefront of Black feminist thought. Patricia Hill Collins connects the strategy of coalition building with transversal politics, which emphasizes seeking solidarity across difference while maintaining individual positionality.[32] Transversal politics was developed by Italian feminists and elaborated by Nina Yuval-Davis in the 1990s in reaction to the isolating effect that second-wave identity politics had on broader movements for justice.[33] bell hooks has also argued for a reassessment of the importance of solidarity among women after the whitewashed version of the concept had been deconstructed by women of color.[34]

Decades before feminist theorists developed the theory of transversal politics, and even before she gave her own trailblazing talk about coalition politics, Reagon prefigured this political work in her musical praxis. This chapter explores Reagon's musicmaking during the period after she left the Student Nonviolent Coordinating Committee (SNCC) in the mid-1960s. Reagon's musical activity during this understudied period in her career offers us a paradigm of the political strategy she would later articulate—a *musical* coalition politics. Reagon used musical coalition politics to facilitate her movement from spaces that nurtured her identity across uncomfortable boundaries in order to build effective coalitions. Reagon's activity in this period also adds to broader discussions about music and the Civil Rights/Black Freedom Movement. Most discussions of Reagon's participation in movement music focus almost exclusively on her participation in the SNCC Freedom Singers; however, if one considers Reagon's later performances and musical activities with the freedom singing framework, her career explodes previously constructed boundaries around freedom song and about the movement itself. Reagon's musical coalition politics were an embodied response to the changing front of the Black Freedom Movement, and they shed light on continuities that the dominant narrative of the movement downplays.

The Harambee Singers: Shaking Loose from Respectability Politics, Shaping a New Freedom Singing Identity

Bernice Johnson Reagon was born in Dougherty County (outside of Albany), Georgia, in October of 1942. She was the daughter of a minister and grew up singing in her rural, Black church. While she was an undergraduate at Albany State College (now Albany State University), she became involved in local civil rights organizing efforts that coalesced into a full-fledged movement in the early 1960s. During that movement, Reagon made a name for herself as a powerful songleader. After being suspended from Albany State for her political involvement in 1961, she entered Spelman College in Atlanta on a full scholarship, but soon discovered that she needed to be more directly involved in the movement. She returned to full-force organizing in late 1962, joining the SNCC Freedom Singers. The Freedom Singers traveled the country, bringing the movement into concert halls, and raising money and consciousness for the cause. Their most famous appearance was their performance at the 1963 Newport Folk Festival, which concluded with the iconic singing of "We Shall Overcome" to close the festival alongside luminaries of the folk revival Peter, Paul, and Mary; Bob Dylan; Joan Baez; and Pete Seeger.

Most histories of music in the Civil Rights era hold up the Freedom Singers as one of the premiere examples of the power of freedom singing. As we saw in the Introduction, however, several strands within the broader Freedom Movement, including many in the younger generation that Reagon was a part of, had begun to sour on freedom song as an effective tool or expression of their political agenda. In 1964, Reagon was back in Atlanta negotiating the raising of a small child, a career as a performer, and the completion of her undergraduate work at Spelman. She says of this period in her life:

> I began to look for ways to continue to be who I was. My life over the next seven years was full of a personal inner searching for balance with all my loves and wants, with a real practical experimentation to see if I could be a wife, mother, singer, and worker sharing the cultural history of my people.
>
> This period was turbulent because it marked a major transition for Black people. From the period of nonviolent demonstrations and "We shall overcome someday," to rebellions in the major cities of this nation, the transition was immersed in demands for acknowledgment of African Americans as a people with a culture and history worthy of being taught to all Americans. It was a time when I and many of our people went inside ourselves and our communities and reconsidered our sense of what was good and what was beautiful about us. The cry of "Black Power" which was first heard on the Meredith March in Mississippi in 1966, became a new breath of life as we struggled to become the people so many of us almost never got a chance to know.[35]

Already, Reagon was carefully considering the intersection of her personal, political, and musical identities, and how those identities interacted with the transitions happening in Freedom Movement activities around the country. She directly related her experimentation and her struggle to "continue to be who she was" with the changing front of the Freedom Movement. Throughout her career as a musician, activist, and public intellectual, Reagon constantly curated her musical and political identity and negotiated her relation to the Civil Rights Movement in the wake of her participation in it. Rather than jettison freedom singing as some of her generation advocated, Reagon expanded her use of music as a tool for exploring new political possibilities.

During this period of experimentation, Reagon was deeply embedded in the burgeoning Black Arts Movement in Atlanta as a logical extension of her movement organizing work and her musical prowess. During her time there, Spelman College hired Vincent Harding, the civil rights activist and historian, to chair the History and Sociology Department. In 1967, Eastern North Carolina native and poet A. B. Spellman—who had been a music critic in New York and a vital part of the Black Arts Movement there alongside Amiri Baraka—came to Atlanta.[36] Spellman, along with other artists in the Atlanta community including Reagon, started the journal *Rhythm*, which was "committed to Revolutionary Pan-African Nationalism" and sought to provide a Black Arts vehicle for local artists and activists.[37] In the wake of the King assassination in 1968, Harding, Spellman, and critic Stephen Henderson collaborated to form the Institute for the Black World (IBW), a think tank that hosted seminars and provided a forum for the discussion of a wide variety of subjects relevant to the Black diaspora. IBW was especially interested in promoting African American art and culture, and included in its statement of purpose that it would exist for the "encouragement of those creative artists who are searching for the meaning of the black aesthetic."[38]

During this same period, Reagon was producing the Penny Festival, a benefit concert and educational program that served as an investment in the local Black community and as a benefit for the Atlanta Cooperative Pre-school Center.[39] The Penny Festival, which only charged a penny for admission but encouraged donors to give more if they could, grew out of Reagon's "awareness of the need for an Afro-American cultural history program in the Atlanta community."[40] The Penny Festival drew from the resources of the Black Arts Movement community in Atlanta beyond Reagon as well; the 1968 festival featured a production about W. E. B. Du Bois entitled "The Black Flame" written by A. B. Spellman.[41] The productions also featured a vast array of Black music, from African American spirituals to African freedom songs, curated by Reagon and performed by artists in the Atlanta community.[42] It was after the first Penny Festival that Reagon formed the Harambee Singers with some of the women who performed with her.[43] The Harambee Singers were something of a riff on the SNCC Freedom Singers for a new time and place and a testing ground for many of the ideas that would come together later in Sweet Honey in the Rock.

The Harambee Singers was a "choral Black women collective" that intentionally nurtured Black history and culture and spoke directly to important Black activist and intellectual networks.[44] For instance, the Harambee

Figure 1. Flyer for "The Black Flame," 1968

Singers were one of several music groups that performed at the opening of the IBW. In the visual aesthetic, political surroundings, musical repertoire, and promotional framing of the Harambee Singers, one can see Bernice Johnson Reagon beginning to differentiate herself politically and musically from the political ethos of the dominant Civil Rights narrative. The Harambee Singers was Reagon's way of exploring "inside herself and her community," as she puts it above; their music and overall style was a deep affirmation of Black womanhood and a step away from the respectability politics that so frustrated younger people in the latter years of the classical phase of the Civil Rights Movement. In the Harambee Singers, Reagon embraced Black Power and the other more revolutionary forms of political engagement she was seeing around the world, without necessarily advocating for Black separatism.

The Harambee Singers sang primarily for Black Consciousness, Black Arts, Black Studies, and Black Power gatherings.[45] These performing contexts place them squarely within the core of a new radical Black politics that was emerging under the leadership of young leaders such as Stokely Carmichael in the 1960s. The Harambee Singers accented blackness with more ferocity than did earlier movement singing groups by participating in the reclamation of African traditional clothing and culture and emphasizing the connection with global postcolonial struggle that attracted the younger generation of Black activists at the time. Gone were the Sunday-best suits, ties, and dresses of the Southern, church-led Civil Rights Movement—in their place were traditional African clothing and hairstyles, a clear identification with younger, more radical politics. The name itself—Harambee—participates in the reclamation of African language and tradition that was active at the time as well. "Harambee" is a Swahili word and references a Kenyan tradition of community uplift activities.

The opening ceremony of Malcolm X Liberation University in Durham, North Carolina, is another example of the types of gatherings at which the Harambee Singers were performing and illustrates the evolution of Reagon's political identity during this period.[46] Malcolm X Liberation University formed as a result of the Black student movement at Duke University in 1969.[47] Rather than push for a Black Studies program that would be controlled by a predominantly White institution, many activists in Durham felt that an independent, Black-run, revolutionary institution of higher learning would better serve the Black community. Malcolm X Liberation University designed its curriculum around the pursuit of Black freedom and the dissemination of Black history and Black pride away from the insidious impact of institutionalized White supremacy.

On opening ceremony day, the people of Durham and gathered guests marched from Hayti—a historically Black neighborhood in Durham—to the new university's campus in downtown Durham singing "power to the people" accompanied by African drumming. In front of the university—which was painted black, red, green, and yellow and featured a prominent mural of Malcolm X with a raised fist—speakers, including activist, scholar, and founder of the school Howard Fuller and Betty Shabazz, Malcolm's widow, laid out the purpose and program of the school. The Harambee Singers, led by Reagon, performed in celebration of the school's opening and the ideals it represented. Their performance of the song "The Black Magician" is very much in keeping with Reagon's evolving singing and performing style. The women stand in a tight semicircle around Reagon wearing colorful, traditional African garb. The singing is accompanied only by handheld percussion instruments. There is a rhythmic drive and vocal tenacity to the performance that buoys the politics of the event and goes beyond the

Figure 2. People Marching to Malcolm X Liberation University's Opening Ceremony

Figure 3. Bernice Johnson Reagon and the Harambee Singers Performing at MXLU's Opening Ceremony

singing Reagon did with the Freedom Singers, prefiguring the style she would later master with Sweet Honey in the Rock. The lyrics eschew the Christian-centric themes of traditional freedom singing for an emphasis on African spirituality.

This performance at the MXLU opening was typical of the Harambee Singers at the time. In their musical repertoire, they frequently took on a more revolutionary edge than the Freedom Singers. According to Jamila Jones, one of Reagon's partners in the Harambee Singers, they never sang the types of songs that were typical of the Montgomery Trio and other groups spawned by the Civil Rights Movement.[48] Instead they took on a pan-Africanist, Black Power leaning in their repertoire and performance style choices. The repertoire they sang at Black Consciousness gatherings included songs such as "Move on Over or We'll Move on Over You," "Hands Off Nkrumah," "I've Known Rivers," "Joe Willie," and "I Am Black and I Have Beauty."

"Move on Over or We'll Move on Over You" was written by Len Chandler Jr. in 1965 and used at protests in the Civil Rights Movement, but it takes a much more aggressive stance than most freedom songs. It is sung to the tune "John Brown's Body." As is suggested by its evocative title, the tune was originally associated with the armed resistance to slavery and has a colorful history of text pairings, including "Battle Hymn of the Republic" by Julia Ward Howe and "Solidarity Forever" by Ralph Chaplin. Chandler's lyrics hark back to the original context of the tune and hold up John Brown as the freedom fighter exemplar. *Sing Out!* magazine printed the lyrics above an illustration of the January 1966 occupation of Greenville (Mississippi) Air Force Base by around seventy tenant farmers demanding land, food, jobs, and shelter. The protest was organized by SNCC and led by members of the Mississippi Freedom Democratic Party such as Unita Blackwell.[49] The illustration in *Sing Out!* features the looming figure of John Brown above the Greenville Air Force Base occupiers. This visual signifier connects the tone of Chandler's lyrics and the Greenville occupiers to John Brown's fiery and violent freedom-fighting.

The lyrics also explicitly critique the de facto anthem of the nonviolent movement, "We Shall Overcome," saying, "You conspire to keep us silent in the field and in the slum, You promise us the vote then sing us We Shall Overcome." There is a meaningful elision happening over the course of the song with regard to who the lyrics are addressing. Are these freedom singers singing to the White power structure? Are they singing to the U.S. government as verse three implies with its reference to a "dove of peace with bloody beak"? Are they singing to moderate elements within the movement itself as the reference to "We Shall Overcome" in verse two might imply? The lack of clarity is instructive for it reveals the frustration and the building militancy among some within the movement, including perhaps the women of the Harambee Singers. The lyrics are also a direct callback to Malcolm X's critique of "We Shall Overcome," and tie the singing of "Move on Over" with Malcolm's more militant brand of activism.[50]

"Hands Off Nkruma," another of the Harambee Singers' frequently performed songs, was written by Jimmy Collier—a Black folk singer who was a staff entertainer for Martin Luther King—and Rev. Frederick Douglass Kirkpatrick—an associate of King's in the Southern Christian Leadership Conference (SCLC) and cofounder of the Deacons for Defense and Justice, an armed, Black self-defense group. "Hands Off Nkruma" addresses the overthrowing of Kwame Nkruma, who became the first prime minister and president of Ghana after leading it to independence from Britain in 1957. It was widely suspected (and later confirmed) that the U.S. Central Intelligence Agency (CIA) was involved in the coup at the time the Harambee Singers would have been performing the song. The prevalence of "Hands Off Nkruma" in U.S. Black Consciousness circles demonstrates the degree to which young activists in the United States were in tune with events in Africa's freedom struggles and beginning to view their struggle through the lens of postcolonialism. Postcolonial thinkers such as Franz Fanon greatly impacted Black Consciousness in the United States, bringing to bear an entirely different philosophical grounding than the nonviolence of Rustin, King, Parks, et al. The lyrics to "Hands Off Nkruma," as one might expect, take quite a different tack than many traditional freedom songs, overtly critiquing global capitalism and federal law enforcement agencies such as the FBI and the CIA, and connecting the coup with the U.S. government's opposition to socialism and communism around the world, including the war in Vietnam.

"I've Known Rivers," "Joe Willie," and "I Am Black and I Have Beauty" were all songs of deep affirmation for Black culture and Black people. "I've Known Rivers" was a setting of the Langston Hughes poem, "The Negro Speaks of Rivers," which muses on the depth of the soul of Black people, on the connection of all Black people to Africa, on the greatness of the accomplishments of African civilizations, and on the deep connection to the land that people of African descent often feel. "Joe Willie" is a love song to African American men, a powerful reversal of the demonization they experience in U.S. culture writ large. "I Am Black and I Have Beauty" is a reference to a passage in the biblical book Song of Solomon. It affirms the unique beauty of Black features in a world that had attached (and continues to attach) negative connotations to Black physicality.

In keeping with their more revolutionary tone, the Harambee Singers worked to establish a musical persona that eschewed associations with commercial enterprise. There are no commercial recordings of the group, despite the fact that they continued to perform long after Reagon left. Their performances were solely for the empowerment and encouragement of the small groups of Black activists and politically engaged young people with whom they associated. A review of a performance of the group that kicked off the University of Michigan's Black Liberation Week in March of 1971 makes clear their antagonism to having their music consumed as entertainment:

> Stemming from African origins of voice inflection and the gospel tradition of employing the feet and hands as the base of the rhythm, their music is far from the Motown realm of music as a commercial venture. Instead it is music of the black revolution, a giving of the total soul in expressing black goals and values, without regard to white concepts of what music should be. "We talk to our people through music. We can't say it's entertainment because it's gotta be more than that. You can go to the movies for entertainment," explained Mattie Casey, one of the five Harambee Singers.[51]

In this excerpt, the reviewer and Harambee Singers member Mattie Casey connect the commercial sensibilities of Motown with White expectation, and the historically and culturally minded rhythm and singing style of the Harambee Singers with a deep expression of blackness that goes beyond entertainment. Anderson and Casey are tapping into a long-established dichotomy between Berry Gordy's Motown as the personification of Black, patriarchal middle-class bourgeois mobility and other, less overtly commercialized forms of Black popular expression such as the early soul music of Stax Records as "authentic" and inherently more in tune with resistant and revolutionary elements. While this perception is subjective and may be oversimplified, the meanings invested in certain types of cultural production are significant for evaluations of freedom singing, as evidenced by the reference to Motown as a way to enhance the revolutionary credibility of the Harambee Singers in the review above. Freedom song is typically given pride of place as an authenticity-bearing and authenticity-granting Black music, given its roots in the Black Freedom movement extending back to the resistance to slavery.

Even the visual markers of early soul, the natural hair and traditional African clothing with which the Harambee Singers signaled their affiliation with a more radical politics, eventually succumbed in part to the commercializing impulse they were initially resisting. This passage from Mark Anthony Neal is revealing in this regard:

> Generally associated with the genre of music that bore its name, throughout the 1960s soul became primarily linked to evocations of black communal pride. In this regard soul came to represent an authentic, though obviously essentialized blackness that undergirded the Black Power and Civil Rights movements that soul has come to be associated with . . . . With the subsequent annexation of black popular music, in which the soul genre was then the dominant popular form, the larger meanings of soul were also deconstructed for use within mass culture. Divorced from its politicized and organic connotations, "soul" became a malleable market resource merchandised to black and white consumers alike.[52]

It is this very process that the Harambee Singers were working against in their insistence on not becoming "entertainment" in a capitalist society. They saw their music and their mission as far too important to be deconstructed for use within mass culture. Not only were the Harambee Singers taking up the visual icons of early soul before they had been commercialized, they were also insistent on the specificity of their audience and their message. They were speaking affirmation of blackness to Black people as Black women and drawing from the deep well of the African American experience. This experience included the music of the struggle they had just come out of, but also had its eye on a new day of struggle where new identities and new resources would be necessary.

In their single-minded purpose, the Harambee Singers did not shy away from setting up boundaries and defining the scope of their project. In the same review of the Black Liberation Week performance quoted above, Harambee Singers member Jackie Howard explained that "Black people cannot be concerned with women's liberation because they are trying to be liberated as a whole."[53] This statement contains the complexity of the idiosyncratic issues facing the Black community, as well as the racism that Black women had already faced from White women in the feminist movement. It reflects the need for a safe space to have experiences of affirmation and nurturing before being asked to contribute to a movement that does not necessarily have the same goals and may not necessarily lead to liberation for Black people. It is also in keeping with one of the requirements of coalition politics. Patricia Hill Collins argues that private conversations and internal processes of affirming self-definition must happen before building coalition.[54] The Harambee Singers provided the space and the soundtrack for these conversations of self-definition in the Black Consciousness circles in which they moved. They, however, do not seem to have been ready during this period to do what Hill Collins describes as the next step in building coalition. Hill Collins says, "[T]hese internal processes of self-definition cannot continue indefinitely without engaging in relationships with other groups."[55] White feminists were a coalition partner Bernice Johnson Reagon would later figure out how to collaborate with, even if the relationship was at times challenging and contentious as the excerpts from Reagon's talk from the West Coast Women's Music Festival above indicate. But at this moment, Reagon was content to be "nurtured and reborn through the rich sands of Black Nationalism."[56]

In the progression from the Freedom Singers to the Harambee Singers to Sweet Honey in the Rock, one can see Reagon working through a strategy for nurturing blackness while also encouraging cooperation and participation across boundaries. The Harambee Singers offered the same critique that Black Power offered to old-guard Civil Rights Movement leadership—rejection of respectability politics; concern about the pace of change; and a lack of concern about the anger the younger generation of activists felt. At the same time, they saw themselves as offering a "voice calling for unity."[57] This unifying voice was first and foremost a call to unify Black people. It seems that at this moment, Reagon knew that Black people must be unified around positive affirmations and articulations of blackness rather than placate the expectations of whiteness or champion a Talented Tenth–style refutation of the negative stereotypes Whites had constructed.[58]

Reagon demonstrated in her musical commitments that freedom singing was an ideal venue for this unifying work. Her freedom singing with the Harambee Singers shows us the beginning of Reagon's articulation of a developing political identity that embraced some aspects of Black Power radicalism and Black nationalism, but which went on to critique the alienation of potential coalition partners. With the Harambee Singers, Reagon took the first step in the process toward coalition politics. The Harambee Singers allowed Reagon to explore musically not only the roots of her Black identity, but also the nurturing womb of Black nationalism, as she described it. In this process she began to refine her own identity as a political person through musical performance of freedom singing in the wake of the Civil

Rights Movement. Reagon's exploration of this new identity through her freedom singing was a "reconsidering" of blackness as inherently good and beautiful that would animate her next steps as a performer. The Harambee Singers were the narrowing and deepening that must occur before one can enter into coalition properly grounded. Reagon's next musical projects restarted the musical dialogue with other groups with a new understanding of what it would take to build meaningful partnerships without compromising one's cultural and political self.

The Southern Folk Cultural Revival Project: The First Steps Toward Musical Coalition Politics

During the same year Harambee Singers was formed, Reagon was busy—in addition to that work, she also released her first solo album, coordinated workshops on her work in the Civil Rights Movement with Guy Carawan, continued her academic training, and began a collaboration with White activist and folk singer Anne Romaine. Reagon's collaboration with Romaine, eventually named the Southern Folk Cultural Revival Project, shows Reagon experimenting with the next step toward embodying a musical coalition politics, where through musical performance Black and White identities are deeply explored, differences are acknowledged, and areas of solidarity are discovered and emphasized. Reagon was still forging a relatively unique stance in the post–Civil Rights era, one that did not compromise on its embrace of the new Black aesthetic, but intentionally remained open to allies and places of potential coalition as well. This stance made her a challenging presence for people such as Anne Romaine. Romaine was left transformed as a result of the encounters generated by musical and political partnership with Reagon, revealing the potential of such musical coalition work and paving the way for Reagon's later musical endeavors. In her work with the Southern Folk Cultural Revival Project, Reagon also began to incorporate her academic studies in a way that would bear fruit throughout her career.

Anne Romaine grew up in the segregated cotton mill towns of North Carolina. Her grandfather was a weaver at the Cannon Mill and her grandmother owned a beauty shop downtown in Kannapolis. Her father earned a law degree and opened a practice in Gastonia, where Romaine made music in her small, Presbyterian church and developed a love for country and bluegrass. Romaine went to Queen's College in Charlotte, and took a job at an all-White prison for girls called the Arkansas Girls Reform School. In the fall of 1964, she began graduate school at the University of Virginia and met Howard Romaine, who had just returned from participating as a SNCC volunteer during Freedom Summer in Mississippi.[59] It was through Howard that Anne was introduced to civil rights work, and eventually to Bernice Johnson Reagon.

Romaine reached out to Reagon in early 1966 about organizing a concert tour to fundraise for the Southern Student Organizing Committee (SSOC), the largely White counterpart to SNCC. SSOC leaders had met with SNCC leaders and others at Highlander Center to discuss future individual and joint endeavors. Bob Moses proposed that the SSOC consider something similar to what the Freedom Singers had provided SNCC: publicity, recruiting, and fundraising through a touring musical group committed to disseminating the message of the movement. At the time, the suggestion was to employ the group most representative of White musical engagement with the movement—Northern, White folk musicians. Anne Romaine was chosen to spearhead the tour.

Romaine spoke first with Guy Carawan and Gil Turner, who encouraged her to consult with Reagon because of Reagon's experience organizing similar musical events with the Freedom Singers. The two women discovered that they shared a passion for history, Southern folk traditions, and using musical performance to further the cause of justice in the South. They quickly revised the original plan for the concert tour to include Black and White folk music performers, and decided that they should all be from the South. They named it Southern Folk Festival, and it was the first venture of the larger umbrella organization called the Southern Folk Cultural Revival Project (SFCRP).

In a pamphlet produced about the history and performers of the tour, Reagon explains their intentions:

> We were high on idealism, thinking that by using songs that had jumped cultural, racial, social, and economic boundaries, we could entice audiences to see where the songs and cultures had gone, maybe even to follow. The concerts we developed had as their strong center the integrity and independence of the cultures, rooted in the life experiences of people singing of the world from their personal point of view.[60]

One can see the foundation of coalition politics informing the project. Reagon and Romaine developed the concerts with the "integrity and independence of the cultures" at the center, "rooted" in the experiences and identities of the individual performers. Nira Yuval-Davis explains that dialogue according to transversal or coalition politics "should be based on the principles of *rooting* and shifting—that is, being centered in one's own experience while being empathetic to the differential positioning of the partners in the dialogue [emphasis added]."[61] Both of these quotes use the same metaphor of rootedness to describe the importance of exploring and articulating one's own identity within the process of building coalition. What is often left underexplored in the feminist literature about transversal/coalition politics is how this rootedness can and should be demonstrated, or through what media the process of cultural and political exchange can flow. Reagon and Romaine show us one such real world example in the concerts they organized for the SFCRP.

For Reagon and Romaine, the selection of performers for the concert tour became a political statement in and of itself, regardless of the lyrical and musical content of the songs they would perform. They would stage and embody what they hoped the audience would take away: that the vernacular music of the South could lead to the realization that different races have

Figure 4. Promotional Brochure for the SFCRP

always been deeply interconnected and inter-reliant. They began recruiting performers willing to travel through the South as an integrated troupe, performing concerts to integrated audiences designed to celebrate the differences between, but also to proclaim the fundamental interdependence of, White and Black Southern folk culture.

Their promotional material made this clear, as well as emphasizing the educational or historical aspect of the project. A grant proposal written by Romaine and Reagon for the SFCRP states: "The theory behind the encouragement of the two cultures separately and then combined is that only an individual with pride and respect for himself and his traditional heritage can then become a part of the larger functioning society, pulling his own weight."[62] This quote directly parallels the cultural work being done in the Civil Rights Movement that culminated in the Black Power and "black is beautiful" emphases of the late 1960s and the 1970s. Indeed, Romaine and Reagon saw their work in direct continuity with the Civil Rights Movement. Many of the experiences they had across the South as they performed mirror the experiences of organizers in the movement. In the first couple years of the tour, they were refused service, they were picketed by hate groups, and they were pulled over and harassed by police. At one point, they were nearly killed by White thugs who ran into their bumper and pushed their car up to an unsafe speed while a second car pulled alongside them with a pistol drawn.[63]

One such experience made a particular impact on Romaine. After a show in Arkansas, the group was preparing to drive overnight to East Tennessee for a concert the following day. They decided that Rev. Pearly Brown, a Black bluesman who was traveling with the tour, would ride with Anne Romaine and another White woman. Romaine protested, fearing for everyone's safety if two White women were seen riding in a car with a Black man at night. Reagon yelled back at Romaine, "You better decide what's more important: your life or doing what's right!"[64] Romaine reports that she was angry for a while after she got into the car, but later realized that the confrontation with Reagon was a turning point for her. The truth that Reagon had the courage to speak to her in that moment caused her to recommit to accepting the consequences of what they were trying to accomplish.

Over the years of their collaboration, Reagon and Romaine had several run-ins like this one that illustrate the challenge of this type of musical coalition politics. In a letter from September of 1974, Reagon complains that her name appears on a poster without her having given consent. She says:

> I have gone over our various conversations re: the meeting this coming weekend. At no point was I definite about the concert, only "might be interested" or "maybe," certainly nothing that would warrant my name appearing on a poster. By the way, it's the second time it's happened this summer. Either I own myself or I don't . . . . Somehow after the conversation, everything I said "maybe" about you turned into a definite and acted on it. I will not be present this weekend—definitely. See this as a protest against the way I was handled in this matter.[65]

In October of 1974, Reagon wrote another letter to Romaine about being put on a committee when she was absent from a board meeting. It reads:

> I cannot imagine being put on that committee when I was not present. Was there really no one else who would agree to it? I reluctantly accept. I am not sure what's going on, but it does not seem healthy to me to put someone on a committee of this type when that person has not been able to, for ideological reasons, participate in the program.[66]

Although Reagon's "ideological" reservations about this specific program are uncertain, in a 2004 interview she explained that by 1969 she had become frustrated with the Southern Folk Festival because the burden of singing about racism fell entirely on the Black performers, while the White performers continued to sing about working hard and labor organizing. In the interview, she said:

> We performed all over the South wherever courageous people would dare to, and sometimes this was like church groups or this was labor groups, more often than not it was small programs on college campuses. By '69 I had stopped that work. I had become uncomfortable with the fact that in the festival, in the concert we were doing racism was represented only in the Black material. So the white singers got to sing about working hard, labor organizing, but they really didn't have any songs about racism. And I started to ask Anne, I said, "when you all gonna start," I said, "we didn't create racism" [laughs]. Why is the only representation of racism coming from the Black side of southern culture? And I said, "some of you need to start to write songs as southern white progressive people about racism." And so I stepped out of it.[67]

Reagon is not reacting to the discomfort of difference here. According to Reagon, Romaine and the other White performers were not pulling their weight in the coalition, which led to a breakdown. Despite the clear tension evidenced here, communication between the two women returned to normal until May of 1981, when Reagon wrote the following letter to Romaine on the letterhead of the Smithsonian Institution:

> Dear Anne:
>
> I have received the brochure on the Southern Grassroots Artists and Tours. You had called me after the fact, informing me that Sweet Honey's picture would be included. Please consider this letter a statement of policy regarding the use of my name or any organization I am associated with. You are hereby requested to refrain from using my name, photograph without my written consent.
>
> I am sorry to be pushed to this point, but I have lived through more than ten years of you taking liberties with my commitment and belief in your work. And it does not extend to the extent you have taken it.
>
> Sincerely,
> Dr. Bernice Johnson Reagon
> Director
> Program in Black American Culture[68]

Reagon's honesty reveals the seriousness with which she approached her musical and political identity and the importance she placed on her collaboration with Romaine. She remained in coalition with Romaine but did not hesitate to draw the line when her priorities were violated. It is precisely these types of uncomfortable confrontations that Reagon argues give coalition politics its power to transform. You must know who you are, have it embedded in your bones and seeping from your pores, and then you must figure out how to share that with other people without losing it or allowing someone else to compromise it. Then you must work in the spaces where your vision of justice overlaps, all the while remaining open to being changed by your encounters with others. The coalition of Reagon and Romaine demonstrates that music can be an effective forum for such encounter, even when lines are crossed and boundaries must be enforced in order to continue the collaboration in a healthy manner.

Two musical examples demonstrate the type of musical coalition politics that was at the heart of the SFCRP's efforts: "On the Line" performed by Anne Romaine and "Joan Little" by Bernice Johnson Reagon.[69] Although I have been unable to locate set lists for the early Southern Folk Festival tour concerts, one can imagine these two songs being sung in tandem as a powerful illustration of the ideals behind Reagon's and Romaine's project. Reagon's "Joan Little" is a cappella, save a percussion instrument and some audible foot stomping in the back of the mix. It is squarely in the idiom of

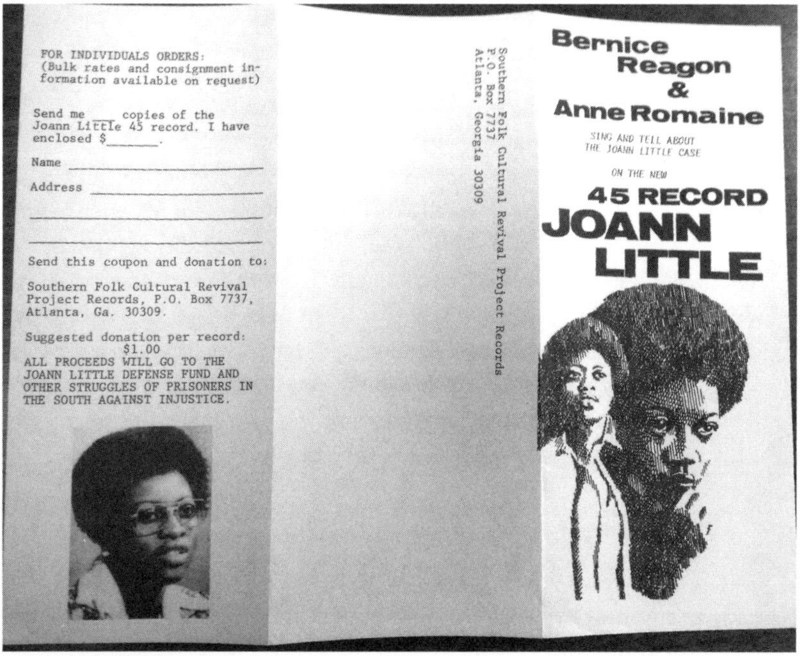

Figure 5. Reagon and Romaine's Joann Little Brochure

the African American spiritual or gospel song, featuring vocal techniques such as slides, runs, and heterophonic improvisation. Frequently, in recorded live performances, Reagon told the story of Joan Little and explained the solidarity she felt with her and expressed in the lyrics before singing the song. Romaine's "On the Line" is in the classic honkytonk style, with a heavy backbeat, acoustic guitar, and a very prominent steel guitar playing winding improvisations throughout.

Both of these songs maintain distinct musical styles rooted in White and Black Southern folk forms but they address a common political concern: justice for Joan Little, a North Carolina woman who was charged with murder after killing in self-defense a prison guard who raped her. This is musical coalition politics embodied. From the depths of their own cultural experience, these two women who do not come from the same place or always agree on the way forward unite their distinct voices in the struggle for freedom. Both songs call their listeners to empathy and solidarity with the women whose stories they are telling. "Joan Little" identifies with Joan by equating her with the listener ("Joan is you"), the singer ("Joan is me), and those with whom the singer is in intimate relationship ("Joan Little, she's my sister," etc.). "On the Line" universalizes the experience of Joan

Little and Inez Garcia by suggesting that human rights in general are on the line if we allow these injustices to go unaddressed. They are both in the spirit of the more narrative freedom songs, the effect of which Reagon has described as a "newspaper in song."[70] Reagon's "Joan Little" gets more personal, however, and narrates Reagon's own experience growing up and her inner feelings as she heard the story of Joan Little. It expresses her outrage despite the ambiguity her raising may have imbued in her. It articulates a clear cultural identity and responds to an injustice in the present.

The case of Joan Little may have offended the sensibilities of the old-guard Civil Rights leadership. Little would not have been selected by the SCLC as a suitable "civil rights subject" in the way Rosa Parks was—her story was too complex, her status too ambivalent for the types of media narratives the traditional civil rights organizations tended to craft, which dramatized the victimization of "worthy beneficiaries" of the movement's goals.[71] Little's mother asked the state to declare her a truant and commit her to a training school, from which she fled. Later in her life, Little was arrested several times for theft and eventually convicted of felony larceny and breaking and entering.[72] It was while serving her time for this crime that Little killed the guard who was attempting to rape her and fled the prison. Reagon, however, does not shy away from standing with Joan Little. Instead she identifies with her and clarifies her position forcefully, but in a way that invited Romaine to respond in kind. It is this clarity of expression and purpose and the ability to elicit response from a diversity of actors that Reagon would continue to hone in her next major performative undertaking—Sweet Honey in the Rock.

Sweet Honey in the Rock: The Musical Culmination of Reagon's Personal and Coalition Politics

Reagon's academic pursuits led her to Washington, D.C., in 1971 where she formed Sweet Honey in the Rock, a group that intentionally nurtured the uniqueness of the African American experience while fostering coalition building in its musical activities. Sweet Honey's performing career provides the medium through which Reagon articulated her mature political and musical identity, combining all that she had gleaned from previous musical experiences in her upbringing, in the Civil Rights Movement, in the Harambee Singers, and in the SFCRP. Sweet Honey in the Rock is perhaps the best example of the continued thriving of freedom singing in performance. Through these performances, Bernice Johnson Reagon inhabits a political persona that combines her commitments to work for freedom and justice, to be a cultural worker for Black American people, and to interact with other groups truthfully in hopes of establishing fruitful coalitions.

In 1973, Reagon was working as the vocal director of the D.C. Black Repertory Company (the Rep); Sweet Honey came out of one of its vocal workshops. Sweet Honey gave her first performance at Howard University in November of 1973.[73] They performed at a commemorative centennial event for W. C. Handy. Shortly thereafter they put on their first full concert at the Rep, which featured the breadth of music that would define Sweet Honey—spirituals, blues, gospel, freedom songs, and all manner of African American vernacular music.

Reagon's commitment to drawing deep from the well of the Black experience is evident in Sweet Honey's performances but in a way that is more open than the Harambee Singers' approach without compromising the specificity of the identities being articulated. The concept and sound of Sweet Honey are steeped in their African ancestry and African American traditions. As a largely cappella ensemble, Sweet Honey joined the ranks of Black ensembles such as the Fisk Jubilee Singers, the Fairfield Four, and the SNCC Freedom Singers. Sweet Honey emphasizes the range of the human voice, accompanied only by the occasional African percussion instrument. Their vocal style was distinct from a predominantly White choir, however. Rather than sublimating the individual colors of each voice to the sound of the larger group, Sweet Honey allows each woman to explore the full color and strength of her voice. The arrangements, most of which Reagon created, often treat each voice independently—they are more polyphonic (and sometimes heterophonic) than homophonic.

Sweet Honey's music is a logical extension of the freedom work that Reagon had been doing and represents a continuing and broadening of the freedom song tradition. Richard Harrington says that "Sweet Honey's repertoire is filled with what Reagon, the group's chief writer and music director, once called 'songs that take care of business that needs to be taken care of'—addressing racial, sexual and political oppression; celebrating black heroes and heroines; yet thriving on cultural connections, not distinctions."[74] Reagon points to Ella Baker, Harriet Tubman, and Sojourner Truth as the mothers of the group and Frederick Douglass, W. E. B. Du Bois, and Paul Robeson as their fathers.[75] In Reagon's words, "Sweet Honey is a group of women who come out of that legacy of the Civil Rights Movement, coming out of slavery and the spirituals. All of those musics put issues on the table."[76] In addition to performing medleys of traditional freedom songs and the spirituals from which they came, much of Sweet Honey's musical performance fits into this book's expanded framework of freedom singing. Sweet Honey songs more often than not address topics of freedom and justice and frequently tell stories meant to inspire empathy and movement participation. Songs such as "Joan Little," "Ballad of Harry T. Moore," and "Ella's Song" illustrate this practice.

"Ella's Song," which Reagon composed using excerpts from civil rights organizer Ella Baker's speeches and sayings, is a clear example of the mature articulation of Reagon's identity and political commitments. Reagon wrote the song for a 1981 documentary film on Ella Baker.[77] Reagon refers to Baker as her "political mother," and intentionally modeled Sweet Honey after the decentralized community of support that Baker cultivated among the young activists of SNCC.[78] "Ella's Song" remains a frequently sung freedom song in contemporary movements; it is included in the new Poor People's Campaign songbook, discussed in chapter 4, and has been sung at Poor People's Campaign mass meetings and protests.[79] Toshi Reagon, Bernice's daughter, performed "Ella's Song" with her band and others at the Women's March on Washington in 2017.[80] I have led the singing of it outside of an Immigration and Customs Enforcement office with new verses pertinent to the sanctuary and immigrant rights movements.

In "Ella's Song," Reagon holds up an example of a figure who challenged the male-dominated culture of Civil Rights Movement leadership, who advocated against the "great man" model of organizing that was prevalent among traditional civil rights organizations in the 1950s and 60s, and who understood the value and the process of building strong coalitions. The lyrics in the refrain and first verse express the tenacity and passion Reagon discovered in the Black Consciousness movement. Verses two and three discuss the importance of passing "the reins" to the young and incorporating them into coalition. Verses five and six implicitly critique the overly centralized leadership model by affirming being "one in the number" who "stand against tyranny" and "teaching others to stand up" rather than needing the "light just to shine on me." The final verse rejects the respectability politics for which the older generation of civil rights leaders frequently advocated, and makes it clear that, as Black women, Sweet Honey will not be tone-policed and are committed to justice regardless of whether or not they have to be "difficult" to achieve it. In a performance from the Voices Festival in 1990, the song develops a driving momentum that enhances the lyric's commitment to pushing forward. This drive is achieved through a constant subdivided rhythm played on the *shekere*, and the increasing rhythmic activity of the backup singers, which climaxes in a section sung on vocables.[81] The vocables section features the most polyphonic complexity in the performance. It sounds as if the singers are improvising in their own voices, joining the choir of women such as Ella Baker who believe in freedom, after having affirmed their identities and commitments in the first half of the performance.

Sweet Honey also performed several songs in solidarity with the South African struggle against apartheid, recalling the Harambee Singers' performance of "Hands Off Nkruma." Sweet Honey's performance for Nelson Mandela's 1990 Thank You Tour in Oakland, California, illustrates their continued commitment to freedom singing, drawing out their distinctiveness as African American women, and welcoming others into the struggle. They sang two songs—"Crying for Freedom in South Africa" and "State of Emergency"—back to back to a crowded coliseum. The women of Sweet Honey were dressed in colorful, traditional African garb and jewelry. From the group's body language to their energetic singing, the entire performance contains within it the urgency and weight of the struggle whose end was in sight, along with the exuberance of celebrating the success of the movement to get Mandela released and pass anti-apartheid legislation.

Sweet Honey has moved fluidly through more and less commercial spaces and modes, showing an openness to engage people with a diverse array of genres and approaches. They cultivated a commercial ambiguity that allowed them to reach a large audience while simultaneously maintaining legitimacy with that audience. They did not wholeheartedly embrace the commercial marketing of their music, but they also did not operate with an antagonism toward commercial venture in and of itself. The position they carved out with respect to commercialization is neutral in stance but positive in result—although they were not fundamentally anticommercial, they and their fans used their lack of commercial radio airtime as an indication that Sweet Honey was delivering a message that was too political and too honest for widespread airplay. Reagon stated, "I don't do music to scale Top 40 charts and neither does Sweet Honey, although there is no reason she, Sweet Honey, should not be there."[82] Writing about Sweet Honey's recording of "Joan Little," Reagon said "[it] was also the first song of Sweet Honey in the Rock that played on the radio—and it was on a news broadcast. That should have given me some clues about how we would fare on Top 40 Black radio."[83] Kojo Nnamdi himself said of "Joan Little": "For Sweet Honey in the Rock to do a song about Joan Little, they were clearly indicating that this group was going to chart a path that was not necessarily going to be compatible with commercial radio or anything else, but it was going to be their path."[84] Sharon Farmer, who frequently photographed Sweet Honey, said, "That was a very tough thing that happened and for it to be heard on the airways . . . . I was thrilled to death because that meant that you could really talk about the truth. To me, Sweet Honey is the truth."[85] All these comments subtly set up the expectation that when given the choice between speaking the truth and achieving commercial success, Sweet Honey was going to choose the truth. However, they engaged fully with the music industry apparatus and were always willing to explore whatever new commercial genres came to the forefront of Black culture, including hip hop. They demonstrate that one does not need to eschew commercial enterprise altogether to maintain legitimacy as a freedom singer in the eyes of one's audience and the activist community.

Sweet Honey was also explicit about coalition building and their widespread impact is evidence of their effectiveness on this front. Sweet Honey began by sinking their roots deep into what it meant to be Black and female. "We sing to offer a look at the world from the Black woman's voice," said Reagon. "The world needs to know what it looks like to us. And that's why we exist."[86] In 1977, Sweet Honey hired scholar and activist Amy Horowitz as their artist representative. By this point, they were using the language of coalition politics to frame their musical projects.[87] In a booklet for an album Horowitz helped produce with Sweet Honey and Holly Near for Redwood Records, they said:

> The women of Sweet Honey in the Rock and Redwood Records consider our coming together for this recording project to be a major effort in coalition politics. In our development of the project we have tried to form a political/conceptual base that offers respect for the concerns of Redwood and Sweet Honey, as well as some guidelines of how we work out areas where there may be conflict in our identities and responsibilities to ourselves and our communities. It is with much hope that we all approach this project. We see that the project may in fact serve as a model for ways in which women working in coalition can grow and broaden our boundaries as we identify points of unity while still maintaining our individual political priorities.
>
> For us the idea of joining together in a coalition project means that we share from our political base enough common ground to warrant the union. At the same time, being in coalition means that there may be aspects of our political bases that are not identical. It has been important to articulate our

> personal and political needs and priorities to each other. One of the primary responsibilities we share in building the coalition is constantly articulating and reviewing as we develop. It is only from this communication that we will keep a close sense of what ground we mutually share, and what ground may present conflicts in identity and focus.[88]

As this statement makes clear, by 1977 Reagon was unambiguously couching her musical activity in nuanced terms of coalition building. To this point, Reagon had not been able to find common ground with the women's movement, largely because she found the concerns it was attempting to address to be far too focused on White, middle-class women.[89] Indeed, Sweet Honey had experienced significant tension when they first began performing on the women's music festival circuit. Eileen Hayes recounts that tensions and questions arose about how Sweet Honey identified themselves and whether or not they were feminist enough, to which Reagon characteristically replied, "What is wrong with being a Black radical woman and calling your organization an ensemble of Black women singers?"[90]

Reagon's collaborations with Amy Horowitz and Holly Near solidified for her both the struggles and the benefits of musical coalition politics. Horowitz organized a tour of California for Sweet Honey that had them singing for the "radical, separatist, White-women-dominated, lesbian cultural network."[91] It was during this tour, on which Reagon describes having "constant conflicts" arising from "racism and cultural differences," that the cost of coalition work crystallized for Reagon. About that tour, she said, "We had to learn on our feet how to be who we were, how to own ourselves, and how not to allow anyone else to define who we were. Being in a coalition was not a place to feel at home. Coalition work is hard and often threatening, but necessary to force change within a society such as ours. It is vital in advancing common issues and goals, and most effective if all parties operate from a solid base within their own communities."[92]

As Sweet Honey in the Rock built their fanbase in the mid-1970s, the strategy of coalition politics permeated their work. Reagon framed all of Sweet Honey's live performances in this light:

> In successful cases, there are people in our concerts who do not run with each other in their day-to-day lives. Our concert audience is a coalition. Sometimes people get to a concert and wonder how could they be there if those other people are there. The concert is an answer to that question. We come out and try, in the response, to answer why we have all come together in this place, using the songs and singing of the African American legacy as language.[93]

Fans of Sweet Honey often wax poetic about the experience of attending a live performance. In a 2003 documentary about Sweet Honey's 30th Anniversary Tour, two fans discuss picking out the best outfit they can find and preparing themselves to attend, and comment that going to hear Sweet Honey live "is actually being a part of the performance, because Sweet Honey does involve you in the process."[94] Members of the group and fans describe a profound sense of community that is created at a Sweet Honey performance. To help facilitate interaction and connection between the audience and Sweet Honey, the lights were always kept up in the house at their performances. As an a cappella ensemble, many connect the sense of community with the vocality of the group. Ysaye M. Barnwell says about Sweet Honey's a cappella singing: "There's no barrier between the group and the audience. We are unencumbered by having to walk out in front of a band, we don't have to deal with a band, it's just us. Like we're sitting on our front porch. And it's a musical conversation that we're having."[95] Ethnomusicologist Kyra Gaunt argues, "What is going on during a Sweet Honey concert is that people are actually losing this kind of façade that we usually have. As adults we'd like to keep our composure and singing really breaks down that barrier. They really are developing a sense of community in that moment. It may be fleeting but it is powerful and is something we are missing in our society and culture."[96]

With Reagon's vocal leadership at the helm, Sweet Honey was expert in creating the space for vulnerability and the feeling of communal connection necessary to move people out of their comfort zone and facilitate the types of encounters that build unlikely coalitions. Frequently, Reagon invited the audience to participate in the singing, a practice rooted in her upbringing in the Black church and her experience as a songleader at movement rallies and protests. Another description of Sweet Honey's participatory impulse reads, "As the words of the songs become intense, Sweet Honey accents the meaning through a time-honored African-American practice of standing up and singing. The audiences more than often accept this as a sign for them, too, to show their involvement. They, too, stand, clap their hands and sway to the music. Before long the concert has turned into an ecstatic community revival."[97] This emphasis on ubiquitous audience participation invited all those present at a Sweet Honey performance to invest themselves in the experience and be prepared to grow in the process.

At times, Reagon faced resistance to this level of participation and openness to coalition work from audience members. In Lawrence, Kansas, a stop on Sweet Honey's 30th Anniversary Tour in 2003, the group's ability to stand firm and lean into the tension that coalition work creates was tested. About this stop on the tour, Reagon said, "Sweet Honey exists to present our perspective in music and culture to anybody who will listen. Therefore, we have to be prepared to go anyplace. Sometimes we'll go into a place where people have no history of Sweet Honey in the Rock. That was certainly true on this particular weekend."[98] The crowd at the Lied Center in Lawrence was predominantly White and largely ignorant of who they were coming to hear, as evidenced by the preconcert interviews. One woman responded to what she was coming to hear by saying "Some music . . . I think!" One young man said he came to hear "Traditional African . . . something like that" with a confused look on his face. An especially excited woman proclaimed that she and her friend were there "to hear Sweet Honey on the Rocks."[99] During the singing of "I Remember, I Believe," Reagon invited the audience to apply their memory to current events.[100] In typical freedom singing fashion, Reagon improvised over a song that had little to do explicitly with sociopolitical events of 2003. Through her improvised additions, she focused the meaning of that particular performance of the song on a contemporary freedom struggle. As the other members of Sweet Honey maintained an open-sounding, cyclical background progression at a quiet dynamic, she mused in speech about how it was often difficult to put words to the feelings she had as she saw the dead bodies of Americans returning from the war in Iraq. But when she felt that she could not talk about what was happening, she said, "I do remember that I don't believe I've been told everything about our policy in invading Iraq."

As she got this sentence out of her mouth there was scattered applause, as well as concerned and uncomfortable stares from the audience. Thanks to Sweet Honey's practice of leaving the house lights up, the audience could see each other's reactions and Reagon could see them as she spoke. It heightened the tension of the moment; it was clear that many in the room were not prepared to have their political beliefs confronted directly. In her bid to have the audience draw from their memory, Reagon went on to call attention to the inconsistency in the idea that the United States was in Iraq solely to liberate the Iraqi people from a dictator that we had supported in the not too distant past. As she calls the audience to memory work, she paces back and forth on the stage with her finger against her temple, suggesting with her body language that she has a thought to offer if the audience is willing to engage. She finished her spoken interpolation by saying "I have to remember that I *know* that even as I listen to everything that they are telling me" before seamlessly transitioning back into singing

"I don't know how my mother walked her trouble down. I don't know how my father stood his ground. I don't know how my people survived slavery. I do remember that's why I believe." Reagon raised the dynamic slightly as she began singing but the group maintained a relatively soft and gentle tone as they concluded the song. On the final chord, Reagon assumed a posture of openness with her arms spread and her palms pointing toward the audience. It is a gesture that recalls a Christian church service where a pastor raises her hands to offer a blessing at the end of the hour. Several audience members interviewed afterwards described their discomfort in that moment, again indicating that those people had not come prepared for their part in the coalition building. However, the way Reagon and Sweet Honey performed the song opened up the possibility of reception and transformation in a fairly hostile and unexpecting environment.

Reagon's final performance with Sweet Honey in the Rock is another example of performative coalition work where the full display of her prowess as a freedom singer and political actor were on display. The performance took place at the Warner Theatre in Washington, D.C. Earlier in the tour Reagon had announced that she would be retiring after that final concert. The encore at the Warner Theatre was the last time an audience would hear Reagon sing with Sweet Honey. For the encore, Sweet Honey, along with Toshi Reagon and her band, sang the spiritual "Old Ship of Zion."[101] Earlier in the performance, Sweet Honey had performed a rock-inspired collaboration with Toshi Reagon's group in a show of cross-generational and stylistic solidarity. This final a cappella encore showed Toshi's band returning the favor by singing with Sweet Honey on their home turf. Visually, the group is striking. The Sweet Honey women are dressed in red and gold *bubas*, while Toshi's band—which includes a Black man, two Black women, a White woman, and a White man—are dressed in black tuniclike shirts with gold stoles. The group also represented a variety of gender expressions and sexualities, along with acknowledging the deaf community by including interpretive signing. The lyrics invite all present to get on board the old ship of Zion before it's too late, which in the context of Reagon's and Sweet Honey's work is an invitation to join in freedom work while you have breath. Reagon immediately invites the audience to indicate their willingness by encouraging them to "sing along; take the song right out of my mouth."[102] Judging by the enraptured expressions, raised hands, and committed singing, the audience was moved to accept Reagon's invitation.

The performers stood hand in hand at times, carefully following Reagon's lead as the spiritual moved from quiet assurance to full-throated exuberance. Rather than remain in lockstep hymnic harmony, the background singers often resolved at different times, and trailed off into collective improvisation. Each individual voice remained unified but present and assertive, never sacrificing their own color or disappearing into the mix but sounding together beautifully. Reagon's improvisations over the harmonic foundation were at times ecstatically dissonant. Several times as the song reached its climax, Reagon jumped to the fifth, then very slowly slid down to the fourth through the flat third and back to the tonic, touching almost every microtone in between. She also frequently employed growling as a vocal technique to add color and emotional weight. In the dissonance and grit of her performance, you can hear the pain and hard-won victories of a life in freedom work, as well as the ever-present tensions of doing that work in coalition. The buoyancy and euphoria of the climaxes communicates the joy of the struggle in the vocal language that Sweet Honey and Bernice Johnson Reagon pioneered in their thirty years of freedom singing together.

Rethinking Performance and Performers of Freedom Song

The questions about the legitimacy of Beyoncé as a freedom singer raised at the beginning of this chapter came to life for me at a meeting of the Society for American Music. I was presenting a paper on my theorization of freedom singing as an expanded interpretive framework with which to analyze music of the Black Freedom Movement. One of my colleagues asked a question about a benefit concert Beyoncé had held just before the conference. Raising the specter of Beyoncé led to a ten-minute discussion about whether her music can be considered in the same breath as traditional freedom song. Critics in the room argued that her perceived lack of involvement on the ground and the distance of her music from the traditional genre's sound and definition disqualified her music from being considered. I was taken off guard by the level of resistance to considering a Beyoncé performance to be freedom singing under the right circumstances. I was open to exploring the question of Beyoncé as freedom singer but many in the room were not. Even those scholars in the room amenable to an expansion of the terms of what we consider "freedom song" were hesitant to grant carte blanche to a pop star such as Beyoncé. I do, however, understand what is at stake in these discussions. How the story of the Black Freedom Movement is told, what connections to contemporary politics are emphasized, and who is telling the story, matters a great deal for how cultural memory is shaped.

These stakes are elevated on a platform as large as the viewing audience of a Super Bowl. My insistence on circumventing the question of genre in favor of the action of freedom singing allows for performances such as Beyoncé's to be considered in light of the tradition, which in turn opens a pathway to discuss the ways a performance such as Beyoncé's mobilizes the memory of the movement and what it says about the place of freedom singing now.

Freedom singing after 1968 provides fertile musical ground for musicians such as Reagon to articulate their own political positionality and their relationship to the memory of the Civil Rights Movement and to contemporary movements for justice. Over the course of her career, Reagon mobilized freedom singing with the Harambee Singers, the Southern Folk Cultural Revival Project, and Sweet Honey in the Rock to curate an evolving political identity that moved from the nonviolent Black church-based activism of the classical Civil Rights Movement through the "rich sands of Black Nationalism" referred to above to the honing of musical coalition politics. Reagon used her time with the Harambee Singers to reassess her identity and deepen her commitment to Black people. Reagon's experiences with Anne Romaine and the SFCRP provided her first opportunity to experiment with the efficacy of a musical coalition politics, which she would continue to articulate in her later musical, activist, and academic work. The SFCRP was also a vital component of Reagon's exploration of her own political and musical identity post–Civil Rights Movement, giving her the space to explore what an extension and evolution of the movement's musical activity might look like in practice. In Sweet Honey in the Rock, the academic, musical, and political identities Reagon had been crafting throughout her career came into focus. Sweet Honey's performances offer a corpus of cultural work that reveals a freedom singer drawing from memories of struggle to inform her work in crossing boundaries and building good will and honest reflection between people of differing identities and political commitments. As she articulated her identity and worked to achieve a musical coalition politics using freedom singing, Reagon issues a counter-memory to the dominant narrative that people no longer found freedom song, and the type of movement building that used it, a meaningful tool in the struggle after 1968.

We can see elements of Bernice Johnson Reagon's freedom singing in Beyoncé and in Rhiannon Giddens. Rather than seeing these two examples as oppositional, we can view them as different ways of inhabiting a relationship to the Civil Rights Movement and contemporary movements for freedom. Beyoncé's Super Bowl performance shows a similar impetus to Reagon's exploration of the nurturing quality of militant Black Consciousness. The fact that Beyoncé's career has been marked by hypercommerciality is cause for interrogation; however, it should not exclude her performances from being considered in the light of the larger Black Freedom Movement (to include contemporary iterations such as Black Lives Matter). In such interrogations of Beyoncé's commercial success, we must also be constantly aware of the gendered ways in which commercial appeal tends to lessen the validity of some performers and not others for listeners embedded in a patriarchal culture. By considering the performances of artists such as Beyoncé in this light, we can discern what political relationships and identities they are articulating and how those relate to freedom struggles. If we dismiss Beyoncé's performance as outside the realm of freedom singing, then we are unable to notice its continuities and its discontinuities with streams of Black political thought and what those dis/continuities say about the state of contemporary freedom movements. For instance, Beyoncé's embrace of capitalistic endeavor does not fit within many people's understanding of Black radical politics. However, there are precedents for resistance that are not so hostile to capitalistic and commercialistic engagement that can help root Beyoncé's performance and provide a context for understanding it within a broader, more nuanced Black freedom struggle.

Reagon's performing career also illuminates Rhiannon Giddens's Greensboro performance. Giddens's performance style recalls Reagon's initial involvement in the Civil Rights Movement as a songleader in the Black church idiom. In addition to her performing style, Giddens has articulated a personal proximity to Reagon that tightens the connection. After Reagon died in July of 2024, Giddens shared Toshi Reagon's comments about her mother's passing, and added her own comment, saying, "Sweet Honey in the Rock forms the base of one of my formative memories, and getting to know and work with her daughter Toshi Reagon has turned into ongoing memory making—I am so blessed to have been near this beautiful soul."[103] Giddens's curation of her intimate connection to the freedom singing tradition not only elucidates and reinforces her political commitments but also grants legitimacy to her performances of her own music, which she frames in light of African American identity and political struggle. The less commercial posture Giddens assumes grants an air of authenticity to her musicking that is reinforced by her historically minded repertoire. This conferred authenticity can be a double-edged sword—it comes with a certain amount of cultural and political capital to be leveraged but it also tends to more directly recall the aesthetic of the classical Civil Rights Movement, thus putting it in danger of losing its disruptive edge in contemporary struggles.[104]

Part of the complexity of the identities and the relationship to the Black Freedom Movement that these three Black women are articulating through freedom singing is a result of their gender. Despite the fact that some within Black nationalist circles in the late 1960s began to paint freedom singing as an effeminate response to the violence and oppression of Black people in the United States, many men in the popular sphere (Sam Cooke, Marvin Gaye, Curtis Mayfield, etc.) were able to successfully sing songs related to the movement while facing little criticism that they were too commercialized to have a legitimate voice in the struggle.[105] This pattern has continued in the post-1968 United States, where male artists are often given much wider clearance to make political statements in their music than their female or gender-nonconforming companions. The path for women performers such as Beyoncé to enter the struggle in the popular sphere is much narrower than it is for men. Either their contributions to the movement have been downplayed, or a very specific persona bound up with cultural notions of authenticity must be cultivated in order to garner legitimacy. This acceptable and legitimized cultural persona for a female political artist looks and sounds more like Rhiannon Giddens singing old freedom songs at a protest in a sweatshirt than Beyoncé singing "Formation" at the Super Bowl in a body suit and a beret. The problem is that both of these artists are articulating a connection to the Freedom Movement as a part of their identity, and an argument over legitimacy obscures those articulations. This is in keeping with bell hooks's diagnosis: "The notion that somehow black males are more committed to racial uplift and black liberation struggle than their female counterparts is an idea that has its foundation in patriarchal assumptions of gender values. Black women's roles in struggles for liberation have always been and continue to be subordinated to those of black males."[106]

More than many, however, Beyoncé, Rhiannon Giddens, and Bernice Johnson Reagon exemplify the propensity to serve as "archivists, excavators, and agitators" for their people who "use sound and musicality to galvanize and disturb historical memory in the public sphere."[107] They bear and transmit through their singing not only the memory of the freedom struggles of Black people, but also the memory of what it means to navigate those struggles as women. Their singing provides a flexible and creative avenue by which they are able to carve out a place within a movement that does not always recognize their contributions. It is more valuable to listen to how and why they are drawing connections to the movement in their singing than to discuss whether they should.[108]

Another Beyoncé performance illustrates her continued use of freedom singing to clarify her political stances and commitments. Beyoncé's 2018 performance at the Coachella music festival in Indio, California, quickly achieved singular status in the minds of fans in the United States. The performance is affectionately known as "Beychella," it has its own Wikipedia page, and Netflix released a documentary on the production of the performance called *Homecoming*. In an at times humorous and breathless review of *Homecoming* for the online Black magazine *The Root*, Corey Townsend called the documentary a "spiritual baptism into black excellence."[109] The documentary discusses Beyoncé's goal of putting the vigor and variety of Black life on display, and affirming it in all its diversity. The performance drew heavily on the culture of historically Black colleges and universities (HBCUs), featuring a full marching band and elements of Black fraternity and sorority practices.

Beyoncé constructed the Coachella performance itself in such a way that the connection of her music to the Black Freedom Movement, and the continued vitality of that movement in contemporary Black culture in the United States, becomes undeniable. Early in the performance, Beyoncé moved from a version of "Freedom," a collaboration with Kendrick Lamar from her album *Lemonade*, to singing "Lift Every Voice and Sing" from on top of the large risers constructed on the stage to house the full marching band in HBCU regalia. She updated her version of "Lift Every Voice and Sing" with characteristic runs and atmospheric instrumental accompaniment. She then transitioned to "Formation," during which she marched with a group of Black women dancers out onto a catwalk in the middle of the audience and performed an extended dance sequence. Throughout the performance and in the documentary, Beyoncé gestures toward the power women in general, and Black women in particular, have when they come together to affirm each other's goodness and strength. As she sings "come on ladies now let's get in formation, prove to me you've got some coordination," it is as if she is channeling the musical coalition efforts of Black women such as Bernice Johnson Reagon before her, who used their musical performances to generate an affirming and challenging picture of the relational and political reality they hoped to create. Both the 2015 Super Bowl performance of "Formation" and the 2018 Coachella performance opened up the space for people to engage not just with Beyoncé as an artist, but with the history of the struggle she referenced and the contemporary world she is attempting to foster in her performances.

Freedom singing allows for fruitful interpretations such as these of the myriad instances in which this performance vein continues to provide meaningful political engagement for artists and audiences. Beyoncé, Rhiannon Giddens, Bernice Johnson Reagon, and many others have used freedom singing to craft and curate a political identity, and to negotiate a relationship to freedom struggles of the past and the present. The broad diversity of the modes of freedom singing they represent raise a counter-memory of a much more contoured movement than the consensus memory typically allows. The subtleties of their performances show us the ways in which this tradition is alive in performance and help to explain the spaces where the movement and its memory are alive as well. The diversity of performative musical engagement with the Black Freedom Movement confirms that it has always been a coalition-building endeavor, one that sings the truth, challenges White supremacy and other oppressions, and encourages partners to join in the struggle.

4

Warren County, Environmental Justice, and Freedom Singing in Protest

On July 15, 2013, protestors filled the rotunda at the North Carolina General Assembly in full knowledge that they would be leaving the building under arrest.[1] There was a palpable defiance among the fairly diverse crowd. A police officer pulled out a megaphone and sternly warned, "This is an unlawful assembly. If you do not disperse in five minutes, you will be arrested." On hearing this, the crowd cheered, indicating their lack of fear at the officer's threat. The protestors, led by the Rev. Dr. William Barber II, gave three more brief speeches about the ways in which the state government had failed its people before the officer announced through the megaphone, "The five minutes are up. Everyone in this area will be arrested." At that moment, the protestors launched into a somber and determined rendition of "We Shall Not Be Moved." The police began to give directions to the media, and then moved in and began zip-tying the protestors' hands and placing them under arrest. As "We Shall Not Be Moved" finished, a chant leader shouted, "What do we want?" and the people responded, "Justice!" "When do we want it?" "Now!" "Forward Together!" "Not One Step Back!" When the chant died down, a voice within the crowd began to sing "Ain't Gonna Let Nobody Turn Me Around," ironically (and perhaps intentionally) just as the police are turning people around to handcuff them. This interweaving of singing and chanting continued for the next thirty minutes, as protestors filed forward to be arrested.

This scene is from one of the civil disobedience actions of the Moral Mondays movement, spearheaded by the North Carolina NAACP. The Moral Mondays movement relies heavily on the toolkit of the Civil Rights Movement, including well-orchestrated, nonviolent civil disobedience full of freedom singing. Their collective actions are often planned in detail down to who will be arrested that day. The Moral Mondays movement is also led by a Martin Luther King Jr. figure—the Rev. Dr. William Barber II—who, in addition to being president of the North Carolina NAACP from 2006 to 2017, pastored a church in Goldsboro, North Carolina, from 1993 to 2023. In 2017, Barber stepped down from leadership in the NAACP to codirect a new Poor People's Campaign, the intention of which is to pick up where King left off in 1968 and organize for policies that benefit poor people across racial, regional, and religious boundaries. After quoting King extensively on the "History" webpage of the new Poor People's Campaign, the organizers go on to state:

> This commitment is needed from all leaders interested in taking up King's mantle. He demonstrated the difficulty and necessity of uniting the poor and dispossessed across race, religion, geography and other lines that divide. In our efforts to commemorate and build a Poor People's Campaign for our times, we will undertake an analysis of the 1967–68 Campaign. We aim to stand on the shoulders of those who came before and put effort into learning lessons and getting into step together.[2]

In both the Moral Mondays movement and the Poor People's Campaign, Barber articulates, in commitment and tactics, his deep connections to King's activism in the 1960s and his understanding of the protests he leads as the continuation of that activism. Cornel West has called him "the closest thing we have to Martin Luther King Jr. in our midst."[3] In October of 2018, Barber received a MacArthur Fellowship for his work "providing a faith-based framework for action that strengthens civic engagement and inspires the country to imagine a more humane society."[4]

Along with these intentional and explicit connections to King and the activism of the 1960s, activists that have participated in Moral Mondays and in the new Poor People's Campaign produced a songbook that illustrates their synthesis of many streams of Freedom Movement activism. The songbook—entitled *We Rise: A Movement Songbook* and subtitled *Social movement music, both old and new*—was produced by Yara Allen, a theomusicologist who is the campaign's primary songleader. The songbook is an artifact of the living tradition of freedom singing; it contains within it all the canonic songs of the Civil Rights Movement; songs that have joined that canon in intervening years, such as Bernice Johnson Reagon's "Ella's Song"; and new freedom songs that have come to prominence in the Occupy movement, immigrant rights movements, environmental movement, and the new Poor People's Campaign, such as "Rich Man's House," "We Are the Protectors," and "Unsettling Force."[5] *We Rise* contains artwork and pictures of participants, and quotes from various activists, all of which reinforces the idea of freedom singing as a coalition builder between different people and even different movements with very different goals. The book seems concerned with accessibility and utilizes the technological and communicative tools available; there is no musical notation within it but there are links to various social media sites and online music streaming services so that one can learn the songs by listening.

In keeping with the breadth represented in *We Rise*, the Moral Mondays movement has intentionally eschewed the championing of one issue, opting instead to mobilize broadly the rhetoric of morality to criticize all three branches of the North Carolina government. Because of this expansive scope, many other movements and movement leaders found occasion to intersect and organize with Barber and the North Carolina NAACP. One of those intersecting movement leaders was Deborah Ferruccio of Warren County, North Carolina. After participating in a Moral Mondays rally and demonstration, Ferruccio wrote:

> As we had marched into the rotunda, the voices of protestors rang clear with the same civil rights songs that have buoyed protestors throughout movement after movement, and I could feel the thread of people seeking justice weaving us together into the moment—past, present and future. I heard our own PCB movement singing, the deep-timbered voice of Roc Steverson and the mingled voices of all the black, white and Native Americans who sang in unity and marched for six-weeks as 10,000 truckloads of PCB-contaminated soil were buried just above our groundwater in a landfill we knew would fail.[6]

In this quote, Ferruccio draws out her lived connection between contemporary movements and a movement she helped to lead at the turn of the 1980s—the movement against locating a dumpsite for PCB-contaminated soil in rural Warren County, North Carolina. This anti-PCB movement in Warren County became the largest civil disobedience action in the South since the march from Selma to Montgomery in 1965. The resemblance of the Warren County movement's demonstrations to those of the Civil Rights Movement was no accident. Early on, the residents began conceiving of their movement as not simply an environmental protest, but a civil rights struggle in continuity with the movement of the 1950s and 60s. It was the "marriage of civil rights activism with environmental concerns," as the *Washington Post* aptly described it in an article titled "Dumping on the Poor."[7] Since 1982, the environmental justice movement, as it is now called, has gained traction both nationally and internationally by calling attention to "environmental racism"—the link between environmental abuse and marginalized communities.[8]

The Moral Mondays vignette raises the following questions: Has the function of freedom singing changed in any way in protest movements after 1968? If so, do those changes tell us anything about how contemporary freedom movements negotiate their relationship to the Civil Rights Movement? Do the particular concerns of each protest find their way into the singing (e.g., does ecological concern change the practice of freedom singing in any way for the PCB protest movement)? What role does memory and nostalgia play in freedom singing at protests after 1968? Do protest movements that rely on more traditional freedom singing show evidence of the ideological and political evolutions of the late 1960s and beyond? If so, how do these evolutions realize themselves in the musicking? And finally, what frictions arise in the practice of freedom singing after 1968 that may have been latent in the 1950s and 60s?

The PCB protest movement in 1979–82 in Warren County, North Carolina, which catalyzed the international environmental justice movement, will be the focus of the rest of the chapter. Events in Warren County both reinforce and undercut the master narrative of the Civil Rights Movement that props up the 1968 lens, and demonstrate that freedom singing has continued to be a meaningful and prevalent feature of protest in the United States after 1968. Protest and its attendant praxis maintain certain continuities that make examining it a fertile endeavor for understanding how the Freedom Movement has evolved and continues to traffic in the memory of the past. Using the Warren County PCB movement as a case study, this chapter argues that post-1968 protest movements adapt protest praxis from the entire spectrum of the Freedom Movement, attempting to synthesize the supposedly contradictory streams of the "good" and "bad" 1960s, and challenge the terms by which the 1968 lens understands protest in the post–Civil Rights era. It further argues that a protest movement's freedom singing gives the clearest window into the ways in which its participants are synthesizing and adapting these streams, and when and how they are undergirding or challenging the 1968 lens. At the heart of this chapter is an interrogation of what cultural memory in the United States has decided "good protest" and "bad protest" *sounds like*, and how those ideas—filtered through the 1968 lens—often sabotage social movements in the contemporary United States.

The chapter details the history of the Warren County PCB crisis and the ensuing protest movement, and analyzes how the Warren County movement came to grips with post-1968 realities of freedom struggle, including the synthesis of the Black Freedom Movement and environmentalism, the fusion of Black Consciousness and freedom singing, and the problem of White participation. It draws upon ecomusicology to explore the first point, suggesting that an ecomusicological approach to freedom singing further supports the expanded notion of freedom singing's relational impact. It concludes by discussing what can be extrapolated from the Warren County case study and applied to protests that freedom-sing in the post-1968 United States, such as Moral Mondays. Ultimately, freedom singing during the Warren County movement shows how its practice progressed in movements after 1968 and the ways in which those movements grapple with the memory of the 1950s and 60s in song.

Dumping on the Poor: Warren County and the Beginnings of the Environmental Justice Movement

The Warren County PCB crisis began in the summer of 1978 when Robert Ward, owner of the Ward Transformer Company in Raleigh, hired Robert Burns and Burns's two sons to illegally dump PCBs along the shoulder of rural roads in thirteen counties, as well as in remote sections of the Fort Bragg Military Reservation.[9] Because the contamination was on state property, North Carolina was responsible for remediation. The state eventually settled on a parcel of land in Afton, North Carolina, as the remediation site. The owners were facing foreclosure and were willing to sell the land to the state. The other option in contention was a section of the Chatham County landfill. Because this was public land, however, county residents had to approve the plan and the state met fierce resistance when it was proposed.[10]

The Warren County site, on the other hand, as a sale of private property, required no such approval. When the state government announced plans to site the PCB-contaminated soil in Warren County, residents reacted with the typical first response: not in my backyard. The PCB dumping in North Carolina came a decade and a half after Rachel Carson's *Silent Spring* woke the country up to the dangers of environmental pollution and negligence. As Edward Wilson says, "When it appeared in 1962, *Silent Spring* delivered a galvanic jolt to public consciousness and, as a result, infused the environmental movement with new substance and meaning."[11] *Silent Spring* also elicited a ferocious response from Monsanto and other chemical pesticide companies, who poured their vast resources into ill-fated attempts to discredit Carson and the newly galvanized environmental movement.[12] The Warren County PCB dumping also came directly on the heels of the dramatic national revelation of the Love Canal tragedy.[13] Love Canal happened so close in fact, that national news coverage paired the stories together as one segment.[14] Although Warren County residents voiced strong resistance at a public meeting in January 1979, the individual in the state government responsible for planning the remediation effort communicated that the landfill construction would go on with or without the consent of the residents.[15] In response, members of the community formed Warren County Citizens Concerned about PCBs (Concerned Citizens) and began mobilizing a campaign against the state's plan.

Litigation was the first resistance strategy Concerned Citizens employed. It brought lawsuits against the state and against the Environmental Protection Agency in an attempt to stop the progress of the dumpsite. The grounds on which the cases were built were scientific and reason-based. The groundwater at the potential dumpsite was a mere five to seven feet below the surface, well short of the required fifty feet stipulated by the EPA's contemporary regulations. In fact, the state initially requested waivers from the EPA for three of the five regulatory categories: the distance to groundwater, the underliner leachate collection, and the artificial liner.[16] North Carolina argued that the "low permeability rate" of the particular clay at the Afton site would protect the groundwater, but the residents argued that there were plenty of other, more suitable sites in North Carolina to consider, not to mention a perfectly suitable, operational, federally approved site in Alabama. Transportation and disposal of the contaminated material to Alabama would have cost the state several millions more than building the Warren County site.[17] As would occur more than three decades later in Flint, Michigan, residents were disturbed by the suggestion that saving money was more important than the health and welfare of the people of Warren County; however, the state never admitted that cost was a significant factor in the decision.

From 1979 to 1982, the lawsuits made their way through the court system. In the end, the courts ruled that the choice of this particular site was within the purview of the state. Governor Hunt's victory was clinched when he convinced the North Carolina General Assembly to pass the Waste Management Act in 1981, which "gives the governor the right to choose the site of a hazardous waste facility prior to a public hearing, reduces the public hearing to a cosmetic function, preempts local sovereignty rights, and gives the governor the power to site with force if necessary."[18] Late in the process, the local NAACP brought a suit against the state, citing race as a factor in the decision to locate the landfill in Warren County. At the time, Warren County had the highest percentage of African Americans in North Carolina and was one of the five poorest counties in the state. The court rejected the argument based on its belated admission into the proceedings.

After its defeat in the court system in the summer of 1982, Concerned Citizens—the leadership of which was predominantly White—and local civil rights leaders from the Black community solidified their coalition. Two of Concerned Citizens' prominent organizers, Ken and Deborah Ferruccio, had moved to Warren County from Ohio several years before the events of 1978–82 with no previous involvement in direct action campaigns.[19] In tandem with local clergy, local civil rights leaders who had experience with direct action, and support from national civil rights organizations, they shifted their focus from litigation to disruptive collective action and civil disobedience. As the state began construction on the dumpsite, the coalition began disruptive action. The rhetoric of the movement moved from highlighting general concern about the toxicity of PCBs and the safety of the community to accusations of environmental racism, accompanied by an adaptation of the collective action praxis of the Civil Rights Movement.

In addition to adopting the mass meetings, marches, sit-ins, and freedom singing, which is discussed in detail below, the Warren County residents also made effective use of the media, intentionally managing the narrative and keeping the story alive as long as possible. Ken Ferruccio, who was president of Concerned Citizens, and Jim Lee, a local radio-station owner, farmer, and activist, took the lead on communicating with media outlets. Ken says that he considered it his role as the spokesperson for Concerned Citizens during the movement to "sing the songs of justice in prose."[20] "Whether it was a press conference or a press statement," Ferruccio said, "what I tried to do was craft the 'music' in the statements in a way that would be clear, simple, memorable; in a way that would appeal to the head, to *logos*, to

Figure 6. Warren County Residents and Civil Rights Leaders Marching in 1982 (Ken Ferruccio can be seen on the front row to the right.) © Jenny Labalme. Used by permission.

Figure 7. Warren County Protestors Singing in Police Custody. © Jenny Labalme. Used by permission.

logic, to the heart, to the passions, and also to a kind of moral and ethical framework."[21] Ken Ferruccio holds a PhD in English literature and brought his understanding of rhetoric to bear on the fight against the landfill in Warren County. He also understood his role as the primary mouthpiece of the citizens of Warren County to be in connection with the freedom singing of the people. He considered the arguments he and others were crafting in the media beginning in 1978 as the "meta-music" undergirding the freedom singing that accompanied the civil disobedience campaign of 1982.[22]

This level of rhetorical and narrative strategy harks back to the classical phase of the Civil Rights Movement. As Julian Bond, Vanessa Murphree, and Aniko Bodroghkozy have established, various individuals and organizations such as SNCC understood the importance of controlling what was reported in the media as best they could.[23] The mainstream media played a large role in advancing the goals of the movement until 1966, when with the rise of Black Power, the mainstream media turned on the movement and began working against it with just as much force as it had exerted to support it previously.[24] Despite this dramatic shift in the media's stance toward the Black Freedom Movement in the late 1960s, Warren County citizens were able to mobilize media response in their favor. In the same way the relatively new medium of television projected images of Black protestors and their allies being beaten by White police officers in Montgomery, Alabama in 1965 to great effect, the national news media projected images of the people of Warren County being mistreated at the hands of a state government intent on forcing its will on them. During this classical phase of the movement, the media campaigns were also connected to the people's musicking—a vital part of SNCC's public information campaign came in the form of the Freedom Singers, who Bernice Johnson Reagon called a "singing newspaper."[25]

The campaign from 1979 through the summer of 1982, powerful as it was, was unable to prevent the installation of the landfill. On September 15, 1982, trucks filled with the toxic soil made their way toward the dumpsite in Warren County. Simultaneously, residents and activists marched the two miles from Coley Springs Baptist Church to intercept the trucks. As they arrived, the State Highway Patrol, dressed in riot gear, met them and prepared to arrest anyone who obstructed the opening of the site. The sounds of "We Shall Not Be Moved," "Which Side Are You On?," and "Kumbaya" filled the air as protestors lay down in the street to block the trucks from entering the site. The highway patrol began forcibly removing the protestors from the road and placing them under arrest. Similar acts of civil disobedience continued for six weeks in 1982, with the arrest count reaching nearly five hundred.

At the end of the six-week period, the trucks hauled the last of the sixty thousand tons of contaminated soil into the dumpsite. Along with assurances from the EPA that the landfill would be safe and the toxins contained, Governor Hunt gave his word that he would protect future generations of Warren County residents by ensuring economic strength and that as soon as it was feasible, he would order the detoxification of the Warren County landfill.

In 1993, state officials discovered that more than one million gallons of water was trapped within the landfill, threatening to rupture the lining and leach contaminants into the groundwater and surrounding soil. Warren County residents negotiated with the state to include in any plan to drain the water the establishment of a joint committee of Warren County residents and state officials to address the problem going forward and to discuss permanent detoxification. North Carolina continued to deny the results of several independent studies that suggested that PCBs were present in groundwater at unacceptably high levels and stalled repeatedly on detoxification. Finally, from 1999 to 2003, the state engaged in a "half-priced cleanup" that did not include oversight and spent significantly less than the projected need to adequately rid the area of contamination.[26]

The most remarkable aspect of the Warren County PCB protests is not that the state ran roughshod over a poor community, but that in the face of that quotidian occurrence, the local community managed to catalyze a movement and raise the issue of environmental racism into the country's consciousness for the first time. The consequences of environmental racism have been documented and repeated since the Warren County protests, from the impact of climate change on the Global South to the water crisis in Flint, Michigan. The most important founding document of the environmental justice movement was a report called *Toxic Wastes and Race in the United States* that was prepared by the United Church of Christ's Commission for Racial Justice. The commission's executive director, Dr. Benjamin Chavis, is the most prominent member of the Wilmington Ten—nine men and one woman who were wrongly convicted and imprisoned for nearly ten years after an incident in Wilmington, North Carolina in 1971.[27] Chavis had only had his unjust conviction overturned in 1980 before he returned to his work with the Commission on Racial

Justice and showed up to participate in the first week of the Warren County protests in 1982.[28] Chavis writes in the preface of *Toxic Wastes and Race*:

> Since 1982, we have investigated and challenged the alarming presence of toxic substances in residential areas across the country. These investigations led us to examine the relationship between the treatment storage and disposal of hazardous wastes and the issue of race.
>
> Much of the data exhibited in this report has never before been compiled for public review. It is our hope that this information will be used by all persons committed to racial and environmental justice to challenge what we believe to be an insidious form of racism . . . . This report is intended to better enable the victims of this insidious form of racism not only to become more aware of the problem, but also to participate in the formulation of viable strategies. Too often African Americans and other racial and ethnic peoples are the victims of racism but are relegated to a defensive or reactive response, rather than a proactive position . . . .
>
> We realize that involvement in this type of research is a departure from our traditional protest methodology. However, if we are to advance our struggle in the future, it will depend largely on the availability of timely and reliable information. We believe this data should be utilized by federal, state and municipal governments to prevent hazardous wastes from becoming an even greater national problem. No residential community, regardless of race, should be left defenseless in the midst of this mounting crisis.[29]

The findings of that research—as well as many studies since—show that the United States has systematically shifted the brunt of the negative impacts of environmental devastation onto communities of color, creating yet another oppression from which people must seek freedom through organizing and movement building.[30] As the *Toxic Wastes and Race* report shows, when class intersectionality is also considered, the disproportional impacts become even starker. In the years following the Warren County PCB protests a recognizable movement developed that would come to be called the environmental justice movement. Several organizations such as People for Community Recovery were started to explicitly combat environmental justice, and traditional civil rights organizations such as the SCLC and the NAACP began incorporating environmental racism into the constellation of concerns they sought to address.[31] In the same way that the combined forces of mainstream environmentalism and civil rights movements brought environmental justice into relief, training the methodological toolkit of ecomusicology on the study of freedom song is also revelatory.

Ecomusicology and Freedom Singing in Warren County

A frequent and ongoing critique of the environmental movement is that "traditional" environmentalisms have been marked by a persistent whiteness that erases the knowledge, contributions, and idiosyncratic concerns of people of color in the United States.[32] Carolyn Finney argues that popular media has created a "racialized perception that when it comes to concern for the great outdoors, participation in outdoor recreation in our forests and parks, and the environmental movement in general, African Americans and other nondominant groups are on the outside looking in."[33] Finney goes on to say that "[a] 'white wilderness' is socially constructed and grounded in race, class, gender, and cultural ideologies. Whiteness, as a way of knowing, becomes the way of understanding our environment, and through representation and rhetoric, becomes part of our educational systems, our institutions, and our personal beliefs."[34]

The dominant narrative of the environmental movement operative up to the time of the Warren County protests in the United States was largely shaped by White understandings of the "environment" and White concerns for its preservation. As stated by Edwardo Lao Rhodes:

> The environmental movement, both in and out of government, is primarily white and to a large extent indifferent to issues of social justice. Minorities are virtually absent from mainstream environmental organizations. As noted by Donald Snow of the Conservation Fund, in his survey on the challenge to the leadership of the environmental movement, "Practically none of the mainstream conservation environmental groups in the United States—regardless of location, scope or size—works effectively with or deliberately tries to include people of color, the rural poor, [or] the politically and economically disenfranchised."[35]

Rhodes goes on to argue that the history of the environmental movement in North America contains a strongly anti-urban bias, and has placed the blame for increasing pollution after industrialization at the feet of the urbanites. Within mainstream environmentalism, the urban is something to be escaped, not reconsidered and transformed. It would therefore be surprising if the environmental movement of the 1960s and beyond was able to quickly shed that bias and incorporate the concerns of the urban.[36]

Within this dominant understanding of environmentalism, the movement moved from wilderness preservation, wildlife/habitat protection, and outdoor recreation in the wake of industrialization to a reform-oriented agenda in the mid-twentieth century, made more urgent by Carson's *Silent Spring* and highlighted by the adoption of Earth Day. However, this narrative "describes only one of several pathways of environmental activism."[37] Although this narrative leaves out other avenues of participation in environmental activism, it was the dominant understanding of participation in the environmental movement in the United States. Environmental movement participants and commentators on the movement largely ignored the activities and concerns of people of color, or did not conceive of them as a part of the environmental movement proper. A prime historiographical example of this ideological segregation is the Memphis Sanitation Workers' Strike of 1967–68, which Martin Luther King Jr. supported. Examining the impetus and demands of the strike places it at the intersection of labor, civil rights, and environmental activism. However, that movement has largely been considered outside of the realm of environmental activism.

Because whiteness dominated environmentalism before Warren County, Warren County's multiracial coalition and the freedom singing that accompanied it offer an early challenge to the ways environmental concerns have been inscribed in the White imagination. Warren County also disturbed the overly simplistic categories operating within environmentalism. The county is rural but largely African American, confusing the anti-urban bias of environmentalism and troubling the conflation of the urban with the African American. The effort to site PCBs in Warren County was, on its face, a cleanup effort; the chemical was dumped throughout the state. But the choice of where to move the contaminated soil revealed the structural discrimination that was already present before the dumping. Not only do the musical practices in Warren County both reflect and generate the relationship between the human participants of different races in the movement, but they also reveal freedom singing as a musical pathway for people who have historically been excluded from environmentalism to articulate their connection to, and concern for, the environment around them. This section of the chapter mobilizes methodologies from the field of ecomusicology to help illuminate this idea, ultimately showing that it was the practice of freedom singing in the context of the environmental concerns that forged the "marriage of civil rights and environmental activism." To put it another way, Warren County sang the environmental justice movement into being.

Scholars and activists have often argued that freedom singing's power and efficacy during protest is about the relationships it affects between human persons and between or against sociocultural structures. For example, freedom singing builds solidarity and morale between protestors, freedom singing allows the protestors to channel nonviolent energy toward the powers they are struggling against, and freedom singing dispels fear among protestors and reminds those being protested of the power of their foes. Freedom singing in Warren County, however, performed an additional function: it built solidarity between people and the place in which they resided. Freedom singing helped the people of Warren County better understand how they fit into a larger ecosystem, and therefore gave them power to pursue the righting of an injustice, or an imbalance, in that ecosystem.

Jeff Todd Titon's definition of ecomusicology as the "study of music, culture, sound, and nature in a period of environmental crisis" is compelling for conceptualizing freedom singing in Warren County as an ecomusicological endeavor.[38] There is an obvious element of crisis at work in the events of the Warren County PCB struggle. Deborah Ferruccio describes how, over the three-year period of litigation before the state began transporting the contaminated soil to Warren County, it was difficult to mobilize into any organized opposition force.[39] Concerned Citizens had to constantly work to keep the crisis in front of the people as they lived their daily lives so that when the moment came to mobilize for their acts of resistance, they would be ready. Alexander Rehding's observation that the ecomusicological endeavor has an "inherent bent toward awareness raising, praxis (in the Marxian sense), and activism" is also relevant.[40] Similarly to Travis Stimeling and Aaron Allen, part of the goal of doing this work is to seek to "confront the cultural problem underlying the environmental crisis."[41] However, this book embraces the activist stance vis-à-vis the environmental crisis facing Earth through the narrower lens of the disproportional impact of said crisis on people of color in the United States.

Two of the prominent songs sung at protests in Warren County—"We Shall Not Be Moved" and "Our Road to Walk"—demonstrate how freedom singing not only affected relationships between human persons but also reconfigured connections between the protestors and the place for which they were fighting. "Our Road to Walk" was a newly composed version of "Come by Here/Kumbaya" written by Deborah Ferruccio during the civil disobedience campaign in 1982. The song shows the continuation of the processes of freedom singing as developed during the classical phase of the Civil Rights Movement. Newly composed verses with specific references to the concerns of the PCB movement keep the singing relevant to the moment, while the chorus (having come from a spiritual that was taken to Liberia and then reimported) ties the singing to a long struggle for

Black freedom.[42] This balancing between the specifics of the contemporary movement and references to the past comes poignantly within the newly composed verses of the lyric as well. Ferruccio incorporates a reference to one of the popular chants of the Warren County movement—dump Hunt in the dump!—in verse one and references the traditional freedom song "Ain't Gonna Let Nobody Turn Me Around" in the final verse. For Ferruccio, using "Kumbaya" also connects her to the White radical tradition of singer-activists such as Pete Seeger and Joan Baez, who frequently sang and recorded versions of "Kumbaya."

The verses are clearly written by an amateur songwriter—the syllabic tracking of the tune is awkward at times—however, this exemplifies the democratic ethos of freedom singing. One of the reasons freedom singing is so prevalent at protests is because the barrier for entry is low. Anyone, anywhere, and any time, can (theoretically) participate.[43] As Bradford Martin explains, "the process of inventing verses created an equality of opportunity between" people of different classes and races in the movement.[44] The song also contains an interesting allusion to international justice movements. Verse two concludes with the line, "A people united can never be defeated." That particular phrase was a chant used often in several revolutionary movements in the 1960s in South America, which were accompanied by a folksong revival termed *nueva canción*.[45] This intertextual allusion speaks to the interconnectedness and solidarity between the proliferation of social movements in the post-1968 world. The U.S. Black freedom struggle feeds into, and is then fed by, movements around the world, a dynamic that began as the Black freedom fighters began to look to the struggles on the African continent to throw off their colonial oppressors. One of the rallying cries of the *nueva canción* movement was *Venceremos!* or "We shall overcome!"[46]

One of the Warren County movement's favorite songs to incorporate into protests was "We Shall Not Be Moved."[47] Frequent performances of "We Shall Not Be Moved" during their marches and protests best encapsulate the forging of this relationship between the protestors and their environment. The chorus of the song asserts, "Just like a tree that's planted by the water, we shall not be moved." The comparison made in the song is environmentally conscious, referring to the stability of a well-located, healthy tree and the nourishing impact of water on growth and life. By singing this lyric over and over, through this specific, contextual act of musicking, the people established their connection to the land and redefined their relationship to nature by extending the concept of beloved community to include the nonhuman aspects of their environment. The image of the tree signaled to the protestors and those they were protesting that they saw themselves and the other living things around them as permanent fixtures of the place, asserting their commitment to long-term rootedness in this community threatened by the possibility of contamination. The song also calls to mind a choice facing the protestors—if/when they lose the fight to keep the state from dumping the chemicals in their community, how many of them are able to uproot their lives and move elsewhere in order to guarantee their safety?

When the protestors sang "Come by Here, My Lord" as they stood in the place they called home and tried to protect it, the "here" is brought from the abstract into the concrete. They were invoking the divine to be present with them and nature in this specific place, so that that divine force might see what is happening and intervene. As Deborah Ferruccio describes, this type of spirituality that comes out of the Black Freedom Movement tradition was new to her in relation to the environmental movement:

> They knew it was a spiritual thing, and I think between the prayer and the singing and the music, it almost encircled this movement in a way that made it different than most movements, at least environmental movements. Not that there had been that many environmental movements, still, the environmental [movement] had been largely educated people who don't open up meetings with prayers.[48]

By calling attention to the trees and the presence of the divine in the environment around them, the Warren County protestors made it clear in their singing that the degradation of the environment in their community and the struggle for Black freedom were interconnected. This sung connection invites new understandings of freedom singing; namely, scholars and commentators can and should be more attentive to the ways in which relationships beyond the interpersonal are being affected in the act of freedom singing. Warren County shows us that the Black Freedom Movement has expanded its fight beyond its traditionally prioritized issues and that the environmental movement is now coming to grips with issues of social justice and inequality. The music draws out these connections and is an important site for exploring them in their intricacy.

The next section explores further how the repeated singing of these songs, especially "We Shall Not Be Moved," articulated and developed a sense of place that strengthened the resolve of the Warren County protestors. This sense of place did not develop completely during the PCB crisis, however. The currents running through activist communities in North Carolina in the wake of the Civil Rights Movement, along with various other cultural dynamics beyond Warren County, enhanced the uniqueness of Warren County as a site where such a catalytic event might take place.

We Shall Not Be Moved: Freedom Singing, Nostalgia(s), and the Importance of Place

What does it mean to participate in a "movement" that is largely about staying put? Bernice Johnson Reagon argues that a different meaning of "movement" and a different understanding of the importance of "place" developed over the course of the Black Freedom Movement of the 1950s and 60s:

> During the nineteenth century, being on your way out of slavery usually meant leaving a place to go to another place, covering geographical territory. You actually had to put distance between where you were and where you were headed. During the twentieth-century Civil Rights Movement, being on your way often meant staying where you were and wreaking havoc in your local community, insisting on its transformation so that a new construction could be possible. Black people were determined to rearrange *space* for themselves and their future. We knew that as tax paying citizens we deserved access to opportunities and resources provided by our organized governing bodies. It really was well overdue, this standing up and taking up new space—we had to move![49]

This evolution in the understanding of movement and commitment to rootedness continued in the work of the citizens of Warren County and their freedom singing. The movement in Warren County began because the people of the area were committed to the health and well-being of that local community, even under threat of state-imposed toxicity. They resisted the state forcefully because of their rootedness. The larger problem of environmental degradation and contamination requires wider vision but the focus on the particular that can be found in the Warren County case study was the only way to bring to light the environmental racism that undergirds shifting the impacts of pollutants onto poor people of color. Their rootedness and their commitment to a specific and localized vision of well-being allowed them to accurately diagnose a systemic and widespread injustice that was affecting many localities around the country.

In keeping with Reagon's emphasis on claiming space, the marching and singing in Warren County called attention to the nature of public space, forcing observers to recognize the protestors as people who had the right to physically and aurally occupy that space. As Reagon and Ray Pratt have argued, singing fills a space sonically with the presence of the people and confronts those in power who would manage access to the space.[50] The kind of routine march performed in Warren County, from the church as the gathering place of the community through the streets, asserted the ownership of the local people over the place in which they marched. The noise of their singing gave them the power of sonic representation in a soundscape dominated by the noise of state-owned dump trucks carrying toxicity, of sirens, and of boots on the pavement. In this sense, freedom singing functioned for the people of Warren County as a counter to the state's sound imperialism.[51]

The philosophy of the Southern branch of the Civil Rights Movement that King and others spearheaded clearly guided the Warren County activists in 1978–82, ten years after King's assassination. The people of Warren County were, for the most part, deeply religious and socially conservative.[52] In addition to the fact that many of them were farmers and contamination threatened their livelihoods, they needed a moral reason to join the struggle and justify breaking the law. King's nonviolent, Christocentric vision of "beloved community" provided a compelling argument for participation for many of them. The presence of clergy, the ritual/liturgy of the mass meeting, the use of spiritual rhetoric, and the adaptation of musical practices from the church helped the people of Warren County connect this movement to the spirituality of earlier civil rights struggles in the South, and to the morality seen as central to the foundation of community life.

At the same time, many activist types had begun a kind of exodus to the rural after years of difficult battles in more populated areas. Several of these activist types descended upon Warren County in the years before the PCB crisis. Floyd McKissick, a civil rights attorney and proponent of Black nationalism in the 1960s, founded Soul City in the 1970s just a few miles down the road from the Warren County dumpsite. McKissick envisioned Soul City to be a thriving beacon of Black self-governance, self-reliance, and entrepreneurship. Although McKissick had secured a federal Housing and Urban Development grant, he faced significant resistance from the notoriously racist North Carolina senator Jesse Helms. McKissick's leadership in Warren County was also complicated by the fact that he had taken a conservative turn in the 1970s, leaving his leadership position in the Congress for Racial Equality (CORE), endorsing Richard Nixon in 1972, and championing Black capitalism. Despite all of this, McKissick participated in the first weeks of the protests and was arrested.

Two other community leaders that participated in this exodus to the rural were Jim and Valeria Lee. The Lees were activists involved with Durham's Malcolm X Liberation University in the late 1960s, who relocated to Warren County in 1973 to start a rural empowerment organization called Andamule. Andamule existed to reverse Black land loss by investing in sustainable farming.[53] Valeria describes their impetus for returning to Warren County (she is from Warren County originally) as in sync with a general interest at the time in "finding more natural ways of living."[54] After many years fighting for civil rights in Durham and Greensboro, Jim and Valeria combined their experiences in the freedom struggle, that impulse toward "the natural," an interest in small farmers in predominantly African American areas, and a concern about the decreasing amount of acreage in the hands of Black landowners, and developed the concept for Andamule. Jim incorporated Andamule and then began leasing land from Floyd McKissick's Soul City to begin the work of developing sustainable farming practices among small, mostly Black farmers in Warren County.

This collection of Black activists in rural Warren County in the 1970s was no accident. Valeria Lee notes that she and Jim were participating in a larger "back to the land" sentiment that was prevalent at the time within Black activist circles, as well as more generally in U.S. society.[55] Robin D. G. Kelley argues that land (and the ability to sustain oneself on it) was of vital importance to the conversation happening within the ongoing Black Freedom Movement.[56] Kelley reminds his readers of the Republic of New Africa (RNA) and its demands for the U.S. government to turn over the territory of South Carolina, Georgia, Alabama, Mississippi, and Louisiana to African Americans to become a self-governed autonomous state (along with reparations for the initial funding of this new nation). Kelley highlights the RNA in order to point out that land is more than controlling territory and the movement of people back and forth—it is part and parcel of the "black radical conception of freedom." "Land," Kelley argues, "is wealth, pure and simple. Historically, it has been fundamental for economic independence and sustainability, not to mention a central source of heritable wealth in the United States . . . . Second and perhaps more importantly, land is space, territory on which people can begin to reconstruct their lives. The dream, after all, is to create a new society free of the overseer's watchful eye."[57]

Although some may perceive the movement from urban centers to sleepy rural places such as Warren County as a form of retreat, for activists like Jim Lee it was exactly the opposite. They saw the future of the Black Freedom

Movement in the acquisition of land and in learning to live off that land. If the U.S. government was never going to offer reparations to Black people in the way of forty acres and a mule, the most radical way forward that many saw possible was to begin to make it happen for themselves and others.[58]

Kelley's idea that land represented "space to create a new society free from the overseer's eye" was in the bloodstream in Warren County, and had been before the 1970s. The memory of Black resistance during the era of de jure segregation was very alive in Warren County and was referenced many times during the anti-PCB movement in 1978–82. Frank Balance, a Black lawyer in Warrenton, raised the memory of the Warren County resistance to segregation at the public hearing where the citizens of the county lodged their vocal opposition to the state's plan to site the landfill in their community, saying, "[Y]ou may have black folk and white folk and Indians marching together in the streets this time."[59]

Along similar lines, Deborah and Ken Ferruccio had also relocated to rural Warren County in a Thoreau-inspired attempt to live a simpler life.[60] This motivation is in keeping with the White radical impulses of the 1960s, as well as the dominant form of White environmentalism prevalent at the time. What connects all of these stories of people coming to Warren County and the people who had always lived in Warren County was a respect for the land and a willingness to see investment in the rural as a way forward to a future of freedom. All of this heightened the appeal of returning to the freedom singing tradition, which had deep connections to musical practices of Southern and rural churches. For these activists, freedom singing represented the musical equivalent of the return to, or reinvestment in, the rural, among other things. In the years since 1968, and in the coming decade, this attitude would be cultivated through extensive documentary work on the music of the Civil Rights Movement, the result of which was the construction of an "authentic" sonic blackness surrounding traditional freedom singing that is part and parcel of its perceived connection to roots, spirituality, land, and primitive identity.[61]

All of this raises questions about whether or not nostalgia played an active role in the Warren County movement and other protest movements that freedom-sing after 1968. Mark Anthony Neal argues that within the ravages of the post–Civil Rights order there developed a "postindustrial nostalgia" within Black popular culture, "loosely defined as a nostalgia that has its basis in the postindustrial transformations of black urban life during the 1970s." He notes that "the prevalence of nostalgia-based narratives in black popular culture would have particular effects on the maintenance of intra-diasporic relations at once providing the aural and visual bridge to reaffirm diverse communal relations, particularly those across the generational divide."[62] The Warren County movement, for its part, trafficked in two different strands of nostalgia, which were often operative simultaneously during protests. The first is related to what Bode Omojoa calls the "strategic deployment of nostalgia" and what Badia Ahad-Legardy calls "afro-nostalgia." Omojoa argues that the singing of marginalized societies often uses nostalgia as a powerful tool, especially as the task of interpreting the past becomes more difficult in the face of "social and political developments of foreign domination."[63] Ahad-Legardy theorizes afro-nostalgia (as it relates to the musicking of Black Lives Matter) as a restorative nostalgia that can "enable, rather than foreclose, the [Black] radical imagination."[64] Tia DeNora also articulates the ways in which memories, even nostalgic ones, can contain momentum for the future:

> The telling is part of the work of producing one's self as a coherent being over time, part of the producing a retrospection that is in turn a resource for projection into the future, a cueing in to how to proceed. In this sense the past musically conjured, is a resource for the reflexive movement from present to future, the moment-to-moment production of agency in real time. It serves also as a means of putting actors in touch with capacities, reminding them of their accomplished identities, which in turn fuels the ongoing projection of identity from past into future. Musically fostered memories thus produce past trajectories that contain momentum.[65]

This type of strategic, restorative, momentum-producing nostalgia worked for the protests in Warren County. The circumstances surrounding the siting of the landfill in Warren County are part and parcel of the types of nonconsensual usurpations that characterize settler colonialism: land that is sacred to the local people is taken by the state or a foreign body to use for their purposes, against the protests of the people. The people and organizers who participated in the Warren County movement mobilized this productive nostalgia to develop a deeper sense of history and connection to the land and the place for which they were fighting, and to define themselves over and against the state that was acting to erase them.

The second type of operative nostalgia in Warren County was a longing for, and a recreation of, a racially unified movement of the past. Nostalgia is necessary in order to mobilize the memory of this movement because (1) it never really existed exactly as it is remembered, and (2) even if it did exist, the consensus memory of the 1960s argues that the more radical and racially specific developments of the latter half of the decade worked to disintegrate the movement of the former half.

At times, freedom singing in Warren County could be interpreted as conjuring a utopia that never existed. As Chérie Rivers Ndaliko points out, this type of conjuring, especially when art is involved, can sometimes substitute the "euphoria of utopia for objective critical scrutiny."[66] This nostalgia for the protest of the "good" 1960s crosses racial lines, but it is more prominent among White Americans who have absorbed the mainstream narrative of the developments of the 1960s and 70s much more fully. This type of nostalgia is often counterproductive because, consciously or subconsciously, it considers the developments of the later 1960s to be negative disruptions to some idealized period before, thereby erasing the contributions of a spectrum of Black freedom fighters and cultivating an unrealistic and stagnant understanding of what good protest sounds and looks like. When discussing nostalgia for a past era in Warren County, however, it is important to remember that although it had been ten years since the ostensible end of the Civil Rights Movement, desegregation and busing fights continued well into the 1970s in most parts of North Carolina. The work of the movement certainly did not feel complete.

The association of the orality of traditional freedom songs with nostalgia, productive or counterproductive, is a phenomenon that was present during the classical phase of the Civil Rights Movement but is more prevalent in protest movements after 1968. For instance, although the spirituals and hymns that formed the musical reservoir from which traditional freedom songs came were commonplace in the churches of the Southern United States in 1954, for the young generation of university students and activists, they already sounded like the music of a bygone era. Freedom singing as a practice has always maintained a tension between its *sound* and the *forward momentum* it encouraged. Most of the traditional freedom songs, lyrically and musically, compelled people forward. Whether through the rhythmic drive generated in performance, the sermon-like climax produced by improvisatory practices, or the lyrical calls to "keep on walking/marching," "get on board the freedom train," join me "on my way to freedomland," or "overcome someday," freedom singing has always combined the deep wells of Black musical memory with the imagining of a just future and the encouragement to move toward it. In Warren County and in all protests after 1968, we have the added layer of active remembering of the Civil Rights Movement through freedom singing.

Not all nostalgia is the social disease that many critics of nostalgia assume it must be. Indeed, both of these operative nostalgias are more complex than a binary understanding of nostalgia can contain. The productive nostalgia, if it loses its future-imagining component, can cease to generate action and begin to facilitate apathy and resignation. On the other hand, the counterproductive nostalgia can, with some honesty and intentionality, become a catalyst for a more inclusive multiracial movement that honors and learns from the complexity of the past and moves into the future with a clarified vision of beloved community. Even though the latter is counterproductive, it does not fall into what Ahad-Legardy defines as "white nostalgia" that "reflects the desire to return to an imagined past of unfettered white supremacy."[67] However, it is crucial to acknowledge that humans often use music as a tool for expressing nostalgia and that freedom singing—because of its specific aural connotations and connection to the mythic, "good" 1960s—is even more prone to an unnuanced nostalgia that reinforces, rather than deconstructs, the 1968 lens. In both cases, the people of Warren County used freedom singing whether nostalgic or not as a way to connect with each other, with the environment around them, and with the idea of the place they were defending.[68]

Ain't No Stoppin' Us Now: Freedom Singing and Black Consciousness

In keeping with the complexity of the operative nostalgias discussed above, the freedom singing of the Warren County movement incorporated elements of rising Black Consciousness, thereby folding the innovations of more radical expressions of the Black Freedom Movement into the tradition. This synthesis of Black Consciousness into the freedom singing of Warren County protestors complicates narratives of rupture and decline surrounding 1966–68 and reveals a way in which the Warren County movement acknowledged in a nuanced way its place in the post-1968 moment.

One of the primary musical practices that the Warren County movement adapted from the Civil Rights Movement was the addition of new lyrics pertaining to the immediate context to old songs and melodies.[69] Inserting Governor Jim Hunt's name instead of Bull Connor or referencing PCBs and pollution instead of segregation became common practice. This type of improvised lyrical change was typical of the freedom singing of the 1950s and early 1960s as well. But freedom singing in Warren County also harked back to musical and cultural developments of the later 1960s. One

Figure 8. Which Side Are You On? → Ain't No Stoppin' Us Now

of the most intriguing updates was the replacing of the lyric to the refrain of "Which Side Are You On" with the lyrics to McFadden and Whitehead's "Ain't No Stopping Us Now." This creative use of a popular song lyric and a freedom song tune loads the performance with intertextual meaning and interpolates a rising Black Consciousness into the freedom singing tradition that challenges the idea of freedom singing as a solely historicized activity.

McFadden and Whitehead's "Ain't No Stoppin' Us Now" was released in 1979, during the midst of the PCB disaster in Warren County. Like many R&B/soul songs of the 1970s, it made general reference to growing Black Consciousness that came directly from the cultural work of the Black Freedom Movement of the previous decade. Although the protestors only used the refrain of "Ain't No Stoppin' Us Now," the image of the duo, the context of Philadelphia International Records (PIR) during the 1970s, and the full lyric provide some of the intertextual flavor that invested the singing with meaning for the protestors.[70]

The lyric expresses a general feeling of optimism and determination in the face of the challenges faced by the Black community in the 1970s. By singing this lyric, the protestors communicated their commitment to positive change in oppressive circumstances, but in a way that specifically accented blackness as associated with the aesthetic of popular styles such as R&B, disco, and soul. "Ain't No Stoppin' Us Now" provides a slight corrective to the vague optimism of "We Shall Overcome" that had drawn criticism from figures such as Julius Lester and Malcolm X by shifting the expectation of change from "someday" to "now."

Despite the fact that Warren County protestors adopted "Ain't No Stoppin' Us Now" to invest a traditional freedom song with more Black Consciousness, the song in its recorded form could be misread as apolitical. However, within the context of second-wave Black Power and the narrative of community empowerment sold in the form of dance anthems that comprised PIR's modus operandi during the 1970s, the political connotations of "Ain't No Stoppin' Us Now"—and by extension the Warren County protestors' adaptation—come into focus. As many have argued, being political as a musician is more complex than one's presentation or one's overt advocacy might initially suggest.[71] Although the double-breasted white suits and wide collars folded over the lapels is a different kind of coding from the dashikis and afros that often signaled radical politics earlier in the decade, McFadden and Whitehead's image had nonetheless been invested with a political potency for Black communities that functions subversively.

Mark Anthony Neal utilizes Henry Louis Gates's concept of signifyin(g) to describe the ways in which the commercial sound and image of artists such as McFadden and Whitehead and labels such as PIR resonated within the diasporic Black community of the mid- to late 1970s while simultaneously turning large profits in U.S. culture writ large.[72] Neal specifically places "Ain't No Stoppin' Us Now" within a collection of dancefloor anthems that "conveyed rich narratives of community, hope, and tradition as well as trenchant critiques of life within and beyond the Black Public Sphere."[73] "Ain't No Stoppin' Us Now" represented a broader movement within Black popular culture, which expanded the notion of what type of music interacted with the ongoing Black Freedom Movement.

It is significant that this lyrical update likely came from the collective improvisation of the protestors at the site of protest, investing the musicking with an urgency that begins to balance the charge many critics leveled at freedom singing—namely, that it is too passive and does not demand change quickly enough. The return to militant but nonviolent civil disobedience in Warren County, in combination with a multiracial coalition adopting the practices of the Civil Rights Movement synthesized with elements of Black Consciousness, powerfully updated freedom singing as a practice and demonstrated its continued vitality in post-1968 protest. By appropriating "Ain't No Stoppin' Us Now," the protestors were also confirming the political significance of such songs and such artists as McFadden and Whitehead.

Other musical practices that accompanied the protest movement introduced further Black Consciousness into Warren County's freedom singing. Chief among them was Warren County's Black-owned public radio station WVSP (Voices Serving People), which was known for its progressive politics and its radical musical programming. In the same way that protestors in Warren County absorbed and used music from Black popular radio, they also absorbed and used the music and politics of lesser-known Black public radio outlets such as WVSP. The music of WVSP provided a soundtrack for people's daily lives, and during the PCB protest movement, the station was the primary bidirectional information outlet—the people received news and updates from WVSP, and WVSP gave the people a voice, ensuring that their activities were broadcasted to the Associated Press and other national media organizations. In this way, WVSP is related to freedom singing in Warren County as well. To understand the full breadth of meaning invested in the people's freedom singing, we must listen to the entire musical culture of the Warren County movement, which included WVSP as well as the private consumption and public performance of popular music and gospel.

In her description of the Black student movement at the University of Missouri in 2015–16, Stephanie Shonekan notes that the student activists collectively sang old staples and new movement songs and chants, but also that they constantly accompanied their actions with individual soundtracks:

> I noticed that when the Mizzou activists were resting or not in strategy meetings, that their headphones were always on their heads, and their earbuds were in their ears . . . . Intrigued by what personal choices were bringing them through the storm of a tense period in their lives, I asked them what they were listening to. Without exception, they said they were deliberate in choosing the music that would get them through each next day.[74]

This dynamic is not new to the Black student movement at the University of Missouri, as Shonekan notes. Indeed, as Brian Ward, Peter Guralnick, and others argue, the popular music of the Civil Rights Movement era accompanied the actions of the music, provided a source of encouragement for those in the struggle, and as I have argued, provided musical material for the continual process of freedom singing.[75] The same was true in Warren County. "Ain't No Stoppin' Us Now" is but one example of popular music listening that infiltrated the protest practices of the Warren County movement. Those musical protest practices combined with WVSP's musical programming and other popular and gospel music give a fuller picture of the soundscape of the Warren County movement and how it negotiated the memory of the Civil Rights Movement and the unique struggles of the present.

WVSP was started by Jim and Valeria Lee, who knew of and had listened to WAFR in Durham, the first public, community-based, Black-owned radio station. WAFR went off the air shortly before the Lees started WVSP, but Valeria was inspired to start something similar in Warrenton. WVSP would be a tool for "political and cultural empowerment" and be committed to "community development and justice work."[76] In addition to news and educational programs, the station also played jazz, blues, popular, gospel, and roots music, along with volunteer programming offered by the people of Warrenton.[77] They saw it as their mission to put back into the community the culture that defined it.[78] WVSP was a point of pride for the community, and it shaped the way they received and disseminated information and understood their world. During the PCB movement, one of WVSP's roles was to record all official conversations so that the community could hold state officials accountable for what they said and promised. Then, as WVSP shared the day's news about the PCB movement, they would intentionally select "politically appropriate" music to frame the struggle, including "a whole lot of Nina Simone."[79]

Overall, the freedom singing of Warren County reveals an interesting truth about the Warren County coalition—while the coalition was multiracial and crossed class lines, the solidarity built during freedom singing was Black-led and foregrounded the experiences of the group that was most impacted by environmental racism and the group with prior experience in movement leadership. White farmer Jim Ward remarked, "If anybody had ever told me whites and blacks would get together in this county like this for anything, I wouldn't have believed it. We decided we had to march, but most of us in [Concerned Citizens] were white and we didn't have any experience marching. We had to call in somebody who did."[80] Once the civil disobedience campaign began, control over the movement, including nonviolence trainings, mass meeting programming, and marches, was ceded to local Black activists such as Dollie Burwell, Black clergy such as Revs. Willie Ramey and Luther Brown, and civil rights leaders such as Golden Frinks from the SCLC.[81] This may explain how the White hog farmers of Warren County ended up participating in freedom singing suffused with Black Consciousness, even though it is unlikely they would have been comfortable with the general political stance such freedom singing articulated.

This integration of Black Consciousness into the practice of freedom singing raises important questions about the nature of, and power dynamics within, the coalition of Black, White, and Native American that Deborah Ferruccio described above. Did the Warren County protest movement, in its freedom singing, ignore the critiques of freedom singing as a practice—and White leadership and participation with the movement by proxy—that came out of the late 1960s? If so, what does this say about freedom singing after 1968? If not, how did Warren County manage the problem of White participation in its musical and organizational practices?

Encourage, Empower, Harmonize? The Problem of White Participation

There was (and is) a significant amount of rhetoric surrounding the Warren County movement that held up the interracial and interclass cooperation as remarkable, even a "flashback to the 1960s."[82] Frequently, those who witnessed or participated in the PCB protests recall Black, White, and Native American participation, and some of them (the Ferruccios in particular) argue that freedom singing was central to those acts of solidarity and unity. This is in keeping with much of the traditional understanding of the function of freedom singing and cultural production within social movements in general. T. V. Reed argues that three of the typical functions of cultural forms in social movements are to encourage, empower, and harmonize:

> Encourage. Individuals should feel the strength of the group. Singing in mass rallies can move a person out of the individual to feel the strength of the group.
>
> Empower. Individuals should feel their own strength. Responsibility for performing a movement text can empower an individual to feel more deeply his or her own particular commitment.
>
> Harmonize. Smooth differences among diverse constituencies. Cultural forms can sometimes cut across lines of age, class, region, even ideology, providing a sense of overarching connection that, at least for a time, subordinates differences.[83]

Reed is careful in his qualifications of the "harmonize" function of cultural forms such as freedom singing in social movements, adding "sometimes" and "at least for a time" to the idea that singing can cut across lines of identity and subordinate difference. Indeed, many movement participants and scholars have discussed the encouraging, empowering, and harmonizing impact of freedom singing, especially in the pre-1968 movement. Ron Eyerman and Andrew Jamison argue that music during the Montgomery bus boycott "served as a source of strength, solidarity, and commitment. It helped build bridges between class and status groups, between blacks and white supporters, and between rural and urban, northern and southern blacks."[84] Bernice Johnson Reagon makes a similar argument about the community that forms in the moment of freedom singing. She says, "[T]he songleader is the galvanizer, the person who starts the song and thus begins to pull together a temporary community formed in the process of that specific song rendition. A good songleader must manifest a strength energy, and enthusiasm that calls each voice into wanting to join in the singing."[85] Beyond this functional reading of freedom singing, Brian Ward argues that protestors were articulating in song the movement's goals and highest aspirations:

> While many classic freedom songs like "Keep Your Eyes on the Prize," "Oh Freedom," and "Ain't Gonna Let Nobody Turn Us Around" were drenched in black sacred musical traditions, it is worth reiterating that many songs, like "We Shall Overcome," were forged in dialogue with, not in isolation from, white hymnal and folk-music influences. At a time when integration and biracial cooperation were touchstones for the movement, this musical miscegenation—also apparent in early rock-and-roll music, which boasted black and white artists and black and white fans, and which drew on both black rhythm-and-blues and white country influences—symbolically reproduced the best hopes of many activists.[86]

Stephanie Shonekan shares an optimistic vision of the power of Black music in overcoming racism, arguing that "the rich layers of [Black music] offer a priceless lens through which black life is illuminated so that #BlackLivesMatter may become valid for those who live inside and outside the community."[87] Scholars working on other types of singing have also noted music's propensity for facilitating unity. Edith Turner's concept of *comunitas* describes well the feeling that many freedom singers articulate—"inspired fellowship" facilitated through the act of singing together.[88] Steven Connor argues that the potential for, and generation of, solidarity is at the heart of joint vocalization:

> Choric utterance is almost always concerned with the establishment of solidarity. This may be what joins prayer and protest, which otherwise may seem, as Fred Cummins has observed, "odd bedfellows." If humble imploring seems to be at the opposite extreme from hortative demand, the two have in common the need for a bracing intensification of common purpose, one which can both enlarge the uttering collectivity and solidify it, sealing in and rounding up all the variations of belief and feeling which might allow the diffusion of common purpose.[89]

However, fault lines in this experience and understanding of freedom singing developed in the late 1960s that cannot be papered over if we are to fully analyze the function and effects of freedom singing after 1968. As the goals of the movement evolved and the challenges of synthesizing the movement against de jure segregation with the movement for broader social and economic justice and Black dignity have emerged, the aspirations of classic freedom songs have been reevaluated.

For instance, communications scholar and activist Chenjerai Kumanyika described an experience of freedom singing at a vigil in the wake of the Mother Emmanuel shooting where the encouragement, empowerment, and harmony was experienced unevenly:

> A reverend led a prayer for the Emanuel AME victims, asking people to take the hand of the person next to them and join in singing "We Shall Overcome." The person next to me was a kind-looking white woman with a small white rose pinned to her T-shirt; lots of people were wearing white ribbons in honor of the victims. She offered me a sad smile and a gentle nod, lifting her hand . . . .
>
> I have reached across the aisle. I have broken bread. I fully believe we all need healing in these moments, and that night, the symbolism was clear: a white person and a black person holding hands in the face of horrific racial violence, singing songs of freedom. What could be more comforting?
>
> But thanks to something I experienced the previous night in Charleston, I couldn't shake a paralyzing feeling: When black people and white people clasped hands in the arena that night, the comfort wouldn't be evenly distributed. The healing wouldn't flow both ways.[90]

Kumanyika proceeds to describe an encounter with a White police officer, where the officer wrongly assumed the smell of marijuana was coming from the group of Black men nearby instead of the group of White college students down the street. Kumanyika felt the familiar urge to appease this White officer, conditioned by generations of violence and racist tone-policing. He compared this urge with the decision he eventually made to grasp the hand of the White woman next to him at the vigil and sing "We Shall Overcome." In this case (and many others) White comfort was prioritized over Black comfort, and freedom singing provided the context in which this cultural power dynamic was unequally enforced.

Similar questions have arisen in the musicological scholarship as well. Andrew Aprile's discussion of appropriation and musical gentrification as it relates to the song "We Shall Overcome" provides a powerful antidote to oversimplified understandings of freedom singing as the silver bullet for generating racial harmony during a protest.[91] Aprile suggests that Pete Seeger's understanding of a "neutral folk process" whereby "improvements" conforming to mainstream taste are made over time is a sort of musical gentrification that does not take into account what is being left behind and why, or the power dynamics at work in this transmutation over time.[92] Musical gentrification is a useful concept for interrogating the discomfort that develops around freedom singing and why many Black activists felt the need to leave the practice behind altogether.

Cornel West's discussion of rap explains the process by which African American ingenuity stays a step ahead of White musical gentrification and appropriation. West argues that rap "combines the two major organic artistic traditions in black America—black rhetoric and black music" and thereby "resists nonblack reproduction, though such imitations and emulations proliferate."[93] In a similar sense, freedom singing's virtuosity, which lies in its improvisatory transformations and elements of Black vocal production at the heart of its efficaciousness, "resists nonblack reproduction, though emulations proliferate." West is also fond of saying that "Martin Luther King Jr. was the most significant and successful organic intellectual in American history."[94] In keeping with the writings of Antonio Gramsci, it can also be argued that songleaders such as Bernice Johnson Reagon, Fannie Lou Hamer, and Roc Steverson (of Warren County) are organic intellectuals of the Black Freedom Movement, articulating the experience of the masses through their expertise in the language of the culture. Freedom singing is one of the primary pathways for that type of communication both within the classical phase of the movement and after 1968.

The case of the Warren County protest movement illustrates this ongoing contestation in the post-1968 Freedom Movement: the problem of White participation. Black activists expressed this problem early in the classical phase of the movement and increasingly began to articulate it as the 1960s drew on. This contention has been represented as a generational conflict because of the primary spokespeople; however, the arguments for and against the inclusion of White allies and leadership frequently crossed generational lines. In addition, very few actors within the Black Freedom Movement argued for complete exclusion of White participation; rather, leaders such as Stokely Carmichael were critiquing the conditions under which this participation often happened. In *Black Power*, Carmichael argued:

> SNCC has often stated that it does not oppose the formation of political coalitions *per se*; obviously they are necessary in a pluralistic society. But coalitions with whom? On what terms? And for what objectives? All too frequently, coalitions involving black people have been only at the leadership

> level; dictated by terms set by others; and for objectives not calculated to bring major improvement in the lives of the black masses . . . . [A]dvocates of Black Power do *not* eschew coalitions; rather, we want to establish the grounds on which we feel political coalitions can be viable.[95]

Carmichael and others who pushed back against the unfettered leadership and participation of White people in the movement were concerned about who was controlling the objectives, the tactics, and the pace of the Black struggle for freedom. Their qualm was not with coalition work in general but with the type of capitulation to White liberalism they perceived in the arguments of figures such as Bayard Rustin, and organizations such as the SCLC and the NAACP.[96]

In the intervening years since the 1960s, as T. V. Reed notes, "representations of the Civil Rights Movement have frequently exaggerated the role of white people" in movement activities.[97] Reed argues:

> There is certainly a partial truth in this, in terms of both the goals of the movement (which included an end to racial segregation) and the practice of the movement, in which white people sometimes played important roles and exhibited great courage in fighting for a cause that did not directly benefit them. But the civil rights movement was fundamentally a movement by black people themselves, many of whom remained highly skeptical about the possibilities of racial harmony even if the legal basis of segregation could be brought to an end. A focus on the role of white people is too often used to cover the continuing racism in U.S. society in the name of the fiction that if we stop talking about race, we will suddenly be transported into a colorblind utopia.[98]

Reed makes clear that Carmichael's desire to check White leadership in the movement was more widespread than the consensus memory allows, and his suspicions of the impacts of ceding too much of the narrative to White concerns was warranted given the ways in which the consensus memory has been used to obscure the complexity of Black political discourse/work and reinforce the 1968 lens.[99] Many historians have overemphasized Carmichael's and Black Power's separatist impulse, implicitly or explicitly blaming them for what these commentators have narrated as the breakdown of the movement's great coalition and the stagnation of its progress. This narrative of decline has been exaggerated and the nuances of the intra-movement negotiations have been lost in the process. Freedom singing both contributes to this oversimplification and challenges it, depending on how singing is mobilized, practiced, and interpreted after 1968.

Other historians and commentators, including many within the activist community, have tried to describe how positive White participation looks and sounds. Regarding musical participation specifically, Brian Ward has argued that White consumption of and participation in Black music opens up the potential for positive transformation:

> It is interesting to consider whether such biracial musical tastes and exchanges really did translate into more progressive racial attitudes among whites, or in some other way prepared the ground for the civil rights movement of the 1960s. Clearly, there has never been any necessary causal connection between white admiration for black cultural forms and performative excellence and more enlightened racial attitudes. Nevertheless, such white predilection for black culture could at least open up the potential for more progressive racial views. Movement historians should not ignore a time when black musical infiltration of white consciousness, consciences, and pop charts was considered a very important dimension of the broader attack on white racism and its institutions.[100]

Although Ward acknowledges the potential for positive movement as a result of these types of exchanges, he is clear-eyed about the fact that the opposite result is just as possible. In the case of Warren County—and all protests after 1968 that utilize the practice of freedom singing—questions must be raised: What kind of impact did White participation have on the movement and what role did freedom singing play? To what extent did freedom singing facilitate solidarity, and under what circumstances did it reify the very power relations it intended to dismantle? Given what we know about the history of songs such as "We Shall Overcome" and the Black Freedom movement itself, what happens when groups continue singing without taking such frictions into account?

To begin to answer these questions we turn to two examples of freedom singing in Warren County, one of which has already been mentioned. While analyzing these examples we should be attuned to the fact that as Bernice Johnson Reagon puts it, "the songs are free," meaning there is no one meaning generated by freedom singing within a protest context such as the Warren County movement.[101] The various moments of freedom singing within this movement are always fraught—they can simultaneously perpetuate problematic and oversimplified memories of the Civil Rights Movement, as well as challenge those oversimplified memories and provide a site for truly democratic engagement to occur. Especially interesting is how freedom singing as cultural production both highlights this problem of White participation as well as becomes a site in which to negotiate the power dynamics inherent in it.

Although the previous section discussed the ways in which the Warren County protestors incorporated Black Consciousness into their musicking and protesting, the overwhelming majority of the freedom singing happening in 1982 was remarkably similar to freedom singing one could have heard in Montgomery in 1955 or Albany in 1961. However, does it have the similar meanings after Julius Lester's declaration that "the days of singing freedom songs and combatting bullets and billy clubs with love are over?"[102] "We Shall Overcome" was a frequent choice of the Warren County protestors. Does their multiracial coalition's singing of "We Shall Overcome" indicate musical gentrification or musical solidarity, or both? Was there a similar dynamic at work in these protests as the one described above by Chenjerai Kumanyika?

Let's revisit Deborah Ferruccio's "Our Road to Walk" as the first prism through which to view this problem of White participation. Deborah and Ken Ferruccio are the type of White leader-participants about whom Stokely Carmichael was concerned. They were from Ohio, rather than Warren County, and they had no civil rights organizing experience when they moved to Warrenton. But they assumed a pivotal leadership role and, by many accounts, very much affected the course of the PCB protests. Deborah viewed her composition "Our Road to Walk" as being in the tradition of folk artist Pete Seeger. She even sent her lyrics to Seeger to ask his thoughts since he was also involved in a movement against PCB pollution in New York.[103]

As Andrew Aprile argues, "Pete Seeger believed that a neutral folk process allowed characteristics of perceived qualitative superiority to be adapted or discarded by the people who sang and performed these songs. This viewpoint might suggest a sort of musical gentrification; subjectively considered 'improvements' conforming to mainstream taste are enacted without regard for that which is displaced."[104] "Kumbaya" is very similar to "We Shall Overcome" in the way it underwent transmutations so it might be "palatable to a white audience."[105] The earliest known recording of "Kumbaya" is significantly different than the versions popularized in the folk revival by the Folksmiths, Pete Seeger, the Weavers, and Joan Baez. This 1926 recording of a Black Georgian man named H. Wylie is striking—the tune is barely recognizable as the campfire version many U.S. Americans have in their memory. Wylie's version is bright and plaintive in tone, featuring syncopated rhythms and microtonal embellishments.[106] Another early recording of a woman named Ethel Best singing with a group offering collective improvisation and harmony to support her provides another picture of the way this song may have first been sung on the Sea Islands of Georgia.[107] The vocal tone is powerful and assertive. The harmonies are often open, and seem more concerned with punctuation than progression. Interjections from the background are improvised throughout. Best often uses microtonal vocal techniques similar to the Wylie recording, including prominent slides.

In Seeger's recording on the other hand, the rhythms are largely flattened. Seeger also lowers the key to D major, placing the melody well within the written range of the vast majority of congregational hymns as recorded by the published hymnals of the major Christian denominations.[108] This flattening in order to compensate for the normative White American voice (what Seeger often has in mind when he assumes what people can sing together and what is too difficult for group singing) fits within the framework Cornel West articulates about Black virtuosity and White imitation of said virtuosity.[109]

Seeger's typical light, airy, calm vocality and relaxed banjo strum pattern that lazily emphasizes the backbeat combine to give the recording a carefree tone that sacrifices the urgency of the early recordings. Seeger's recording, and the other recordings from the folk revival, help to explain the song's "fall from grace."[110] Ysaye Barnwell of Sweet Honey in the Rock expresses frustration at the cultural cliché "kumbaya moment," which typically means to ignore differences and seek superficial consensus, saying, "Anytime you hear someone saying, 'It's not a kumbaya moment,' stop them.[111] 'Kumbaya' is a song that comes out of a spiritual tradition in the Georgia Sea Islands, and it means 'come by here.' People say that as an invocation to get God to come, because he or she is needed—it's a crisis. People are saying, 'There

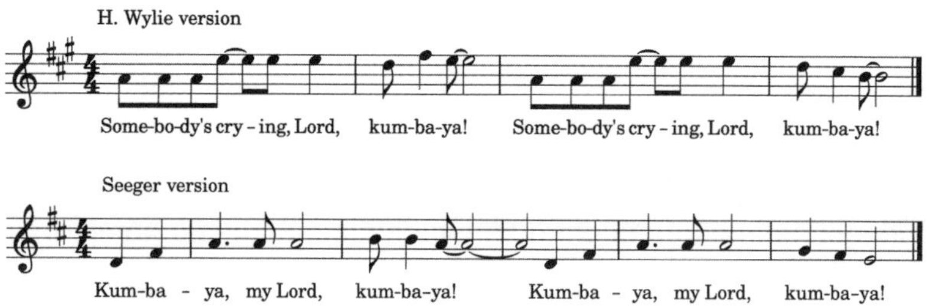

Figure 9. H. Wylie's Opening Phrase of "Kumbaya" (top) versus Pete Seeger's (bottom)

is an urgency here; whatever God is, come and stop here, and help fix it.' I can say that, and people get it, and they start to understand cultural appropriation, and misappropriation."[112]

But if we imagine this "misunderstanding" of "Kumbaya" through the lens of freedom singing as a critique of certain performances of the song (not of the song as an object) and the political stances those performances have come to represent, then we might be able to begin to calculate the costs of such musical gentrification. Deborah Ferruccio's rewrite of "Kumbaya" for Warren County, and the singing of the song in groups at the protests, represents a participation in this musical gentrification, despite the best intentions of all involved. The point, however, is not to lambast such instances, but to examine them closely in order to understand what may be lost in the transmutation.

Singing "Our Road to Walk" in the style of Pete Seeger maintains certain historical problems and unjust power relations that both Seeger and Ferruccio have worked to eliminate. Although it is a song that traces its origins to Southeastern U.S. Gullah culture, Seeger's transmuted version, which provided Ferruccio's blueprint, privileges the aesthetic values of White folk music and the norms of White collective singing. Given the connotations of singing "Kumbaya" by 1982, its singing in Warren County also represents an instance of the counterproductive musical nostalgia mentioned above that tends to flatten difference. At the same time, Ferruccio's song contains the most specificity about the Warren County situation of any of the singing during the protests, and so it does provide the most direct lyrical response to the crisis. "Our Road to Walk," then, falls more into the topical freedom singing tradition than the group participation tradition, which is logical since this was the way many White folk singers participated positively in freedom singing during the classical phase of the movement. The problem arises when that participation becomes usurpation and erasure of the Black musical traditions that are the backbone of freedom singing.[113] Like many examples of White participation in Black freedom struggles, the composing and singing of "Our Road to Walk" is complex.

Another instance of freedom singing featuring Warren County songleader Roc Steverson helps us explore an additional layer of the problem of White participation. Although the protest movement was largely Black-led, the community trusted the Ferruccios to lead Concerned Citizens, and to be their primary liaison to the press. Ken earned the community's trust not just because of his intellect and communication skills, but because he put himself and his body on the line for them on multiple occasions.

One of the most affective examples of this occurred after the landfill was in place and had begun to fail. The landfill was filling with water, and the state was planning to drain out the now contaminated water and dump it into a nearby creek in order to keep the landfill from being overwhelmed. Ken, who was in jail for an act of civil disobedience, staged a hunger strike to protest this latest move by the state to endanger the people of Warren County. Deborah, Roc Steverson, and several reporters went to the outdoor jail yard to visit with Ken through the fence. Roc saw how emaciated Ken looked, kneeled down on the outside of the fence, grabbed Ken's hand through the fence, and sang him an old gospel song. "Have you got down on your knees and prayed today," Steverson intoned in his rich and compelling bass voice. No one, including the media personnel, was left unmoved by Steverson's singing.[114] This buoying of a movement leader through freedom singing has a parallel in anecdotes such as when Martin Luther King Jr. would call Mahalia Jackson to have her sing him "Precious Lord, Take My Hand."[115]

This act of freedom singing reveals a sharing of power and a display of solidarity. Ken's act of civil disobedience was drawing attention to the ongoing furtive movements of the state and captured the attention of the media. In this way, Ken was using his body as a powerful organizing tool on behalf of the community. At the same time Steverson, although he was not physically well enough to go on a hunger strike, used the power of his singing body to buoy Ken's efforts and reinforce the ongoing collaboration occurring in Warren County between White environmentalism and the Black Freedom Movement. There is a danger in this scenario to view Ken as a White savior, sacrificing his body and gaining notoriety for his salvation efforts. However, if you understand that both individuals involved in this anecdote are leveraging the power they have available to them for the good of the coalition with neither benefitting disproportionately, you can see this as a picture of solidarity.

This picture of solidarity is complicated, however, by the Ferruccios' actions in later Warren County political history. In 1993, when the PCB landfill failed and the state-funded remediation process began, a working group of citizens and government representatives was formed to facilitate the remediation. Ken Ferruccio cochaired the group with Dollie Burwell, a Black resident of Warren County who was a leader in the 1982 protests as well. Burwell believed that the best path forward for the Black residents of Warren County was not disengagement from the political process, but a reengagement with government. The Ferruccios, on the other hand, were deeply skeptical of state motivations and resisted government involvement altogether, including locally elected Black leadership. This difference eventually led to what Eileen McGurty calls a "dissolution of solidarity among the black and white citizen activists."[116] Ken resigned as cochair of the working group after several disagreements, the worst of which occurred over the hiring of a science advisor to oversee the detoxification. The Ferruccios and the other White members of the working group favored Joel Hirschhorn, who was White, and Burwell and the Black members of the working group favored Patrick Barnes, who was a Black geologist with a Black-owned environmental consulting firm. The opportunity to hire a Black-owned consulting firm to assess and remediate the site fit well within the continued mission of achieving environmental justice through a Black-led multiracial coalition. However, the Ferruccios had doubts about Barnes's credentials and thought the group ought not to consider race when choosing a science officer.[117]

This tension continued into the twenty-first century. During the planning of a 2012 commemoration of the PCB landfill protests, Deborah resigned from the planning community over disagreements regarding how safe the landfill site was. The Ferruccios' mistrust of the governmental representatives and of Patrick Barnes continues to play itself out in the way the two activists engage politically in Warren County and remember the PCB movement.[118] Both of these incidents reveal that while freedom singing generated solidarity during the 1982 protests, the problem of White participation persisted.

The problem of White participation remains a prevalent concern not just in Warren County but also within justice movements more broadly. The example of Warren County sheds light on the types of intricacies that arise when varying races and classes, who are granted varying levels of societal power and privilege, attempt to organize and act in solidarity. Freedom singing—which combines the notorious malleability of music as a communicative medium with the aural memory of Black freedom struggles of the past—often provides the ground on which these intricacies are negotiated. Warren County has lessons that speak directly to these ongoing movements seeking to negotiate the problem of White participation.

Conclusion

The environmental justice movement has now had global impact. Traditional civil rights organizations recognize environmental issues as central to their task, and environmental organizations that previously ignored the problems of poor people of color have now begun to wrestle seriously with environmental racism. Although its roots extend further back, the movement as a coherent social phenomenon coalesced quickly behind practices and philosophies emerging from Warren County in the wake of the PCB disaster. Affective sounds and images of these practices were broadcasted to a national audience and placed within a narrative of both increasing environmental concern and growing racial inequality. Freedom singing connected this instance to past civil rights struggles, gave the movement meaning and purpose, and carved out a distinct place for it among contemporary social movements. Improvising upon the legacy of civil rights freedom singing, the Warren County protestors emphasized their connection to the place being threatened and synthesized the spiritual and nonviolent aspects of Southern activism with rising Black Consciousness. They provoked an extreme reaction from the state and foregrounded the issue of environmental racism. Studying the importance of musicking to their movement highlights freedom singing as a living tradition rather than a stagnant repertoire, and provides us a more nuanced lens through which to view freedom singing in the present, as well as in the past.

One of the most important lessons of the Warren County movement is that the role of nostalgia within movements after 1968 must be considered carefully. The second form of nostalgia discussed above, the counterproductive, is a much broader phenomenon than just in the protests in Warren County and actively shapes much of the protest after 1968 in the United States and the reactions to it in mainstream U.S. culture. Questions for movements as they sing are: How is nostalgia operating here? Is it serving to preempt the forming of coalitions with certain strands of the Freedom Movement and erase the contributions their members? Does it play into the hands of the consensus memory, which can be destructive to contemporary gains?

As with Warren County, one of the most effective ways to combat counterproductive nostalgia is to actively and intentionally cultivate connections to the entire spectrum of Black Freedom Movement ideologies within contemporary movements. We saw this at work in the Warren County movement in the participation of activist radio, the inclusion of popular music that held up contemporary Black aesthetics, and the connections to radical land-based politics. We can also see this at work in the freedom singing of the Moral Mondays movement/Poor People's Campaign. The *We Rise* songbook is a prime example, where songs, quotes, and images from various standpoints, with various concerns, and from varying aesthetic places are preserved and held up as generative in the continuing struggle.

Environmental justice forms another striking link between Moral Mondays/Poor People's Campaign and Warren County. Yara Allen—who in her musical leadership and her scholarship serves as a Bernice Johnson Reagon figure for Moral Mondays—wrote the song that has become the anthem of that movement, "Somebody's Hurting My Brother." The song uses call-and-response to recruit protestors and listeners as singers. Allen sings "Somebody's hurting my brother, and it's . . . " and the group responds "far too long." The refrain at the end of each verse is "And we won't be silent anymore!" Allen frequently narrates the song's genesis in connection to the coal ash pollution crisis in North Carolina, where Duke Energy dumped coal ash into the state's waterways for decades, leading to vast contamination with wide-ranging deleterious health impacts.[119] Indeed, the song goes on to get more specific than "somebody's hurting my brother/sister," singing "Somebody's poisoning our water and it's gone on far too long." Allen's live remembering of the song's composition rooted in the coal ash disaster disrupts any counterproductive nostalgia that may arise in the singing of such a traditional-sounding freedom song. Instead, freedom singing such as this creates a direct link between this contemporary movement, the original environmental justice movement, and the larger Freedom Movement, and generates solidarity between the singers and those who have been harmed by toxic waste and its negligent disposal.

The Moral Mondays/Poor People's Campaign vignette and the Warren County case study show us that movements in the United States after 1968 have no choice but to negotiate their relationship with the cultural memory of the Civil Rights Movement. The sounds these more recent protestors make are one of the primary signifiers in this regard; freedom singing positions contemporary movements in relationship to the cultural memory of *the* movement. At times, these movements rely on the power of an incomplete narrative of the Civil Rights Movement, but oftentimes, as their freedom singing shows, they incorporate a wide range of practices and references that work to synthesize what are often set up as competing poles within Civil Rights Movement historiography. Through this process of synthesis, in which freedom singing plays a central role, the 1968 lens is contested and the pervasiveness of the misinterpretation and misapplication of the memory of the Civil Rights Movement in U.S. culture is challenged. The Warren County movement participated in this contestation in two important ways: it sang into being the environmental justice movement and it combined the productive nostalgia of freedom singing with the reforms of Black Consciousness, despite the fact that such a combination was risky for its coalition. These two innovations have had cascading impacts beyond the Warren County movement.

The explosion of the environmental justice movement in Warren County shows the natural consequence of the cultural praxis of Black Power in the 1960s and 70s. The roots of the positive reconstruction of blackness extend back beyond Black Power; however, it was that arm of the movement and its attendant cultural production that shouldered the burden of facilitating the reclamation of blackness in the public sphere. That movement succeeded in convincing Black people of their "somebodiness," which made it impossible for them to accept environmental racism without a fight.[120] It has always been a given that White communities would resist accepting the impacts of environmental degradation. White people have always received messages of their inherent worth; the whole of U.S. culture communicates that their lives matter. White communities have always believed that they should not have to accept the consequences of an environmental crisis, even if the White people at the helm of powerful corporations are the primary culprits. The connection made in the environmental justice movement between the consequences of environmental degradation and communities of color would not have been possible without the cultural work of Black Power.

Ken Ferruccio, in a letter to North Carolina governor Pat McCrory, articulated well the synthesis of environmental concerns and social justice for poor and minority communities that took place in the Warren County movement and music's pivotal role in forging that synthesis:

> During my participation in the 1982 demonstrations against the state-forced opening of a PCB landfill in Warren County, I saw that commonality of shared values united a diversity of North Carolinians and those who came from other parts of the state and nation to oppose environmental injustice. Thirty years later, I participated in and witnessed the same unity in diversity when the citizens began to sing their freedom songs and religious hymns in the people's house in Raleigh during the Moral Mondays demonstrations. Although they come from different churches, classes, backgrounds, professions, circumstances, traditions and ways of life, they know the songs. They are inseparable from the songs they sing. You can't understand the significance of civil rights activism in North Carolina, and perhaps throughout the South and nation, unless you understand the significance of the music.[121]

Decades on from the Warren County movement, it is sometimes difficult to tell whether the protests shined only a momentary spotlight on the "slow violence" that environmental degradation visits on poor communities of color.[122] Despite the assurances of the EPA and the promises of Governor Hunt, as mentioned above, state officials discovered in 1993 that more than one million gallons of water was trapped within the landfill, threatening to rupture the lining and leach contaminants into the groundwater and surrounding soil. Even so, the governor's office continued to deny the results of several independent studies that suggested that PCBs were present in groundwater at unacceptably high levels and stalled repeatedly on detoxification. From 1999 to 2003, the state engaged in a detoxification effort that many residents believe did not fully rid the area of toxins.[123] Warren County remains one of the poorest counties in the state. The area around the landfill is still fenced off, and it is unclear to the local people whether or not it is safe.[124] Lip service is often paid to the Warren County movement; in fact, EPA Administrator Michael Regan visited Warren County in 2022 to announce the creation of a new arm of the EPA charged with advancing environmental justice in the United States. He said, "We are finally ensuring that communities who have long borne the burden of pollution see, breathe and feel the benefits of the federal government's investments."[125] Benjamin Chavis commented that this news signals that the government is finally listening.[126] Even if that is true, it's difficult not to notice that it took forty years for this listening to take place. Many of the Warren County protestors lived and died seeing no movement toward reparation and restitution, much less action to prevent future environmental injustices. Toxic waste in the United States is still disproportionately foisted upon poor communities of color. The impact of the climate crisis continues to fall disproportionately on the blacker and browner parts of the globe.

If this sounds bleak, it is. When evaluating such movements, however, it is vital to look beyond typical quantitative means of analysis. Bernice Johnson Reagon suggests, "Th[e] concentration on court cases and integrated restaurants" that characterizes many traditional civil rights histories has "resulted in a lack of recognition of a larger struggle: the transformation of Blacks in terms of their own identity and expectations."[127] When asked "What good was the Civil Rights Movement?," Alice Walker makes a similar point that, in their pronouncements about the success and failure of the movement, White commentators never consider the incredible consciousness-raising among the Black citizenry as a significant gain.[128] In this sense, in order to measure the success or failure of the Warren County movement, one must not look simply at whether or not they succeeded in preventing the siting of the landfill itself, but also at the transformation of the individuals, the Long Black Freedom Movement, and the environmental justice movement that the people of Warren County and their singing facilitated.

Alexander Rehding argues that a balance between "enlisting the commemorative and community-building powers of music in the service of ecological approaches" and the "critical and political angles of ecomusicology" will be the most productive approach for ecomusicology and the activism it hopes to engender.[129] In other words, utilizing music's power to harness nostalgia balanced by the urgency and activism of apocalypse is a recipe for musicking that contributes to solutions amid ecological crisis. The Warren County protests exemplify this approach. Drawing from deep cultural memory with the music, calling to mind history and memory, and mobilizing the feeling of that nostalgic gesture to highlight the rupture in the sociological present, they generated urgency and momentum to stop the bleeding and to begin to make things right.

5

Documentary Media, Freedom Song, and the Construction of Sonic Blackness

The penultimate segment of the 2009 documentary *Soundtrack for a Revolution*, directed by Bill Guttentag and Dan Sturman, covers the 1965 march from Selma to Montgomery, arguably the height of the classical phase of the Civil Rights Movement. The film moves directly from the speech King gave on the steps of the capitol building in Montgomery to discussing attempts to take his life. Although the film to this point (1:08:10) had focused on the campaign in the South, the narrative breezes through an anecdote about King being stabbed at an appearance in Harlem, New York. The only comment on this disjuncture is that the scar left from the letter opener was in the shape of a cross, and King once remarked to Andrew Young that he looked at it every morning and thought about how he had to be willing to die to continue with his work. Then, as a point of transition to King's Memphis assassination, the film shows a short clip of some White men waving Confederate flags, bloodthirstily shouting, "We want King! We want King!," followed by King ducking as he hears what sounds like a gunshot.[1] The viewer is left to assume this comes from the similar scenes we have been shown across the South; one would have to be well versed in visual civil rights history to know that this five-second clip comes from a march in Chicago, Illinois, in 1966.

Immediately, a period recording of "Woke Up This Morning with My Mind Stayed on Freedom" sounds while the interviewees introduce King's participation in the Memphis Sanitation Workers' Strike in 1968.[2] As King's friends and associates recall his assassination at the Lorraine Motel in Memphis, a woman begins to sing "Precious Lord, Take My Hand," which was King's favorite gospel song.[3] The recording of "Precious Lord" fades out and footage of marchers in King's funeral procession singing "Woke Up This Morning" enters briefly.[4] The film then cuts to studio footage of John Legend as he performs his new version of "Woke Up This Morning," accompanying himself on the piano. The film then alternates between shots of Legend at the piano, King's funeral, and short clips of King during his life and work, all set over Legend's singing.

As the film concludes, the interviewees reflect on the continuation of King's work and the legacy of the Civil Rights Movement in the United States. Sentimental guitar and synthesizer music enters softly under the final remarks. The last line of the film is "You can kill the dreamer but you absolutely cannot kill the dream." At that moment, a black and white image of people on the National Mall that at first appears to be the 1963 March on Washington transitions to color. An image of Barack Obama taking his oath of office crossfades in as the music reaches a cadence, and the viewer realizes the image is of Obama's first inauguration in early 2009.[5] The screen cuts to black and the credits begin to roll, as all of the musicians featured in the film sing a collaborative rendition of "We Shall Overcome."

This vignette from *Soundtrack for a Revolution* illustrates well the complexity and potential predicaments involved in telling the story of the Civil Rights Movement. The documentary attempts to "tell the story of the American civil rights movement through its powerful music" and features a narrative of the movement centering around King's activism, and punctuated by contemporary versions of traditional freedom songs recorded for the film.[6] Artists such as The Roots, John Legend, and Angie Stone arranged versions of "Ain't Gonna Let Nobody Turn Me Around," "Woke Up This Morning with My Mind Stayed on Freedom," and "Wade in the Water," respectively.

The scene above is the conclusion of the film and the sequence that makes the most suggestive (and problematic) historical and interpretive moves. Reception of the film reveals how pervasively and deeply the tropes of the Civil Rights Movement's dominant narrative have rooted themselves in the U.S. imagination. A reviewer for the *Seattle Times* proposed that *Soundtrack for a Revolution* "may well be the finest broad history on film of the Southern Movement."[7] While several reviewers lamented the film's brevity and tendency to gloss over important events, none questioned the integrity of the narrative being presented, the overly simplified conception of the music, or the suggestions made in the film about the movement's connections to contemporary politics.

This vignette raises questions: What role have documentary films and sound recordings played in constructing the post-1968 meanings of freedom singing? What can close readings of these documentaries tell us about the unique ways this medium uses music in general—and freedom song in particular—to construct meaning? How do history- and meaning-making in documentary film and sound recording—as nonfictional presentations of the history of the movement and its music—interact with the other contexts in which freedom singing occurs in U.S. society? These broad questions will guide the remainder of the chapter as it seeks to understand documentary media as a final context in which freedom singing has played an active and meaningful role in U.S. political and cultural life. As with performance and protest, in documentary accounts of the movement freedom singing becomes a site to both actively shape the cultural memory of the movement as well as leverage the power of its memory for ongoing political effect.

In this chapter, we explore how documentary media (including film, sound recording, and print) depicts the freedom singing of the Civil Rights Movement in the period following the traditional end of the movement. It argues that the White folklorists who did much of the early documenting of freedom singing were animated by a form of primitivism—a seeking of truth in the cultural production of an idealized and simplified Other. While their work was valuable and their legacies broad, figures such as Alan Lomax and Guy and Candie Carawan curated an "authentic" sonic blackness in their documentation of freedom singing and helped to construct the canon of freedom song through their primitivistic filter. This version of an authentic sonic blackness is found in a longer discourse among Black people about the articulation of Black identity through music—a discourse that is often interrupted by White ethnographers, musicians, and commentators.[8] A counterpoint is presented by way of the use of music in Henry Hampton's sweeping documentary of the movement, *Eyes on the Prize*. Over the course of its fourteen hour-long episodes spanning 1954 to 1985, *Eyes on the Prize* presents a nuanced narrative that holds together many of the tensions that are overemphasized in other accounts in movement historiography. On rare occasions it reinforces the 1968 lens; but when analyzed in its totality, its use of music and narrative deconstructs the limitations established by the work of early sound documentarians and the mainstream media in the 1960s, and contests the way the movement is popularly remembered and depicted in the United States. Finally, we return to *Soundtrack for a Revolution* as the chapter concludes, contrasting it with *Eyes on the Prize* and delineating the ways in which documentary presentations on the Civil Rights Movement participate in contemporary political meaning-making as they undergird or subvert the 1968 lens.

Freedom Singing, Film Theory, and the Civil Rights Subject

Critical theory and film theory provide the theoretical underpinnings of this chapter. Laura Mulvey's theorization of the male gaze, and its corollary in critical race and postcolonial theory, the White/Western gaze, are foundational.[9] Stuart Hall has talked about the concept of the gaze as the "imperial eye," an indecisive kind of representation of the Black subject as either a dangerous primitive or a docile servant.[10] Stephen Charbonneau draws on a similar concept that he calls the "racial look" in his work on race and nonfiction film.[11] This chapter uses an aural analog to the White/Western gaze or racial look—White aurality—to understand the way White folklorists approach freedom singing.[12]

In conjunction with Mark Slobin's understanding of super/subcultural expressions, this book's approach to analyzing film has been influenced by apparatus theory, which asserts that film is necessarily ideological on the basis of its construction as reality for the viewer and should therefore be critiqued as either reinforcing or resisting dominant ideology through its production and reception.[13] In the case of freedom song documentation, it considers how a film or other piece of documentary media uses music to subvert or reinforce the ideology of the dominant narrative of the movement and the 1968 lens. White aurality is a central component of the 1968 lens in that the 1968 lens relies on hearing freedom singing from an ideological vantage point—the vantage point of the dominant group that flattens nuance and pigeonholes freedom singing into the U.S. consensus memory of the Civil Rights Movement.

A central theme of this chapter is the relationship of freedom singing in documentary films to what Herman Gray terms the "civil rights subject." Aniko Bodroghkozy argues from the work of Herman Gray that depictions of African Americans on television after the Civil Rights Movement established certain expectations and mores regarding who "deserved" to benefit from the movement:

> [T]elevision in the United States, in its cultural work of reconstructing and remembering the civil rights era, produced as a "necessary, cultural trope," a very particular representation of blackness—middle class, hardworking, successful, willing to sacrifice, individualized—as the worthy beneficiary of the civil rights movement. This "civil rights subject" contrasted favorably in televisual discourse with the poor, disenfranchised segments of the black community who did not fit with the civil rights narrative of achieved equality . . . . In envisioning equality, news and entertainment television gave viewers a representation of blackness that at one point went by the label "white Negro"—a particularly pointed trope signifying "black and white together." Network television premised equality on a largely white definition whereby African Americans were ready for equal time to the extent that their representations conformed to whitened standards of middleclass and professional respectability.[14]

The deployment of music in documentary accounts of the Civil Rights Movement reflects and reinforces the contrast established between the civil rights subject and the "poor, disenfranchised segments of the black community who did not fit with the civil rights narrative of achieved equality." Activists in the early Civil Rights Movement frequently deployed a similar idea in their planned demonstrations and acts of civil disobedience. The NAACP's selection of Rosa Parks as the face of the Montgomery bus boycott rather than Claudette Colvin, and the subsequent erasure of Colvin's role until recently, illustrates this strategy. Parks was a secretary for the NAACP, a well-respected and educated adult, and according to Colvin, had the "right hair and right look."[15] In other words, Black civil rights leaders knew that Parks was a more acceptable representation in the minds of White America of who deserved to have access to integrated services than Colvin. Civil Rights Movement leadership frequently used the media to help construct this civil rights subject and then, in turn, to dramatize the mistreatment of such "deserving" people. This strategy is alternatively known as respectability politics, and it was one of the ideologies that young activists in SNCC began to reject forcefully in the latter half of the 1960s.[16] Indeed, it became clear in the years following 1968 that U.S. society would leverage those who did not fit the image of the civil rights subject against the entire African American population in order to roll back the gains of the movement.

For many curating the narrative of civil rights, the optimistic and determined sounds of traditional freedom songs indexed the "worthy beneficiaries" of the struggle, whereas the lack of singing, or the frustrated, challenging, and militant sounds of funk and some forms of jazz represented those segments of the Black community that did not fit that mold. Because the Civil Rights Movement holds such an idealized position in the U.S. consciousness, these civil rights subjects have been valorized as an acceptable, even truer, expression of what it means to be Black and American. In this way, those who have told the story of the movement (including the media, documentarians, mainstream historians, etc.) to U.S. audiences reinforced through the sounds of traditional freedom singing an "authentic" sonic blackness, implicitly arguing what the gains of the movement sounded like over and against the sounds of those who had not seemed to benefit from it. Ironically, this authentic sonic blackness, especially when constructed and reinforced by White actors, is defined in terms of whiteness, both when it is cast as the opposite of whiteness in its folk simplicity and also when it is used to delegitimize other forms of Black expression as viable expressions of Black Americanness.

The deployment of freedom singing that occurs in many documentaries on the Civil Rights Movement subtly makes a similar claim—*this* is the blackness that was at the heart and soul of the movement and therefore is the expression of blackness that should receive the benefit of the movement's blood, sweat, and tears. In deconstructing this process of representation and simultaneously arguing for an expanded notion of freedom singing, we may be able to explode the limitations placed on who can lay claim to the dividends of the Black freedom struggle.

The Folk Canon, Primitivism, and the Internal Other

Several ethnomusicologists, anthropologists, and cultural studies scholars have detailed the ways in which folklorists and documentarians have approached various Black musics (and Black people) through primitivist lenses.[17] On this topic, four scholars have been particularly influential: Brian Hochman, Ronald Radano, David Garcia, and Jennifer Lynn Stoever. Hochman's *Savage Preservation: The Ethnographic Origins of Modern Media Technology* details the connections between ideas about race and the development of media technology, especially those technologies employed by ethnographers to document so-called primitive cultures that were ostensibly dying and disappearing.[18] Also helpful is the concept of savage ethnography, the central contention of which is that "certain populations [a]re incapable of progressing beyond the primitive social state" and that it is "the duty of the civilized to record primitive life in the face of its certain demise."[19] We will see a similar compulsion to preserve what is "disappearing" below, as it animated many of the White documenters of freedom singing.

In *Music and the Racial Imagination*, Ronald Radano and Philip Bohlman argue:

> Race . . . accrues meaning around spaces of Otherness. In these other spaces, race *sounds* different, that is, foreign and distant—displaced from the familiar. It has nonetheless, an arresting quality because, its foreignness notwithstanding, race enables access. Its "logic of form" seems to sound across temporal and social distances, fulfilling for a legacy of Western observers an appropriative desire for the authentic, the universal.[20]

This dynamic of Western observers drawing close to music of the racial Other, to the sounds of difference, because it is imagined as both foreign as well as accessible and "authentic," is central to the worldview of the documenters discussed below. Radano's explication of the narrative much of the listening public believes about Black music from his monograph *Lying Up a Nation* is also relevant. In *Lying*, Radano argues that although the complexities of cultural production do not bear this story out, many believe wholeheartedly that "the qualities so often affiliated with black music—its soulfulness, its depth of feeling or 'realness,' its emotional and rhythmic energy, its vocally informed instrumental inflections—grow directly out of the depths of social tragedy only to rise miraculously as the voice of racial uplift."[21] This story, according to Radano, does not allow for the intricacy of Black life and Black cultural production that is evident when one considers alternatives to this narrative. As we will see below, the Carawans, Alan Lomax, and other early documenters of freedom singing believed and perpetuated this narrative that Radano deconstructs as limiting the interpretations of Black expression.

In *Listening for Africa*, David Garcia focuses on the ways in which primitivist conceptions of Africa are read onto Black music in the diaspora. He argues that ontological, phenomenological, economic, and political privilege is granted to whiteness in modernity as defined in contradistinction to the "primitive":

> [T]he geographic places where black music and dance were believed to have originated (Africa) and still survived (Caribbean and South America) were separate in every possible way—socially, economically, and temporally included—from the modern city or metropolis. Because of their privileged status in the workings of this logic, then, anthropologists, departments of

> tourism, historians, record company producers, and Africans as well were enabled to navigate the temporalized distantiation separating urban or modern from rural or premodern space. They held the capacity to listen and even travel back in time to the "jungle" or "bush," a fantastical feat that was in fact not fantastical at all but a matter of the spatial practices and becomings endowed to them by Hegelian, Comtean, Darwinian, and capitalist spatialized decipherings of the world and its history.[22]

In Garcia's reading, then, primitivism not only demeans and oversimplifies those subjects on whom it trains its gaze, but it also grants capital to whiteness and White people as normative arbiters of modernity with the freedom to move in and out of spaces they primitivize, while at the same time generating interpretations of the cultural production they are observing that reinforce their ideological and material positionality.

Jennifer Lynn Stoever's concept of the "sonic color line" and the "listening ear" are also intimately related to this discussion. The primitivizing of Black sound by White documenters falls into what Stoever calls "willful white mishearings and auditory imaginings of blackness."[23] Stoever defines the "sonic color line" as "the process of racializing sound—how and why certain bodies are expected to produce, desire, and live amongst particular sounds—and its product, the hierarchical division sounded between 'whiteness' and 'blackness.'"[24] She defines the "listening ear" as "a figure for how dominant listening practices accrue—and change—over time, as well as a descriptor for how the dominant culture exerts pressure on individual listening practices to conform to the sonic color line's norms."[25] In this sense, White aurality overlaps with the listening ear as a description of dominant listening practices, and the documenting of freedom singing discussed in this chapter contributes to Stoever's sonic color line.

This tendency among White listeners to primitivize Black and Southern people is similar in ideology and musical effect to the artistic movement called primitivism within Western art and music history; both are connected by the colonialist mindset that undergirds them. Primitivism was a movement within Western art that trafficked in "the belief that what is least mediated by modern society—children, peasants, 'savages,' raw emotion, plain speech—is closest to the truth."[26] The "primitive" as a resource to be used by composers and artists was seen as pure presence, frozen in time as an expression of historical humanity before it was corrupted by the ills of modernity.

White Europeans and Euro-descendant people sought and perceived this more "natural" humanity among various groups, including those characterized as "savages," the folk, and children. In many ways, the quest for some distillation of folk identity in the music of U.S. Black Southerners was a search for an internal Other, a noble savage caricature, with which to construct a "simpler"—and therefore (in the minds of the seekers) "truer"—path forward for American musicking and identity formation. Similarly to primitivism and exoticism in other contexts, the attraction of White folklorists and musicians to Black cultural expressions and the ideas about blackness those expressions reinforce in the mind of White Westerners represent some combination of fear and desire—what Eric Lott calls "love and theft"—on the part of the White observer/participant.[27] The maintenance of the canon of freedom songs, which has resisted deconstruction, also reveals primitivist, nostalgic impulses behind what types of musicking are privileged.

The similarities between the primitivist impulse in music and art history and the aims of White folklorists and musicians such as John and Alan Lomax, Pete Seeger, Guy Carawan et al., are striking. They too, were looking for truth in the simplicity of the Other, the "primitive" within. They crafted a canon of American folk song partly (perhaps primarily) as a reaction to modern commercialism and its perceived decadence. These White folklorist-musicians harbored a deep suspicion of anything they perceived to be commercial. They romanticized and valorized as authentic that which eschewed modernity, and searched for what they thought was the furthest thing from the decadence of contemporary society as possible—Black communities in the South. At the same time, these White folklorist-musicians enjoyed the privileges modernity bestowed upon them as White, as intellectuals and social scientists, as men, and as cisgender heterosexuals. Although this book deals with efforts to document the Civil Rights Movement through various media, this documentation must never be considered uncritically as objective, despite the fact that documentarians frequently position their work that way. As Benjamin Filene has said, "the Lomaxes, for the most part, have been treated as preservationists who reclaimed an endangered folk-song heritage. But they were creators as much as caretakers of a tradition. As with most canons, the canon of American folk music that the Lomaxes defined says as much about their tastes and values as about the 'reality' they documented."[28]

Aaron Oforlea compellingly argues that Alan Lomax's landmark monograph *The Land Where Blues Began* demonstrates this propensity for primitivizing, romanticizing, and othering those he was recording and studying:

> [Lomax] doesn't know that an authentic black experience doesn't exist and he can't explain to his audience the extent to which the white unconscious is inscribed in racialized discourses about black people. Lomax's white privilege impedes his ability to theorize blues performances as simultaneously taking place within and without white culture. Exoticizing and primitivizing the blues, Lomax writes, with admiration in his book The Land [Where Blues Began], "I was overcome with wonder. How could these worn farm laborers and their slave ancestors, driven, demeaned, and cruelly exploited, have created songs so full of nobility and love?"[29]

Oforlea points out that Lomax's ideological predisposition toward the people and the music he studied prevented him from seeing the blues in its complexity, from understanding how his subject position influenced what he included and excluded from his ethnographic account, and from understanding how his surprise at the "nobility and love" found in the people he was observing trafficked in colonialist and racist tropes. Albeit not as egregious as what can be found in *The Land Where Blues Began*, Guy and Candie Carawan and other early documenters and mediators of freedom song demonstrated a similar propensity to primitivize, creating a dubious cult of authenticity surrounding certain traditional types of musicking and establishing the frameworks through which many (especially White, bourgeois, non-Southern) Americans understood the music of the Civil Rights Movement. This cult of authenticity surrounding traditional freedom song contributes to a broader tendency to reinforce rather than undercut the 1968 lens.

In order to bring the connections between primitivizing impulses and the curation of the freedom song and other Black musics in the United States into sharper relief, we turn to Paul Gilroy, Patrick Mullen, Martin Favor, and David Garcia. Gilroy argues that, within Black political discourse, there exists a tendency to seek a "supposedly authentic, natural, and stable 'rooted' identity" that comes from the Euro-American intellectual heritage, which leads many to deny the "syncretic interdependency" of Black and White thought and in turn to assume that they can describe a "pure and homogenous" cultural expression that is "automatically expressive of the national or ethnic differences with which they are associated."[30]

In his thorough critique of the field of folklore studies (with an emphasis on how White folklorists, including himself, have studied Black culture), Patrick Mullen makes a similar point:

> There was a "historical connection between the Enlightenment and the institution of slavery—the rights of man and his enslavement" (Morrison

1992, 42) so that some important notions about race and the concept of folk originated during the same historical period. White Europeans were imagining an Other who was stuck in the past—in other words, traditional—to better define themselves as modern.[31]

In representations of the Civil Rights Movement, this "imagined Other stuck in the past," with a "supposedly authentic, natural and rooted identity" is realized in the freedom singing Black Southerner. The constructed folk authenticity of this figure is pitted against the "angry" Black Chicagoan or the Black Muslim from Harlem and given an aura of romanticized authority rooted in this construction. As Martin Favor says, "the critical discourse of blackness places the 'folk'—southern, rural, and poor—at its forefront" meaning that "certain utterances . . . are accorded a greater value, a larger measure of 'authenticity' than others."[32] Homi Bhabha argues, along similar lines, that "an important feature of colonial discourse is its dependence on the concept of 'fixity' in the ideological construction of otherness."[33] Fixity is at the heart of the White aurality through which the Carawans and Alan Lomax listen to the subjects they are documenting. In the documentation of the Civil Rights Movement (and its broader historiography), the utterances accorded greater value and a larger measure of authenticity have been the traditional freedom songs, the songs whose interpretations are fixed aurally and ideologically in the imaginations of these documenters. This is not to deny their importance to the movement but to call attention to the ways this valuation, when overemphasized or oversimplified, prevents a multifaceted conception of the musical and ideological makeup of the movement, as well as hindering its continued dynamism.

White Documenters, the Mainstream Press, and the Construction of Authentic Sonic Blackness

As Oforlea highlights above, the legacy of Alan Lomax is not straightforward. The same is true of the people primarily responsible for the recording and disseminating of the freedom song canon during and after the Civil Rights era. Without the tireless persistence of figures such as Guy Carawan and Moses Moon, we would be left with far fewer audio recordings and transcriptions of the freedom singing that occurred during the mass meetings, marches, and protests of the Civil Rights Movement.[34] Without the work of record producers such as Moe Asch at Smithsonian Folkways, these recordings might be inaccessible for most U.S. Americans. However, while the work of the song collectors and folklorists was vital to preserve audio of freedom singing, these same documenters collected and presented the music from a certain ideological vantage point that has played into dynamics with far-reaching consequences beyond their intentions. As Tricia Rose says, "white listeners' genuine pleasure and commitment to black music are necessarily affected by dominant racial discourses regarding African Americans, the politics of racial segregation, and cultural difference in the United States."[35] Their love of the music (and even of the people producing it) should not obscure the cultural dynamics at play.

About John and Alan Lomax—the most prominent of U.S. song collectors and folklorists (and whose work is often cited as foundational for American ethnomusicology as well)—Benjamin Filene argues:

> The Lomaxes' goal, therefore, was both to preserve and popularize folk music. This two-sided mission created powerful contradictions in their work—contradictions that were compounded by their lack of self-consciousness about their role as intermediaries between folk and popular culture. The Lomaxes had a specific conception of America's folk music and ignored any songs that did not fit that conception . . . . The Lomaxes claimed to be impartial folklorists who documented an existing tradition, but they had a personal vision that has powerfully influenced how Americans remember their musical heritage.[36]

Indeed, the following remarkable passage from Jerrold Hirsch's article reveals the extent to which John Lomax imposed his own expectations on the music he valued:

> Modern life threatened the survival of folklore, Lomax maintained, for it threatened the pastoralism, the rural life, and the isolated communities he saw as the necessary conditions that produced folklore. He argued that "the spread of machine civilization is rapidly making it hard to find folk singers." He implied that only "a life of isolation, without books or newspapers or telephone or radio, breeds songs and ballads." From his point of view, the true folksong could only be obtained by finding "the Negro who had had the least contact with jazz, the radio, and with the white man." The old tunes were folksong; later developments were almost regrettable: "Daily association with the whites and modern education prove disastrous to the Negro's folk destroying much of the quaint, innate beauty of his songs." He saw songs abandoned and replaced by what he thought of as "a flood of jazz and of tawdry gospel hymns." He approved of the thesis that jazz was "the debased offspring of Negro songs." Given these developments, he maintained, prison camps were the ideal place to collect Black folksong: "Here

the Negro prisoners were segregated, often guarded by Negro trusties, with no other contacts with the whites, except for occasional official relations. The convicts heard only the idiom of their race."[37]

It should be noted that John and Alan Lomax were very different people with very different motivations and ideological drives. Very often (as one can see reflected in the Filene quote above), they are treated as a singular force; however, especially with regard to racial politics, they had distinct views and objectives. While both romanticized and primitivized the Black Americans they studied, John Lomax was a "nineteenth-century Southern conservative on race issues" while Alan was a "twentieth-century leftist liberal" and a "committed supporter of civil rights."[38] Good intentions or not, this does not exonerate Alan from analysis of the impacts and maleffects of his primitivizing of Black people in the Southern United States.

Guy Carawan's ideological approach to race and folk music maps much more closely onto Alan Lomax's than John's. Guy and Alan were of the same generation of leftist White American folklorists working with Black musicians in the South. When Guy Carawan traveled around to mass meetings and marches recording the musicking that inspired him in those contexts, he operated under similar assumptions and with similar goals as Alan did on the latter's famous song-collecting trips. In addition to a shared approach, Carawan and Lomax were close friends and Guy considered Lomax a profound influence on him. Carawan and Lomax met in London in 1957 and developed a professional and personal relationship that lasted until Lomax's death in 2002.[39] Their professional relationship included the co-production of an album in 1962 called *Freedom in the Air: A Documentary on Albany, Georgia 1961–1962*, which is discussed below. As Kristen Turner recounts, "Lomax's notion that folk music could be used as a way to reshape a decadent American culture resonated with Guy's idealism . . . . As he described it later, 'I learned so much by staying with Alan and it would have a big influence on me once I got back to the United States.'"[40]

Not only did Carawan record freedom singing, but he played an influential role in its documentation and dissemination. He taught songs to activists around the country, organized workshops about freedom singing, and played an active role in framing and distributing the music in print, oral, and recorded form. It is in his capacity as a mediator for White American mainstream culture that one can see most clearly the impacts of the Carawan's documentation efforts on the U.S. cultural memory of freedom song after 1968.

Carawan's ideology about folk music and authenticity limited the freedom song canon he (and other similar White folklorists) helped to define and legitimize, and his tendency to romanticize and even primitivize Southern Black Americans in the Freedom Movement often reinforces the dichotomies on which the 1968 lens relies. This primitivizing tendency in Carawan's documentation places his work in accidental league with the oversimplified narrative told by the mainstream U.S. press in the late 1960s. After the Watts riots in 1965 and the emergence of Black Power, the mainstream U.S. press did an about-face in its documentary coverage of the movement, training a much more hostile eye toward its activities and effectively blaming parts of the Freedom Movement coalition for the violence of the late 1960s.[41] While Carawan himself was committed to the cause during his lifetime, the implicit primitivism in his documentation opens his body of work up to reinforcing this oversimplified narrative, and in turn, to reinforcing the continued influence of the 1968 lens.

The Carawans' extensive documentation of the music of the Civil Rights Movement includes three books of photographs, prose, and song transcriptions, and eight albums of recorded material, all released on the Smithsonian Folkways label. These documentary accounts span the period from 1960 to 1980, a period in which the meanings and relevance of the Civil Rights Movement to U.S. life were actively contested by participants, opponents, and commentators of all stripes.

When you organize the Carawans' documentary accounts of the music and activities of the movement by date, patterns surface. One notices that the Carawans released one project a year from 1960 to 1968, during the most active years of the classical phase of the movement itself. There was then a renewal of their activity in the 1980s, when a simultaneous resurgence of interest in broader Civil Rights Movement history took root in the United States.[42] This resurgence included fifteenth- and twentieth-anniversary commemorations of landmark movement events around the country, the push for Martin Luther King Jr. Day to become a federal holiday, and the release of the first television series documenting the movement (discussed below). Not coincidentally, Bernice Johnson Reagon began her tenure as director of the program in Black American culture at the Smithsonian in 1977 and continued in various positions (including curator of the National Museum of American History) until 1997.[43] In addition to larger cultural trends, her presence and advocacy work at the Smithsonian served to catalyze a large portion of the historical work that occurred during her tenure there.

Figure 10. Documentary Media on Civil Rights Movement Produced by Guy and Candie Carawan

Year	Title	Medium	Notes
1960	*The Nashville Sit-in Story: Songs and Scenes of the Nashville Lunch Counter*	Sound recording	Released on Smithsonian Folkways
1961	*We Shall Overcome: Songs of the "Freedom Riders" and the "Sit-Ins"*	Sound recording	Released on Smithsonian Folkways
1962	*Freedom in the Air: A Documentary on Albany, Georgia, 1961–1962*	Sound recording	Released on Smithsonian Folkways, coproduced by Alan Lomax
1963	*We Shall Overcome: Songs of the Southern Freedom Movement*	Print	
1964	*Sea Island Folk Festival: Moving Star Hall Singers and Alan Lomax*	Sound recording	Released on Smithsonian Folkways
1965	*The Story of Greenwood, Mississippi*	Sound recording	Released on Smithsonian Folkways
1966	*Ain't You Got a Right to the Tree of Life? The People of Johns Island, South Carolina—Their Faces, Their Words, and Their Songs*	Print	Updated edition published in 1989
1967	*Been in the Storm So Long: A Collection of Spirituals, Folk Tales, and Children's Games from Johns Island, South Carolina*	Sound recording	Released on Smithsonian Folkways
1968	*Freedom Is a Constant Struggle: Songs of the Southern Freedom Movement, Volume 2*	Print	
1980	*Birmingham, Alabama, 1963 Mass Meeting*	Sound recording	Part 2 of three-part *Lest We Forget* series for Smithsonian Folkways, source material from 1963
1980	*Sing for Freedom: Workshop 1964 with the Freedom Singers, Birmingham Movement Choir, Georgia Sea Island Singers, Doc Reese, Phil Ochs, Len Chandler*	Sound recording	Part 3 of three-part *Lest We Forget* series for Smithsonian Folkways, source material from 1964
1992	*Sing for Freedom: The Story of the Civil Rights Movement Through Its Songs*	Print	Combined re-issue of *We Shall Overcome* and *Freedom Is a Constant Struggle*; new edition released in 2007

From 1960 to 1968, during which all three books were originally published and six of the eight albums were released, there is a clear trajectory to the framing the Carawans give their documentation. The Carawans emphasize the importance of folk tradition over and against the diversity of musical, cultural, and ideological forms that proliferated in the same period. Scholars have largely viewed their advocacy for folk traditions through a benevolent lens; however, when read through the larger trends in the movement, and when one understands how freedom singing became a site for contesting the future and, later, the memory of the movement itself, their increasing accent on folk tradition takes on new meaning. Because the Carawans loom so large over the documentation and canonization of freedom song, it is vital to interrogate their legacy in light of these dynamics in the post-1968 United States.

An example of how Carawan's and Lomax's ideology shaped the way they documented freedom singing can be seen on the documentary album they produced together, *Freedom in the Air: A Documentary on Albany, Georgia, 1961–1962*. Before a note is heard, the album cover frames the experience as genuine, as "just the facts." It has the look of a newspaper front page: a yellowing black and white image of Albany protestors kneeling beneath the album title in block letters like a headline. The subtitle "a documentary on Albany, Georgia" suggests that the listening experience is meant to be educational and representative of truth, rather than merely entertaining. The noting of Carawan's fieldwork and Lomax's participation lend further credence to this aura of intellectual legitimacy and historical accuracy.

The first sounds the listener hears are older singers performing a slow, lined-out hymn as part of a worship service. While this style of singing was obviously still present and used during some church services, it did not reflect the majority of the singing that accompanied Civil Rights era mass meetings and demonstrations. By making this lined-out singing style the first sound the listener hears, Carawan and Lomax are influencing the listener's entire experience of the sounds that follow, suggesting that everything on the album—music, speaking, retelling of actions—springs from this cultural source. The listener is immediately struck by the disjuncture of these opening sounds in comparison with what follows, and thereby the "folkness" of the people being documented; we hear them from a distanced position first, as historicized objects rather than contemporary people. Listeners, especially consumers of folk music, often invest this historicized position with authenticity and sincerity.

Several contemporary reviews of the album reinforce this investment. In a review in the magazine *Community*, Ella Jenkins contrasts what she characterizes as the "overly-stylized," "much too rehearsed, polished" singing of freedom singers on the album *Sit-In Songs* with the singing documented on *Freedom in the Air*. She says of *Freedom in the Air*, "this recording has a simple beginning: a slow-moving, long-metered, mournful hymn sung in a local church, sung by 'older' people, and sung with a feeling for freedom. As these moving voices continue, you listen with a kind of kinship. Next is heard a powerful, convincing voice, that of a local minister, Reverend Ben Gay . . . ."[44] In a review for *Harper's Magazine*, Eric Larrabee also contrasted the perceived authenticity of *Freedom in the Air* with the recordings on *Sit-In Songs*, which he called "the truth packaged and merchandized by the record business, and thus something less than true."[45] He goes on to remark that on *Freedom in the Air*, the "sound of protest can be heard alive and quick" and the "materials are rich with immediacy and danger."

These reviews reveal the primitivizing paradox—although the subjects are distanced and historicized, they are simultaneously granted an immediacy and closeness to the observer's conception of human nature and emotion. The older style and the older voices on *Freedom in the Air* are crucial to this evaluation for listeners, and the ideology surrounding these older styles and older people would become a sticking point between the Carawans and movement activists later. Carawan and Lomax both articulated strongly that they thought the folk traditions of the Black community were undervalued by the Black community itself, and they frequently emphasized and lifted up older traditions, even paternalistically arguing that Black communities did not understand the value of their own traditions.[46]

Freedom in the Air features eight unique instances of singing (with some performances coming back several times over the course of the record) among the spoken word excerpts. The lined-out hymn fades directly into an upbeat performance of "Woke Up This Morning with My Mind Stayed on Freedom," again suggesting the direct connection of the lined-out singing with singing of a song more prominent in movement organizing. Performances of "Over My Head," "You Better Leave Segregation Alone," "Oh Freedom," "Just a Closer Walk with Thee," "O Pritchett, O Kelly," and "Keep Your Eyes on the Prize" are also used in the documentary. Interestingly, Carawan's unedited recordings from Albany feature two performances that did not make the final album—a song written by the college-aged protestors called "When You See Me Again," and a performance of the hymn "How

Great Thou Art" by Bernice Johnson Reagon.[47] "When You See Me Again" is composed and sung in the style of commercial popular music, complete with doowop background vocals. It could easily have been heard from a jukebox or in a dancehall in 1961. Reagon embellishes "How Great Thou Art" with contemporary gospel stylings. Although in her later writing Bernice Johnson Reagon confirms that most of the singing in mass meetings and gatherings during the classical phase of the movement was in the "older style" (that of the a cappella spirituals and freedom songs), Carawan and Lomax "put their thumb on the scale" so to speak by including the lined-out hymn singing and cutting two of the performances that suggest the Civil Rights Movement participants were listening to and interacting with popular music and culture, rather than existing in some idealized isolation from these broader influences.[48]

The liner notes confirm the ideological leanings with which Carawan and Lomax approached this joint documentary effort. The notes contain an excerpt from a letter written by Lomax to Carawan about his work in Albany, including the following passage:

> I hope they [young protestors in Albany] feel proud of the cultural heritage of their forebears . . . . Tell them that they can search the world over, all the libraries, all the manuscripts, and they will never find a cultural heritage more noble, more vital, more flexible, more sophisticated, more wise, more full of love, more human or more beautiful. Tell them the whole world is shaken by hearing its faint echoes in jazz. Tell them that if they can walk into their free future with the great arts, the great laughter, the wit and the perceptiveness of life that their oppressed but always proud life-enobled [*sic*] ancestors possessed—and add to this their own sophistication, that the culture of the American Negro can become the wonder of the civilized world . . . . If they can accept the folk of the south on their own terms they will build not only an invincible political movement but a bridge of beauty that all mankind will long to walk across.[49]

The language Lomax uses here, while positive, contains some of the paternalism and primitivism that shaped what he and Carawan valued most deeply in their documenting of the music and culture of the Civil Rights Movement. Both Carawan and Lomax feel a need to inform Black Southerners what type of Black traditions they should value most, as can be seen clearly in the opening of this quote. Lomax uses some form of the word "noble" twice when describing the cultural heritage young Black Southerners receive from their ancestors, a nobility that for Lomax and Carawan seems channeled in the lined-out singing scattered throughout *Freedom in the Air*. This idea—that the folk/indigenous/native have some kind of inherent nobility because of their simplicity—ties into a long history of colonial discourse on the "noble savage" and the wisdom and authenticity of his "natural" life. One can also clearly see Lomax's bias against newer forms of African American music such as jazz, as he remarks that the world has been shaken by what he calls mere "faint echoes" of their received tradition.[50]

As the documenting efforts of the Carawans proceeded through the 1960s, they doubled down on this emphasis on an authentic Black folk culture as the lifeblood of the movement, despite the protests of many Black participants in the movement. Guy and Candie moved to Johns Island, South Carolina, from 1963 to 1965 to document and study the Gullah culture of the Black residents of that island. They documented their time on Johns Island in three of the documentary albums/books listed in Figure 10 (*Sea Island Folk Festival*, *Ain't You Got a Right to the Tree of Life*, and *Been in the Storm So Long*). The Johns Island experience also indirectly inspired one of the 1980 Smithsonian Folkways releases, *Sing for Freedom: Workshop 1964*, which is discussed below. Along with these works they published articles, produced folk festivals, and encouraged singers from the island to tour, including appearances at events as large as the Newport Folk Festival.

In a 1964 interview with Studs Terkel on WFMT radio in Chicago, Guy Carawan repeated several of the tropes that formed the backbone of his ideology about the people of the Sea Islands and the freedom singing of the movement.[51] He first contrasted the "cultivated, city-style" music of the denominational churches on the island, with the "real, old-time testimony meetings" of the praise house called Moving Star Hall, where he made the bulk of his musical recordings. He then argued that many people on Johns Island have been "brainwashed" into consuming modern gospel music more readily than the folk culture Guy himself found so compelling. He explained to Terkel that he and Candie were trying to get young people to appreciate the folk Gullah culture in the way they did. He and Alan Lomax frequently reminded the people of the island that tens of thousands paid to hear the Johns Island singers at the Newport Folk Festival; they both seemed to think that the approval of the attendees at Newport should override the aesthetic and political concerns young people and activists had with centering this tradition over the other music they listened to, found meaning in, and performed. In the same interview Carawan went on to say that he was "amazed to find unlettered people dealing with the major points of life" and that Esau Jenkins, one of Johns Island's more prominent residents, "only has a fourth-grade education, but he's got a lot of native wit, he's a genius."[52] This type of rhetoric is similar to the way Lomax marveled at the ability of Southern bluesmen to produce songs so "full of nobility and love." It is a primitivizing discourse that relies on the essentialized stasis of the people being discussed, and reacts with awe when they produce music that addresses themes that human beings frequently address in their cultural production.

The reaction of some of the people of Johns Island to *Ain't You Got a Right to the Tree of Life*, the Carawans' documentary book full of pictures, quotes, and song transcriptions, reveals that some people on or from the island saw the representation of its people as demeaning and inaccurate. Another folklorist who came to the island after the publication of *Ain't You Got a Right* reported that "the subjects of the book and their immediate neighbors are not at all charmed with its beauty. They are insulted, aggrieved, and thoroughly disillusioned with the authors who had lived for a period among them. Their protest and hurt feelings were centered mainly around the pictures, which not only concentrated on one limited section of the population but on their appearance in working clothes."[53] This report describes the limited stance with which the Carawans and Lomax tended to approach these people and their music.

In an article about a folk-song festival that Guy Carawan organized on Johns Island, Alan Lomax wrote:

> We all grew up loving and enjoying the singing of the Negro people. Because it was all around us like the soft air of our land, we took for granted that it would always be there. Only when it had almost entirely disappeared, replaced by the juke boxes, television and book-trained choruses, have we realized how much was disappearing from our lives . . . .
>
> We all know that somehow the Negro has captured in his songs the essence of the pathos, the irony, and the hope of the states of the deep South. The question will be how to nurture this tradition of sweet music so that it would continue into our future . . . . I spent most of my youth travelling around the South and recording the songs in their natural settings for the Library of Congress. There in our national archives are preserved thousands of songs virtually forgotten today. During the same period the Charleston Society for the Preservation of Spirituals faithfully learned the slave songs of the Sea Islands and presented them on records, in books, and in concerts. But neither of these efforts affected the Negro community itself, which

> turned its back on the old traditions on the ground that they were symbols of slavery and degradation. Until recently it appeared that Negro folk music was a lost cause.
>
> My prophecy is that . . . the musical genius of the South, which has helped to give Southern life its flavor in spite of our special problems, will be alive again—that the strong, sweet music of our world will be linking us together and will be one of the symbols by which the South will be known and of which we will be most proud. The seeds have been sown in the live oaks near your city, and my hope is that, because the musical soil is so rich there, the growth will be generous and of benefit to generations to come.[54]

Many of the tropes discussed above are present in this article, including the paternalistic chiding of Black Southerners for not recognizing the value of this tradition for themselves and the assertion that "juke boxes, television and book-trained choruses" are inferior cultural pursuits, evidences of a decadent modern society that must be resisted. Present in this excerpt is also a tendency to associate Black people in general, and the people of Johns Island specifically, with nature. For instance, Lomax juxtaposes the "singing of the Negro people" that is "all around us like the soft air" with the trappings of modern society of which he disapproves. He talks about recording songs in their "natural settings" and argues that the "seeds [of a future built on the musical genius of the South] have been sown in the live oaks near your city" where the "musical soil is rich." All of these nature metaphors and references associate the Black residents of Johns Island closely with nature, while assuming that the unmarked (assumed White) readers of Lomax's article come from the modern and civilized city, which is desperately in need of the natural authenticity of the old culture of Johns Island. Again, all of this is a primitivizing discourse, which locks the documentary accounts of Lomax and the Carawans, and by extension those who consume them, into a limited understanding of the music and the lives of these people. This romanticization and conflation of Black people with nature is particularly ironic given that, as discussed in chapter 4, the Black residents of Warren County, North Carolina, would, in a few short years from the date of this article, reveal that Black communities across the United States disproportionately bear the brunt of the disposal of toxic waste and other environmental contaminants.

As Kristen Turner summarizes, the Carawans participated in and organized several workshops that were intended to be places of musical exchange for songleaders and activists involved in the movement.[55] In 1964, they organized the "Sing for Freedom Festival and Workshop," which was, in Guy's words, intended to present "the full range of Negro folk music and freedom songs to young freedom workers."[56] At this workshop, Carawan had the Sea Island Singers and Black folk singer Doc Reese lead sessions, which elicited an intense debate about the place of this music in the modern Freedom Movement. At the same gathering, Guy taught twenty freedom songs to the more than fifty singers from across the South, as well as several Northern folk singers including Phil Ochs, Len Chandler, Tom Paxton, and Theo Bikel. As Turner mentions, this shows Guy "reinforcing the canonical status of certain songs."[57] Carawan's own biases about folk music affected which songs (and what types of music) he perpetuated in scenarios like these workshops, as well as in his documentary work.

One can see this impulse begin to cloud the way the Carawans interpret the shifting cultural emphases of the Civil Rights Movement over the late 1960s. In their 1968 book that documents the music of the movement, *Freedom Is a Constant Struggle*, they betray their own ambivalence toward the shifts occurring in the singing and the politics of the movement. Although they do include some of the songs from more diverse musical sources and styles rising to prominence within movement culture, they cast doubt as to whether these songs can function as powerfully as more traditional freedom songs. The Carawans begin their introduction to *Freedom Is a Constant Struggle* with Stokely Carmichael's quote: "No more long prayers, no more Freedom songs, no more dreams—let's go for power."[58] They continue:

> Here is a book of Freedom songs—songs that have evolved since the 1963 March on Washington. Already many of them seem outdated in light of the new mood within the civil rights movement. The days of singing, "We love everybody . . . We love George Wallace" have passed. Many battle-scarred veterans of the last six years can no longer stand with arms crossed and sing with great hope and expectation that "the truth will make us free."
>
> . . . Since 1960, there have been tremendous changes in the civil rights movement. The veterans of those six years have experienced disillusionment and growth. With the new demands of Black Power they are trying to grapple with more realistic ways to change our society. Just what forms of expression, musical or otherwise, will accompany these new developments must be left to some future book.[59]

By juxtaposing Carmichael's quote with a paragraph about the importance of singing to the movement, the Carawans make their position clear on where they hope movement participants will come down on the question before them. They go on to rehearse the major successes of the Southern nonviolent movement before finishing with the second paragraph above. This serves to reinforce the idea that the singing played a definitive role in these successes, and that the current strain of skepticism rippling through movement circles is misguided. Interestingly, in 1968 they did not separate Black Power and other new developments from the Civil Rights Movement; there was no sense for the Carawans that the movement was losing momentum—merely changing, and in a way with which they disagreed.

Some of these sentiments can be seen as well in the 2007 edition of *Sing for Freedom*, which combines 1963's *We Shall Overcome* and 1968's *Freedom Is a Constant Struggle*. In it, the oversimplified declension narrative that is deconstructed throughout this book is on full display. In the Preface, the Carawans argue, "This [the 1965 Selma March] would be the last great march with a hopeful spirit of black and white together. Soon the cry for black power would be heard and the singing would give way to chanting and an angrier mood."[60] Here, we find repeated the argument that Black Power silenced the musicking of the Black Freedom Movement altogether to its detriment. As we have seen, this is far from accurate but it does reveal the ideological standpoint from which the Carawans are looking back on the events of the 1960s and beyond. In 2007, the Carawans seemed to have accepted the narrative that the evolutions in the late 1960s led to the end of the movement and its singing. They are calling for the remembrance of what the songs meant at the height of the movement, hoping that new movements will take them up, just as before. Given the assumptions underlying this hope, however, it reads as counterproductive nostalgia. Rather than attending to the music that *has* continued to accompany Black freedom movements since 1968, the Carawans in 2007 seem content to accept what Elizabeth Ellis Miller calls the "rhetorical depreciation" of freedom song as a genre, and make a meager call to preserve these songs from being "lost."[61]

The Carawans' ambivalence about modern developments in the movement that diverged in philosophy and style from their preferred version of protest and freedom singing aligns with Stuart Hall's understanding of the ambivalence of the "imperial eye." About depictions of the colonized by the colonizer, Hall says, "One noticeable aspect about all these depictions is their *ambivalence* . . . . The primitive nobility of the ageing tribesman or chief, and the native's rhythmic grace always contain both a nostalgia for an innocence lost forever to the civilized, and the threat of civilization being overrun or undermined by the recurrence of savagery, which is always lurking just below the surface . . . . Both are aspects—the good and the bad sides—of *primitivism* [emphasis original]."[62] One can sense a fear behind the Carawans' ambivalent statements about the evolutions of the late 1960s. The "new angry mood" as they describe it is the corollary of their romanticized view of the folk culture of Black Southerners in Hall's formulation; nostalgia for the goodness and innocence of "premodern" culture as represented by traditional freedom singing is paired with a lurking, threatening violence as represented by the newer music Black freedom fighters were beginning to find more appealing.

Another aspect of the Carawans' ideological commitments can be seen in the connections they draw between the movement and their concept of folk culture in the late 1960s and beyond. In the Introduction to *Freedom Is a Constant Struggle* (1968), after expressing their ambivalence about the "new mood" in the movement, they write, "An important part of the new mood within the movement is a proud embracing of American folk heritage and its earlier African roots . . . . Included in this development is a growing awareness and appreciation of Negro folk music. This is why we have included a chapter on the roots—old spirituals, children's songs, work songs, and blues—songs that have sung freedom and protested in their own way, some of them since slavery times."[63] The Carawans do not include in this description the significant resistance they faced as they lifted up their folk aesthetic among Black activists. This continued focus can be seen in their production of the album *Sing for Freedom: Workshop 1964* in 1980, which featured music of the Birmingham Movement choir, the Georgia Sea Island Singers, White Northern folk singer Phil Ochs, Black Northern folk singer Len Chandler, and Doc Reese, who, according to the Carawans, was a "masterful singer of prison work songs."[64] It is telling that in 1980, when looking back on the movement and documenting its music, the Carawans emphasized this folk conception of freedom singing.

In the Preface to *Sing for Freedom* (1992), the Carawans write about the workshops that were intended to bring together traditional singers with movement activists: "These gatherings, in addition to focusing on the current freedom culture, also encouraged the reclaiming of a rich Afro-American past. Folklorists—Alan Lomax and Willis James, in particular—met freedom fighters at these conferences and intense discussions took place about the value of older cultural traditions to contemporary struggles." As we saw above, Black activists often took exception to the idea that White folklorists should be imposing their ideas of Black culture on the movement during these "intense discussions."[65]

These post-1968 documentary efforts reveal that the ideology with which the Carawans approached the people of Johns Island continued as they remembered the movement and framed their documentation of it. Despite the fact that they had great admiration for the people of Johns Island, Lomax and the Carawans were operating under the folkloric comparative method, which, as Karl Hagstrom Miller argues, is undergirded by a Darwinian paradigm.[66] We can see by the ways they represented the freedom singing of the people of Birmingham and Johns Island that the Carawans and Lomax believed cultures evolve from primitive to civilized, that isolation gives a window into the "primitive," and that the "primitive" is closer to what it means to be fundamentally human than the mediated forms of engagement in modern life.

On a continuum of approaches to Black folk music, the Carawans would fall partway between Alan Lomax's overt primitivism and the work of Bernice Johnson Reagon, who did emphasize Black folk music as a valuable tradition, but did so without any of the tropes on which Lomax's ideology relied. The Carawans were less explicitly hostile toward forms of Black popular music than Lomax, although occasionally they did articulate their preference for folk music and their suspicion about more commercialized forms of Black music.[67] Unlike Reagon, however, the Carawans went further than simply exploring the positive uses for Black folk music; they cast doubt on the effectiveness of a movement that did not sing traditional music, and heavily emphasized (what they perceived to be) more isolated forms of Black folk music, even as movement songleaders and participants began to explore more popular material for their freedom singing. Although she worked primarily as a folk artist and lifted up many forms of Black folk music in her time at the Smithsonian, Reagon also embraced other forms of music, such as her experimentation with rap and other genres while with Sweet Honey in the Rock, as well as politics that diverged from the mainstream Civil Rights Movement, including her exploration of Black Arts and Black Power with the Harambee Singers.[68]

Aside from its fundamentally demeaning nature, the problem with Lomax and the Carawans approaching freedom singing in this way is that it prevented them from fully documenting and appreciating the complexities of the tradition with which they were enamored. Not only did the Carawans tend to overemphasize the type of freedom singing that conformed to their ideals about the folk, but Guy also performed interventions in the music culture itself, cultivating and reinforcing a canon based on his own framework. Carawan and Lomax demonstrate that, when trained on freedom singing, White aurality desires its own conceptions of blackness—conceptions that often primitivize and reduce rather than illuminate and nuance. White aurality values reduced conceptions of blackness over the demonstrated expressive plurality of Black people. The limited canon of freedom song, which was strongly influenced by Lomax and Carawan's ideology about folk music, created the world in which it was necessary for Tammy Kernodle to argue for an expansion of the canon of freedom song to include Nina Simone, an argument that Black activists in the 1960s and 70s would likely have taken for granted, but one that was a necessary watershed in the context of the post-1968 movement historiography where a canon of freedom song based largely on early documentation by White folklorist-musicians is firmly ensconced.[69]

The constructed authenticity attached to traditional freedom singing in the Civil Rights Movement has political consequences as well. If the folk expressions of the isolated Southern Black church are the "authentic" representations of sonic blackness, then the politics associated with those sounds are granted outsized credence, and other political and musical expressions of the movement are ignored or outright resisted. Because the idea of freedom song has been tethered solely to Kingian nonviolence, the Carawans' documentary approach reinforces the oversimplified consensus narrative of the movement and the 1968 lens, which views with suspicion any musical—and by extension, political—strands that do not align with the one constructed as authentic and truly representative of the people's struggle for freedom.

Curating the Stories, Sights, and Sounds of Freedom in *Eyes on the Prize*

In 1978, Henry Hampton, founder of the film and media company Blackside, Inc., wrote, "There has been no serious, inclusive television project that focuses on the little-known participants and major issues of post-WWII civil rights activity. They have always been done by whites who depicted black folks as poor, downtrodden, and brutalized primitives . . . but it was the strength of blacks that made the civil rights movement happen, with support from some whites."[70] After marching with King in Selma, Hampton had watched the documenting of the movement perpetuate primitivized understandings of Black people and oversimplified understandings of the movement itself. The name of his film company signaled the goal Hampton sought to achieve—to correct the imbalance in the way history was being portrayed by offering the world a view from the "Black side." Hampton demonstrated in word and deed his commitment to amplifying Black understandings of the movement and documenting the history of the Black freedom struggle with its complexity intact.

Blackside's landmark series *Eyes on the Prize* (*Eyes*) is a documentary effort that maintains many of the tensions and troubling details of movement history that are often glossed over and oversimplified. *Eyes* presents a nuanced picture of the interconnectedness of various strands of the movement that challenges the consensus memory that had already developed by its release in the late 1980s. On the whole, the narrative and its use of freedom singing illustrate how movement documentaries can subvert the problematic assumptions that undergird the consensus memory of the freedom struggle. The ways in which liberal institutions interacted with the production of *Eyes* give us an understanding of how these institutions attempted to produce knowledge in alignment with their vision of the world, and how Hampton and Blackside resisted their attempts to control the narrative.

While it may well be possible to follow the example of *Eyes*, the complex narrative it tells has not yet permeated U.S. consciousness. Contemporary documentaries such as *Soundtrack for a Revolution*, along with other ways the memory of the Civil Rights Movement is leveraged in contemporary political life, demonstrate that a mythic cultural memory is still intact, despite Hampton's best efforts to dislodge it.

Henry Hampton decided he wanted to start a film company in 1968. In the year that "everything went wrong," after participating in movement activities, completing his education, and working with the Black caucus of the Unitarian Universalist Church of America, Hampton made the remarkable decision to focus his intellect and passion on educational nonfiction filmmaking.[71] Hampton and the other filmmakers at his company Blackside spent ten years making short industry films and public service spots, before Capital Cities Communications (Cap Cities) gave Hampton the opportunity to begin work on the "serious, inclusive . . . history of post-WWII civil rights activity." Cap Cities was trying to contract minority producers to improve its diversity quotient for an FCC license renewal, and they asked Blackside to propose and "develop a major television project of its choice."[72] That original Cap Cities project, which Hampton titled *America, We Loved You Madly*, was to focus on the Southern Civil Rights Movement from 1954 to 1965. It failed spectacularly, due in part to differing visions of what the project should be (sober and nuanced historical documentary or catchy Watergate-style exposé that would drive ratings) and in part to Blackside's amateur mistakes. In 1985, however, PBS commissioned Blackside to produce *Eyes on the Prize: America's Civil Rights Years, 1954 to 1965*, a multipart history of the movement free from the strictures of commercial television. The first six episodes would air in February of 1987, while the eight-part *Eyes on the Prize II: America at the Racial Crossroads, 1965 to 1985* (*Eyes II*) aired in 1990.

The context in which *Eyes* was developed and released—the United States in the 1980s—was a turbulent and generative time for the production and contestation of the history of the Civil Rights Movement. The decade began with the trial of four Miami police officers who brutally killed Black resident of Liberty City Arthur McDuffie in late 1979. The officers were acquitted by a majority White jury in May 1980, sparking riots in which fifteen people were killed. These were the deadliest such uprisings since the Detroit riots of 1967.[73] At the same time, Ronald Reagan ran for and won the presidency, explicitly stating that he would continue what Nixon had started, rolling back policy gains made by the Civil Rights Movement of the 1960s. In 1982, the six-week civil disobedience campaign that catalyzed the environmental justice movement in Warren County, North Carolina, garnered national attention.[74] The push to fund and establish the Birmingham Civil Rights Institute and the National Civil Rights Museum in Memphis took place throughout the decade. In 1983, Harold Washington was elected as the first Black mayor of Chicago. In December of 1986, just one month before *Eyes* premiered, several young Black men were attacked by a White mob in New York City. The mob chased one of the men, Michael Griffith, onto a highway where a car struck and killed him. Throughout the decade, the fight to establish Martin Luther King Jr. Day raged in Congress, highlighting the continued contestation of the movement's meaning in American life. Reagan signed a bill allowing for the federal commemoration of the holiday in 1983, but it was not officially celebrated until January 1986. Just before MLK Day in January 1987 (the day before *Eyes* premiered) Arizona governor Evan Mecham made it his first act to rescind his predecessor's proclamation of Arizona's commemoration of the holiday, sparking national boycotts of the state. In 1984 and 1988 Black civil rights activist Jesse Jackson ran high-profile campaigns seeking the Democratic nomination for president. All the first major academic publications about movement history appeared in the 1980s, including Clayborne Carson's *In Struggle* (1981), David Garrow's

Bearing the Cross (1986), Howard Zinn's *SNCC: The New Abolitionists*, and the first of Taylor Branch's *America in the King Years* (1988) trilogy. Before the 1980s, a comprehensive history of the movement did not exist. In fact, Henry Hampton had to ask Judy Richardson to create a timeline of Civil Rights Movement events for the *America, We Loved You Madly* pitch to Cap Cities executives.[75]

It was in this climate that Hampton and Blackside developed and released *Eyes* as an attempt to recalibrate how the U.S. public understood the events of two decades prior. *Eyes* participated in a long history of nonfiction filmmaking that acted as "a key medium for narrating as well as managing the nation's escalating engagement with race and racism."[76] Many of the people discussed throughout this book intersect in the late 1980s by contributing to *Eyes*. Bernice Johnson Reagon recorded music for the series, was interviewed for some of the episodes, and served as a contract music consultant. Benjamin Chavis, who was active in the Warren County movement, appeared as an interviewee in the series. Several recordings made by Guy Carawan and Moses Moon were used for the series, and Guy and Candie Carawan served as contract music consultants. Carawan also sent notes about rough cuts and taught a session on the history of the music for the production staff. Many of the activists, freedom singers, and thinkers who had contributed to the early historiography of the movement came together to continue that conversation in *Eyes*.

The *Eyes* production staff was very conscious of how they used music in the series. Before the production of *Eyes II*, Hampton asked the entire staff to participate in several weeks of what they affectionately referred to as "Eyes School," where experts in various fields of movement history were brought in to give the documentary staff a full and nuanced understanding of the history. The staff recorded the sessions, including those sessions on music. Ethnomusicologist Portia Maultsby, Guy Carawan, Odetta, and Bernice Johnson Reagon all led sessions teaching the staff about the music of the movement and the history of African American music more generally. Before one of the sessions, the production staff discussed their conception of how music should function in documentary filmmaking. The comments included that "music is emotional, music is manipulative, music is editorial," and that "music, even if it isn't being sung at the time, is a thread of the politics, a thread of the strategy. It has to be used in the same way that you use shots of film, the same way you use the [ambient] sound."[77] Later in the meeting, while discussing how music should match the context of the footage, someone remarked, "Was that the song of that movement or are you just slapping 'We Shall Overcome' everywhere?" There are copious amounts of notes and letters exchanged between production team members and music consultants that reveal how detailed and labored the decisions they made were over what music to include in the series. These statements and documents reveal a complex understanding of music's role in meaning-making through the medium of documentary film and heighten the importance of the musical choices made throughout the series.

For instance, in a document written by associate producer Llewellyn Smith, Smith shares notes he received from Bernice Johnson Reagon on Season 1, Episodes 1 and 2 with the production team. In one section Reagon critiques the initial choices for the section on Emmett Till. Smith reports that Reagon "strongly suggests we change the music over the shots of Tallahatchie River, feels Jessye Norman humming 'Steal Away to Jesus' is a throwback to slavery that is out of context here."[78] Later in the memo, Smith says Reagon was unhappy with the version of "O What a Beautiful City" they had selected for the end of the Montgomery segment because the "guitar for her was inappropriate for Montgomery."

From the first freedom singing one hears in *Eyes*, a statement about the complexity of the history is made. Appropriately, the entire series is named after a spiritual-turned-freedom-song. The version of "Keep Your Eyes on the Prize" that accompanies the title sequence in each episode was arranged and recorded by Bernice Johnson Reagon, and communicates some of what Hampton aimed to do with the entire series. The text of the verse chosen to accompany the refrain in the title sequence says, "I know the one thing we did right, was the day we started to fight! Keep your eyes on the prize, hold on." Implicit in this line for those who know the music of the movement is the verse that precedes it: "The only thing that we did wrong, stayed in the wilderness a day too long. Keep your eyes on the prize, hold on." Equating the word "fight" with the rightness of the movement gives the singing of this song a more aggressive edge than many other instances of freedom singing. The vocal performance on the recording strengthens this analysis. For an a cappella performance, the rhythmic drive of the twenty-second clip is remarkable. This is achieved by energetic accenting, strategic interplay/call-and-response between the songleader and the simulated congregation, and a level of swing not often achieved without an instrumental rhythm section. The shouted "hey!" after the first line of sung text suggests the inclusion of chanting alongside singing as expressive tools for freedom singers.

With its use of "we" and references to staying in the wilderness and starting to fight, "Keep Your Eyes on the Prize" also foregrounds the communal, decentralized nature of the movement's typical organizing methods, in contrast to the heroic figure narratives often presented. This communal sentiment is amplified by the way the backing vocals enter along with the accompanying images that appear. After the shouted "hey!," the backup singers join in singing "was the day we started to fight." As the clip progresses, more and more voices join as more and more animated marchers appear on the screen. Women's voices are the first we hear, and they lead throughout, with the men's voices joining halfway through the recording, which suggests the often-overlooked leadership of local women in movement organizing. It was one of Hampton's goals to highlight the contributions of the "fan ladies" and "ordinary world parishioners" rather than focusing on the "great men" who had dominated all depictions of the movement to this point.[79] While the background vocals sing largely the same rhythms, the listener can hear the songleader and many within the congregation/choir improvising on their various lines. Little variations can be heard cascading throughout the melody and harmony parts. This kind of collective improvisation simulates the singing that might happen at a mass meeting or on a march and gives a live energy to the recording. The recording is full of what Charles Keil would call "participatory discrepancies"—slight variations in pitch, rhythm, and tone that generate excitement in musicking and encourage the listener to participate.[80]

There are four ways *Eyes* deploys freedom singing that bolster a more complex and complete narrative of the movement and its musicking:

1. When the series features traditional freedom singing, such singing is used in a diverse and interesting way, often showing the conflicted and contested nature of singing optimistic freedom songs while doubting the outcome of the struggle;
2. *Eyes* makes frequent use of various other genres (including popular music) that played an important role in civil rights activities and held deep meaning for the participants;
3. *Eyes* features singing and chanting from unexpected factions that express different tactics than nonviolence; and
4. *Eyes* clearly demonstrates through diegetic and nondiegetic music that freedom singing played a vital role after 1965, when the consensus narrative has movement music waning.

Analysis of the uses of some of the canonic and iconic freedom songs in the series illustrates *Eyes*'s thoughtful depiction of traditional freedom singing. The series emphasizes the contested meanings generated when singing these songs, even during the classical phase of the movement. A frequent note in the production documents suggests finding appropriate recordings of iconic songs that match the specific sound the editorial team is seeking.[81] In a 1989 letter from one of the producers, Sheila Curran Bernard, to sound editor Leah Mahan on the music for "Episode 202 [which would eventually become 'Season 2, Episode 2 | Two Societies']," Bernard notes that they are "still searching for the recording they want" but will definitely be using "We Shall Overcome."[82] In a 1986 letter from Guy and Candie Carawan to the production team, the Carawans insist that the production team select a recording that is contemporary to the time they are depicting.[83] They say, "This version" of "We Shall Overcome" is "appropriate to the time—recorded in early 1961. You should listen carefully and pick out some section that fits." What is clear from these examples and others in Hampton's papers is that the music team labored to incorporate different versions of the canonic songs to show the breadth of the singing that was done and to complicate any oversimplified understandings of what they meant to movement participants.

The uses of "We Shall Overcome" in "Season 1, Episode 4 | No Easy Walk" show a particularly deft hand in accentuating the song's poignancy for the movement as well as its conflicted nature. At 16:00, after a particularly lively performance of "Ain't Gonna Let Nobody Turn Me Around" in Albany, Georgia, Bernice Johnson Reagon discusses how most of the meetings in Albany were filled with singing.[84] She says, "Most of the work that was done in terms of taking care of Movement business had to do with nurturing the people who had come. And there would be two or three people who would talk, but basically song was the bed of everything." The episode then moves directly into a clip of "We Shall Overcome" that Albany mass meeting attenders sang as they exited a meeting. They updated the words and sang "We shall go to jail, we shall go to jail, we shall go to jail someday . . . ." The episode then moves to discussing Martin Luther King Jr. and Ralph Abernathy attempting to serve a forty-five-day jail sentence as a strategic act to win attention and support for the Albany cause. They were thwarted, however, by someone "mysteriously paying their fine." This instance of "We Shall Overcome" then takes on new meaning. It shows the defiance of the song in the right context but also immediately calls into question the strategy and tactics it represented. King's nonviolent approach did not work as well as intended in Albany because the chief of police, Laurie Pritchett, had studied the movement's tactics and often sought to deescalate situations before they became public relations disasters for him and the city government. In the next interview cut, Pritchett admits that he arranged to have King released in hopes that King would leave town. This performance of "We Shall Overcome" is then invested with both the determination and the frustration of working with national movement leadership and negotiating the best strategic path forward.

At the 45:00 mark of the same episode, "We Shall Overcome" is used to frame the March on Washington sequence. We hear the song three times over the course of the sequence. First, the dignified and stalwart SNCC Freedom Singers recording plays over images of protestors gathering in D.C. and heading toward the Lincoln Memorial. About this particular recording, Bernice Johnson Reagon says, "This version's use of cross-punctuating calls from all voices reflects the congregational music tradition of Albany. In Albany's mass meetings, the song was slowed down, providing more space for improvised, spontaneous vocal elisions, leads, and cross-statements of lines."[85] By using the sounds of this particular recording, the documentary makes the statement that the ambiguities and difficulties of the Albany movement (and other local movements) have now come together in unmitigated success. The movement seems to have made the singing of "We Shall Overcome" true in this moment—overcoming felt within reach and, in many ways, the March on Washington was itself an overcoming.

The recording fades out as the narrator talks about "trouble behind the scenes." The narrator and interviewees then discuss John Lewis's planned speech, which criticized the Kennedy administration for its lack of enforcement of civil rights legislation. Bayard Rustin and A. Philip Randolph pleaded with John Lewis and other representatives from SNCC to change the speech and pacify the White House. Lewis and the others eventually decided to compromise and rewrite the speech out of a spirit of unity and out of respect for Randolph. The viewer then hears a clip from Lewis's speech and the narrator discusses King's "I Have a Dream" speech, after which the second instance of "We Shall Overcome" commences. The film shows Black and White marchers engaging in the traditional crossed-arm, swaying performance of the song; the singing is loud, robust, and joyful. The third instance of the song, a version featuring organ and female soloist, crossfades in as the singing of marchers fades out. This final instance recalls the roots of the song (and the movement itself) in the Black church. The music ends as scenes from the aftermath of the march are shown and the narrator and interviewees reflect on its success. This sequence shows the anthemic status of "We Shall Overcome" for the nonviolent movement and suggests that its performance cultivated unity, compromise, and fulfillment of the hopes they had for the movement up to this point.

The episode immediately cuts to footage of the 16th Street Baptist Church in Birmingham, Alabama, with sirens blaring in the background. Less than three weeks after the March on Washington, four girls were murdered and fifteen others injured in a racist attack on the church. The episode concludes with scenes from the funerals of the children who were murdered in the 16th Street Baptist Church bombing. Funeral attendees sing a sober and mournful version of "We Shall Overcome" as the narrator says, "[T]he murder of these children shook the nonviolent movement to its core. They sang 'We Shall Overcome' but in anger and in rage, many wondered how." The credits roll as the funeralgoers sing "God is on our side."

Moving directly from singing "We Shall Overcome" at the March on Washington to singing it at the funeral of the victims of the 16th Street bombing illustrates the fraught and multivalent nature of the song's meanings. The song becomes a site to contest whether nonviolence is a viable strategy, whether the people really believe that "God is on their side." The complex meanings generated from these instances of "We Shall Overcome" are representative of the way traditional freedom singing is used throughout the series. There is almost never a naïve or oversimplified meaning suggested by the placement of these songs/this singing, which is in keeping with Hampton's understanding of the movement and the goal of the series.

The second way *Eyes* deploys music in the series is by frequently incorporating other genres in the narrative, effectively rejecting the idea that traditional freedom singing was the only kind of musicking that was meaningful to movement participants. As is to be expected, the preponderance of traditional freedom singing occurs in the first six episodes, which cover 1954 to 1965, whereas more popular music is used in the latter eight episodes covering 1966 to 1985. However, popular music and other vernacular styles are used in the first six episodes while traditional freedom singing is both used diegetically and depicted nondiegetically in the latter eight, as we will see below.

The music in "Season 1, Episode 5 | Mississippi: Is This America?" is paradigmatic of the diversity of styles that are used to accompany the activities of the classical phase of the movement. The episode begins by introducing Freedom Summer with scenes of children playing at Freedom Schools and young volunteers descending on Mississippi while the 1962 instrumental blues rock track "Green Onions" by Booker T and the M.G.'s plays. Within this episode alone the viewer/listener hears "Green Onions," a blues tune played on harmonica; "We Shall Not Be Moved," a "freedom" chant over organ improvisation; "Ballad of Medgar Evers" by Matthew Jones; Bob Dylan's "Blowing in the Wind"; some fife and drum music; "We Shall Overcome"; "In the Mississippi River" by the Freedom Singers; and "Go Tell It on the Mountain" led by Fannie Lou Hamer. This diversity accurately depicts the complex soundscape of the movement, which was far more ideologically and musically porous than historians and documentarians have typically recounted.

The third way *Eyes* undermines the consensus narrative of the movement with its use of freedom singing is by featuring singing from those factions within the movement that have conventionally been depicted as violent, angry, and opposed to singing, challenging the absoluteness of the tethering of freedom singing to nonviolence. "Season 2, Episode 1 | The Time Has Come," which documents Malcolm X's growing influence on the movement and the rise of Black Power as a powerful rallying cry, features several striking examples of this. At the beginning of the episode, after hearing Malcolm criticize old school movement leadership, the viewer sees and hears a group of protestors sing a new version of "Down by the Riverside" with the lyrics "Gonna lay down my jumpin' shoes down by the riverside, and I ain't gonna shuffle no more!" We then hear Jimmy Collier and Frederick Douglass Kirkpatrick's "Everybody's Got a Right to Live." Collier and Kirkpatrick were advocates of self-defense rather than nonviolence but were also songleaders in the Chicago Freedom Movement (also called the End-the-Slums Movement), which King's Southern Christian Leadership Conference spearheaded.[86] In the next scene we watch a group of Black Panther Party (BPP) members standing in formation, wearing black jackets and berets, many sporting Afros, singing "Black is beautiful, Free Huey! Said I wanna free, Free Huey!" In all senses of the term this is freedom singing, and yet, this footage from *Eyes* is one of the few examples of recordings of Black Panthers singing, and it has not been discussed as freedom song. This song will return in Season 2, Episode 3, where we see some Black Panthers teaching it to schoolchildren during the BPP's free breakfast program.[87] The editorial team decided not to include provocative b-roll footage of the Panthers teaching the same children a call-and-response style song/chant that proclaimed "The revolution has come, off the pigs! It's time to pick up your guns, freedom!"[88] This clip further illustrates the wildly different ideologies that drew from freedom singing as a means of protest and organizing.

At the 43:00 mark of Season 2, Episode 1, the viewer sees footage of some marchers for the Lowndes County Freedom Organization singing an a cappella version of Wilson Pickett's "Land of 1000 Dances" during a voter registration drive in the summer of 1966. “Land of 1000 Dances” had been recorded several times before Pickett’s version; however, Pickett’s was released in July of 1966 and quickly topped the Billboard Hot Rhythm and Blues chart. The marchers’ version featured improvised verses that inject the one-word refrain with a much different meaning. The clip shows the marchers singing “Freedom’s got a shotgun (hey hey!), I said Freedom’s got a shotgun (hey hey!) and Freedom’s gonna shoot it (hey hey!), at those segregated bigots! (hey hey!) Nah nah nah nah nah. . . .” Although the songleader is a young man, the crowd singing is of varying ages and genders. When the refrain arrives, the songleader is lifted up on the shoulders of some other marchers, and the viewer can see some young, sullen-looking White men standing with arms crossed on the steps of a building behind the marchers as they sing “nah nah nah nah nah!” The Pickett recording then fades in over footage of continued voter registration activity. This performance is quite telling, because it breaks down the myths surrounding what types of musicking belong to whom in the movement.

The final way *Eyes* challenges typical freedom song narratives is by documenting that singing occurred and was still meaningful long after the dominant narrative claims singing became obsolete to the movement. Between 27:30 and 36:00 of “Season 2, Episode 5 | Ain’t Gonna Shuffle No More,” we see protestors in the Howard University student movement of 1968 drumming and singing several times. At 27:30, the students are singing an original song, “Are You Ready Now?,” which transitions into a chant accompanied by drumming: “beep beep, bang bang, ungawa, Black power!” At 33:03, students are shown singing “We Shall Not Be Moved” with an improvised verse stating “Tell D.C. cops now, we shall not be moved!” Then at 35:45, a group of students sings the version of “Down by the Riverside” mentioned above with the lyrics “Gonna lay down my shuffling shoes down by the riverside, and I ain’t gonna shuffle no more!” The singing is powerful and forceful—the spirit and technique is in no way diminished from the singing of the Albany movement or other Southern movements famous for their powerful freedom singing. Freedom singing was a vital part of the Howard students’ struggle against a university administration that resisted the rising Black Consciousness on campus.

In the opening montage of “Season 2, Episode 6 | A Nation of Laws,” a protestor being forced into a paddy wagon by riot police outside the 1968 Democratic National Convention in Chicago sings “We Shall Overcome” defiantly into the faces of the police officers arresting her. At 13:38 in the same episode, congregants at a mass meeting sing “Free Fred Hampton,

Free Fred Hampton fascist pigs, Free Fred Hampton, we need our warrior beside us!" to the tune of "Wade in the Water." The episode then shows a White man recounting how he was in the congregation at a Black church in Chicago that welcomed Fred Hampton when he was released on bond. Everything about this sequence challenges traditional narratives of the movement—that freedom singing stopped as Black Consciousness rose, that more militant arms of the movement such as the Black Panther Party did not affiliate with the church-based movement, that militant Black activists did not allow White people to participate in the movement. Later in the episode, Nina Simone's recording of "I Wish I Knew How It Would Feel to Be Free" plays over footage from Hampton's funeral. *Eyes* featured very similar sequences for the funerals of Medgar Evers; Addie Mae Collins, Cynthia Wesley, Carole Robertson, and Carol Denise McNair (the 16th Street Church bombing victims); James Chaney; and Martin Luther King Jr. By treating Hampton's service in the same way and accompanying it by Simone's singing, *Eyes* reclaims Hampton (and Simone's music) as part of the lineage of funeral services for freedom fighters and victims of racist violence accompanied by freedom singing.

A final example of this usage of freedom singing comes in "Season 2, Episode 7 | The Keys to the Kingdom," which tells the story of the school desegregation fight in Boston, Massachusetts in the 1970s. At the 2:00 mark, a large crowd of protestors outside of the Old City Hall building sing "No more segregation, no more segregation, no more segregation over me . . . " to the tune of "Oh Freedom." The performance is accompanied by guitar and shows a singing style influenced by the White Northern folksong tradition. This example continues to deconstruct the idea that when the movement moved North, it went silent. It also challenges the hard date that is typically fixed around 1968 for the end of the movement. If the struggle in Boston lasted through the 1970s and was accompanied by similar organizing, similar sounds, and similar goals as the classical phase of the movement in the South, can it truly be excluded from the timeline?

The most problematic moments in *Eyes*, from the standpoint of musical oversimplification, come at the outset and the conclusion of the fourteen-episode series when the series attempts to summarize and universalize the movement rather than document it in its granularity. The opening montage of Season 1, Episode 1 features a pastiche of traditional freedom song, including the "Freedom Now" chant, "Go Tell It on the Mountain," "Woke Up This Morning with My Mind Stayed on Freedom," "We Shall Not Be Moved," "Been in the Storm So Long," and "We Shall Overcome." This montage gives the impression that traditional freedom singing is the only important music to accompany the journey on which the viewer is preparing to embark.

The relationship between music, video, and narration at the conclusion to the series is more complex. At 51:35, Season 2, Episode 8 transitions from the content of the particular episode to summarizing and concluding the series. Unita Blackwell speaks about going from being denied a seat at the 1964 Democratic National Convention as a delegate of the Mississippi Freedom Democratic Party to speaking from the podium at the 1984 Democratic National Convention. Footage of Jesse Jackson speaking at the same convention shows him articulating his famous idea of America as a rainbow nation. Melba Moore's 1990 recording of "Lift Every Voice and Sing" enters under narration of the movement inspiring other movements around the world and under footage of the Berlin Wall falling, anti-apartheid protestors in South Africa, and protestors in Tiananmen Square in China. Moore's recording of "Lift Every Voice" benefited Black charities and organizations and featured luminaries such as Terri Lyne Carrington, Stevie Wonder, BeBe and CeCe Winans, Dionne Warwick, Jeffrey Osborne, Stephanie Mills, and the gospel/jazz ensemble Take 6.[89] In the music video for "Lift," actor Louis Gossett Jr. narrates the beginning of the track: "There is no wall, no barrier of resistance, that can stop the tumultuous tide of everlasting hope. So through it all, keep hope alive! All over the world as the walls crumble, hope rises. Nelson Mandela glories in the words, the beat, the melody, and the joy, and the victory, and the conquest. There's no turning back. Let freedom ring! Lift every voice and sing, 'til the power comes down!"[90] This preface in the song's music video reinforces the universalizing tropes *Eyes* is drawing on as well—Gossett's narration and *Eyes* even make the same comparisons to international movements.

The concluding thoughts of Season 2, Episode 8 then turn to contemporary issues in the U.S. Black community, but do so in a problematic and surface-level manner. "Use of drugs" and "crime" are mentioned in vague terms without the thoroughgoing and contextualizing analysis that would allow a balanced understanding of the structural causes of these issues. The viewer is left with the impression that the classical movement as represented by "Lift Every Voice and Sing" succeeded in inspiring great struggles around the world but is struggling to bring an ambiguous optimism and unchanged organizing to the same problems it faced as it moved North in the 1960s. Although throughout the series *Eyes* has been careful to depict movement music in all its complexity, it regrettably uses only traditional freedom singing to accompany the moments when it gives ultimate and transcendent meaning to the movement.

This usage of "Lift Every Voice and Sing" can be contrasted with another filmic usage from the same time period: that of the memorable opening sequence of Spike Lee's *Do the Right Thing*. *Do the Right Thing* begins with a stately solo saxophone playing the melody to "Lift." The sax is then usurped by the confrontational sounds of Public Enemy's "Fight the Power" accompanying the visual of Rosie Perez dancing against a red urban landscape. Shana Redmond says of this musical juxtaposition that "the initial verbs that ground the titles of each song [lift, fight] demonstrate the change in context as a politics of respectability gives way to the demands of a postindustrial urban insurgency."[91] Redmond goes on to argue that the transition both disrupts the memory of the "long-passed civil rights victories that the smooth jazz of 'Lift Every Voice and Sing' was meant to represent" as well as marks the politics represented by "Fight the Power" as "contiguous" with the political mobilizations of the 1950s and 60s from which it departs.[92] Lee's usage of "Lift Every Voice" comes from a complex understanding of the continuing interconnectedness of 1960s and 1980s Black protest culture, and effectively undercuts the negative oversimplifications of the 1968 lens. In addition, Lee's usage of "Lift" more closely aligns with the ways in which *Eyes* mobilizes freedom singing throughout the series when it does not feel pressed to make grand and universalizing gestures.

Henry Hampton and his team made an enormous push in the postproduction of *Eyes* and *Eyes II* to market the series for educational purposes. They produced teaching aids and companion documents for the series so that it could be used in the classroom. Five of the historians who served as consultants for the series edited *The Eyes on the Prize Civil Rights Movement Reader*, which collected documents, speeches, and oral history related to what was depicted in the film series.[93] A syllabus and materials for a "telecourse" on the Civil Rights Movement using *Eyes* was created by Toby Kleban Levine and Jacques Dubois with examination questions by historians Aldon Morris and David Stevenson. And yet, the oversimplified dominant narrative of the Civil Rights Movement persisted.

Beyond Primitivism

Returning to the subject of this chapter's opening vignette—the conclusion of the 2009 documentary *Soundtrack for the Revolution*—we can now see the contrasts between its treatment of freedom singing and civil rights history and that of *Eyes on the Prize* more clearly. Where *Soundtrack* obscures the history by glossing over the period between the 1965 Selma march and King's assassination in 1968, *Eyes* expends significant energy contextualizing and complicating common understandings of that same period. Where *Soundtrack* relies on freedom singing to sentimentalize an already misremembered history and fill in the gaps in its narrative, *Eyes* allows the multivalent meanings of freedom singing to speak through the challenging moments in movement history. Where *Soundtrack* problematically reinforces an American progress narrative on race by hastily connecting King's dream to the election of Barack Obama and utilizing "We Shall Overcome" to reinforce an overly realized optimism about that progress, *Eyes* allows the complexity of its subject period to remain unresolved.[94] These differing documentary strategies produce differing knowledge about movement history, which in turn produces differing reactions to contemporary freedom singing and freedom politicking. *Soundtrack*'s methods produce a counterproductive nostalgia and obscure the complexity of the ongoing structural problems in the United States and the ongoing movements to address them. *Eyes*'s methods generate a knowledge that allows for more precise connections and continuations to be drawn out of the history.

With *Eyes*, Henry Hampton set out to refute the kind of primitivist depictions of Black Americans he had witnessed in other documentary work on the period. The documentary work of the Carawans and Alan Lomax contains this primitivist tendency as it traffics in a discourse of "authentic" sonic blackness that disregards the complexity of Black expression. This discourse on Black authenticity and identity is much older and broader than the work of Lomax and the Carawans, and is not confined to White aural conceptions of Black people, but often begins as a negotiation among Black people themselves into which White interlopers insert themselves. Discourses about jazz within the Black community and outside of it are representative of this. The identity work negotiated through jazz continued in the discourse surrounding funk, and eventually hip hop. On one side, authenticity as a value in hip hop, funk, and jazz privileges a blackness that is innovative, transgressive, and spontaneous, while the authenticity discourse surrounding spirituals, freedom songs, gospel, and the blues privileges a blackness rooted in spirituality and folk simplicity.

The dialectic between these two ostensibly opposing sides reinforces the false dichotomies of Southern versus Northern, rural versus urban, nonviolence versus self-defense that the mainstream press had a large role in establishing and that U.S. cultural memory still carries. These dichotomies underpin the 1968 lens's conception of good and bad or acceptable and unacceptable Black protest. In the end, arguing for innovative, transgressive music and politics as a truer expression of Black identity than the folk simplicity of spirituals, freedom singing, and the blues did not remove the primitivizing lens with which White aurality approaches sonic blackness—it merely shifted who the "authentic folk" are. Instead of primitivizing the isolated rural Black person, White aurality now primitivizes the urban poverty-stricken subject of hip hop as the most authentic expression of Black humanity. Exploding the categories and seeking an entirely different approach is necessary if this cycle is to be disrupted.

In addition to critiquing primitivizing discourses in freedom song documentation, the scholarship of Gilroy, Mullen, Favor, and Hagstrom Miller can provide alternative frameworks for scholars, musicians, and documenters alike. These alternative frameworks can lead to new ways of documenting and representing the diverse and varied musical activities of people involved in the Black Freedom Movement. In *The Black Atlantic*, Gilroy describes how two opposing yet symbiotic perspectives, both problematic in their own way, operate in many interpretations of the cultural expressions of the Black Atlantic writ large. The first is an ontological essentialism and the second is a strategic pluralism. Gilroy indicts both Black and White intellectuals in his explanation of the ontologically essentialist standpoint:

> Where it pronounces on cultural matters, it is often allied to a realist approach to aesthetic value that minimizes the substantive political and philosophical issues involved in the processes of artistic representation. Its absolutist conception of ethnic cultures can be identified by the way in which it registers incomprehending disappointment with the actual cultural choices and patterns of the mass of black people. It has little to say about the profane, contaminated world of black popular culture and looks instead for an artistic practice that can disabuse the mass of black people of the illusions into which they have been seduced by their condition of exile and unthinking consumption of inappropriate cultural objects like the wrong hair care products, pop music, and western clothing. The community is felt to be on the wrong road, and it is the intellectual's job to give them a new direction, firstly by recovering and then by donating the racial awareness that the masses seem to lack.[95]

Gilroy goes on to argue that this position often manifests among "uneasy spokespeople of the black elite" who "have fabricated a volkish outlook as an expression of their own contradictory position."[96] We can see in the realm of freedom singing the same tendency, especially but not exclusively among the White (and mostly elite) documenters, to be disappointed with the "actual cultural choices and patterns of the mass of black people" and how they instead attempt to construct a version of the struggle using the music they find more authentic. This imagined history does not do justice to the complexity and plurality of the lives and choices of people involved in the movement. Lomax's and the Carawans' increasing interest and emphasis on folk traditions during the late 1960s and beyond follows the same pattern. They attempted to course correct Black activists as those activists embraced more popular forms of cultural expression, to "recover" awareness of an older tradition that they valued more, and then to donate that awareness to a movement culture that they perceived to lack depth.

Gilroy's description of the second prevalent perspective on Black cultural production gives a further warning, but also opens up a way forward. The strategic pluralist perspective, Gilroy argues, "affirms blackness as an open signifier" where the "polyphonic qualities of black cultural expression form the main aesthetic consideration."[97] "The difficulty with this second tendency," Gilroy contends, "is that in leaving racial essentialism behind by viewing 'race' itself as a social and cultural construction, it has been insufficiently alive to the lingering power of specifically racialised forms of power and subordination."[98] So for Gilroy, the challenge in interpreting the cultural production of the Black Atlantic is to maintain the "polyphonic qualities of black cultural expression" while also ensuring that pluralism maintains a rigorous analysis of how racialized power structures continue to complicate any narrative that relies too heavily on oversimplified utopianism. In the United States, this often manifests itself in a colorblind politics that is now prevalent across the political spectrum, but has its roots in the post–Civil Rights era conservative backlash under Nixon and Reagan.[99]

Similarly, Patrick Mullen suggests that ethnographers doing research should embrace a kind of dialectic. After critiquing the shortfalls of White folklorists such as John and Alan Lomax, Mullen offers a version of reciprocal ethnography as a way to do collaborative research across racial boundaries.[100] However, Mullen confesses that in one of his cross-racial collaborative projects he "did not consider carefully enough issues of power and position" in the relationship.[101] Mullen's suggested model for White folklorists/ethnographers would be valuable for White documentarians of freedom singing as well. For instance, while Guy and Candie Carawan did feature the voices of their Black informants from Johns Island, they were insufficiently aware of the power dynamics at play in the gathering and documenting process, as evidenced by the negative reception of their book *Ain't You Got a Right*. When confronted by the negative reception, instead of interrogating how they could have done their work more ethically, the Carawans tended to get defensive and explain away the critiques.[102] Mullen, on the other hand, models a highly reflexive approach that considers all critiques and frequently includes them in the final version of his work.[103]

Martin Favor argues for a disruption of the "stability of both whiteness and blackness" by understanding race, in the Butlerian sense, as performative, by critiquing discourses of authenticity, and by insisting on the multiplicity of racial identities.[104] Favor then argues that "it is through coalition and an empowerment of diversity that we are to come to the destruction of discrimination," an argument that Bernice Johnson Reagon seems to have intuited and tested performatively in her work after the Civil Rights Movement.[105] What might it look like, then, to acknowledge multiplicity and practice coalition politics in civil rights and freedom singing documentary production? Hampton's diverse but Black-led film company committed to representing the Civil Rights Movement in all its complexity is one example of how reciprocal coalition work can be brought to bear on the work of documentation. Musicologists, folklorists, and documentarians *can* refuse to "attractively fictionalize the sounds of the past," but only if their documentation is marked by a sincere and hard-fought reciprocity that maintains the polyphonic qualities of freedom singing and seeks to build coalition between people of difference.

Conclusion

Freedom Singing into the Future

"We Shall Overcome" is just a song to most
Americans, *but we must do it*. Or die . . .
If the Civil Rights Movement is "dead" and if it gave
us nothing else,
it gave us each other forever . . .
It gave us hope for tomorrow. It called us to life.
Because we live, it can never die.

—Alice Walker

Almost thirty-seven years after the Watts Rebellion, Los Angeles went up in flames again. With awful recognition, Black citizens of Los Angeles had watched the clips of LA police officers savagely beating Rodney King on the side of the road in March of 1991. On April 29, 1992, after the four LAPD officers who had been charged with assaulting King were acquitted by a jury, the injustice was too much to absorb and the "dynamite in the ghetto" exploded again.[1] All told, somewhere between fifty-four and sixty-three people died in the protests, looting, and violence that ensued, some at the hands of the National Guard, Army, and Marine Corps service members who President George H. W. Bush called in to suppress the uprising.[2] The memory of the Watts riots immediately became a powerful interpretive referent, as the arbiters of U.S. cultural memory in the media sought to understand what was happening and place it into a larger narrative.

The 1968 lens was an active participant in this framing. President Bush relied on the 1968 lens to divest the current situation of any relationship to the Civil Rights Movement. In his address to the nation on May 1, 1992, he said:

> What we saw last night and the night before in Los Angeles is not about civil rights. It's not about the great cause of equality that all Americans must uphold. It's not a message of protest. It's been the brutality of a mob, pure and simple. And let me assure you: I will use whatever force is necessary to restore order.[3]

Bush reacted very similarly to Lyndon Johnson, who said this in his statement on the Watts Rebellion of 1965:

> Our conscience cries out against the hatred that we heard last week. It bore no relation to the orderly struggle for civil rights that has ennobled the last decade. Every leader in that struggle has condemned this outrage against the laws of the land.
>
> I hope that every American who believes in equal opportunity for his fellow men, understands this distinction that I have made. For we shall never achieve a free and prosperous and hopeful society until we have suppressed the fires of hate and we have turned aside from violence, whether that violence comes from the nightriders of the Klan, or the snipers and the looters in the Watts district.
>
> And so long as I am your President I intend to preserve the rights of all of our citizens, and I intend to enforce the laws that protect all of our citizens—without regard to race, religion, region, or without fear or favor. A rioter with a Molotov cocktail in his hands is not fighting for civil rights any more than a Klansman with a sheet on his back and a mask on his face. They are both more or less what the law declares them: lawbreakers, destroyers of constitutional rights and liberties, and ultimately destroyers of a free America. They must be exposed and they must be dealt with.[4]

While Johnson tried to leverage his relationship with Martin Luther King Jr. and snippets of King's rhetoric to reinforce his position on Watts, King himself refused to issue a blanket condemnation of the rioting. Instead, he implored Black Americans to resist rioting because of the destruction it brings upon Black people and Black communities, and consistently argued that riots were a logical, if emotional, response to the "contingent, intolerable conditions" experienced by some people in the United States, conditions that sometimes lead them to embrace the "language of the unheard."[5] Bush was able to forcefully put distance between the 1992 LA riots and the Civil Rights Movement only through reliance on a deeply flawed memory of the Civil Rights Movement. As Joseph Darda argues:

> Fixing King in [1964] (the end of the "short civil rights movement") enables the forgetting of his later career, years committed to confronting economic inequality and urban poverty. The LA Riots [of 1992] are incommensurable as a legacy of the civil rights movement in light of this periodization. If 1964 is the end date of King's career in our cultural memory—an argument made in white granite on Capitol Hill—then the riots can represent no more than "the brutality of a mob, pure and simple." The maintenance of this logic relies on and is the product of neoliberalism and its form of racialization, colorblindness . . . . [T]he disremembering of the civil rights era and King does not take place in isolation but establishes "official interpretations" that foreclose on more radical forms of action and structures of knowledge.[6]

Musical responses to the 1992 LA riots became sites that either reinforced "official interpretations" and "foreclosed on more radical forms of action" or sites that challenged such interpretations. As Tricia Rose details, rap artists had been sounding the alarm for many years before the LA uprising and continued to provide U.S. popular culture with a nuanced, insider perspective on the motivations and pressures experienced by people in South Central LA and other similar contexts.[7] Rose recounts: "It was as if the rage that had exploded in South Central had finally validated rappers' nagging, seemingly exaggerated stories of race and class frustration. Overnight, such rappers as Chuck D and Ice Cube, who were once considered social menaces, became prophets and seeing eye dogs for a nation that had just realized it had gone blind."[8] Ice Cube called out the police officers who beat King by name and challenged the official dismissal of riots as legitimate responses to conditions in South Central in his 1992 track, "The Predator." He pulls no punches as he raps "Fuck Laurence Powell and Briseno, Wind and Koon, pretty soon, we'll fuck them like they fucked us and won't kiss 'em, riots ain't nothing but diets for the system."[9] Ice Cube's diagnosis of the LA riots as "diets for the system" calls the listener's attention to a root problem that is systemic and cannot be forced on the people who are on the receiving end of the state's violence and structural racism. Rap artists became the bearers of a counter-memory that challenged conventional U.S. understanding of the riots and of its own progress.

Garth Brooks's song "We Shall Be Free" represents an alternative framing of the 1992 riots. Brooks has reported that the song was inspired by his experience as he flew out of Los Angeles after a performance and looked down to see the smoke rising out of South Central.[10] Brooks's take on the riots repeats and reinforces the official interpretation of such instances of Black uprising, one that mobilizes a mythic memory of civil rights activism to buttress colorblindness and impose nonviolence on the margins from the center. In contrast to rappers who embraced their role as "prophets of rage," Brooks begins his song with the qualification "This ain't comin' from no prophet, just as ordinary man."[11] The false humility of this statement and invocation of the concept of the "ordinary" relies on long-standing tropes of the assumed normativity of whiteness and the views of the "silent majority" in U.S. American society, effectively framing the song as a representation of U.S. consensus memory. Brooks continues to picture what his ideal world would look like. In verse two, Brooks sings, "When the last thing we notice is the color of skin, and the first thing we look for is the beauty within . . . we shall be free." In verse three, Brooks returns to this theme when he sings, "When there's only one race, and that's mankind, we shall be free." Brooks's analysis of the situation and the solution is shallow at best, and maintains the problematic assumption of post-1968 America—that daring to raise the specter of race is the real issue rather than the systemic racism that continues to incite rebellion from those with the boot on their neck.

In the almost sixty years since the events of 1965–68, there have been several moments in U.S. political and cultural life where the anxiety surrounding the crisis of that period was recalled and mobilized to contest and influence the interpretation of contemporary political events. The 1968 lens—which helps to maintain a sanitized consensus memory of the Civil Rights Movement and passes new instances of Black protest and insurgency through that memory—remains a prominent interpretive filter through which these moments are understood. The 1968 lens pervaded responses to the 1992 LA riots, the Ferguson uprising of 2014, the Black Lives Matter movement, and the 2020 uprisings after the killings of George Floyd and Breonna Taylor. The question remains whether the people of the United States will be able to jettison the 1968 lens and integrate the counter-memories that would make the actions of contemporary freedom fighters legible in U.S. culture and political discourse.

The Introduction quotes Jon Michael Spencer, who characterized the end of the Civil Rights Movement and its music as a movement that "progressively waxed silent," going from "nonviolence to violence" and "singing to silence."[12] There is a twofold assumption undergirding this autopsy: that traditional freedom song is/was the only musicking that counts as movement music, and that traditional freedom singing did, in fact, go silent after the upheaval of the late 1960s. As we have seen throughout this book, both of these assumptions are inaccurate. The classical phase of the movement has, at times, been represented as a uni-musical experience when, in actuality, its musicking was far more multivocal than our historiography suggests. The singing of traditional freedom songs also continued after 1968 in vital and meaningful ways. These moments of freedom singing became sites of contestation, nostalgia, and continued organizing, sites of memory where the ongoing relevance of the movement to contemporary life was articulated in sound. When one moves from a repertoire-based approach to a process-based approach, one can trace the continuation of freedom singing into other styles and consider sounds that have been excluded from conventional interrogations.

The ideology of violence and silence that pervades understandings of the late 1960s and the 1970s has been injected into understandings of sound, protest, and meaning in U.S. life. As commentators have invested traditional freedom song more and more thoroughly with the consensus memory of the 1960s, chants and protests that sound different from the cultural conception of "good" protest have been invested with the ominous anxiety of racial violence and the potential collapse of the racial status quo. The vehement reaction to the simple chant "Black Lives Matter!" is evidence of this and echoes the backlash to the "Black Power" chant of the 1960s. At the same time, the chant "Build that Wall!," which thundered across every Donald Trump campaign rally in 2016, engendered little of the same anxiety, even though it has been the harbinger of actual violence carried out against immigrant communities across the United States. The 1968 lens only invests Black sound with violence, although the evidence that this is not only wrongheaded but also dangerous is everywhere. There is a connection between the equation of chanting and violence and the equation of rap—which occupies a similar sound world and cultural space—and violence.

In addition, commentators invest protests that bear no sign of violence and even no sound at all—such as Colin Kaepernick's kneeling during the national anthem at National Football League games to protest police brutality—with the same sorts of ideological objections. Because Kaepernick responds to a moment of compulsive nationalistic singing with silence, commentators have interpreted his silence as aggressive. Kaepernick is accused of forgetting—forgetting how "fortunate" he is, forgetting the people who have fought for his "freedom," etc.—but his silence is not the silence of forgetfulness, but of *counter-memory*. All these meanings and interpretations of sound (and the lack thereof) in relation to Black freedom are legacies of the ways in which U.S. culture has shaped interpretation of freedom singing after 1968.

Listening is the key to this future of freedom and flourishing for all in U.S. society—not a listening that maintains and legitimizes official interpretations of sound and protest, but a listening that is attuned to the voices that are resisting the consensus memory of U.S. history in vigorous ways. This listening will need to attend to all forms of sound in relation to the Black struggle for freedom in the United States, including the "music to which people have stopped listening [and singing]."[13] Rather than resisting the evolving meanings and styles of freedom singing as some documenters have tried to do, this listening will need to broaden its soundscape to include all the forms of musicking that interact with the Black Freedom Movement in the United States in order to genuinely understand its continued vitality. This broadening will "open the movement to genuine engagement."[14] Freedom singing has been, and will remain, one of the most prolific and active sites for such a genuine engagement. Opening our collective ears to the polyphonic meanings of freedom singing in this third decade of the twenty-first century may finally break the stagnation of U.S. consensus memory, allowing us to hear the music's call to build a better world and to make the dream a reality:

Get on board, children!
Ninety-nine and a half won't do!
It doesn't have to be like this!
Today, another world is possible!
We who believe in freedom cannot rest!

Afterword

Every summer my paternal grandmother, Earlene Jacobs Stacks, hosted the Jacobs family reunion at her home in Charlotte, North Carolina. Not only was she the family's matriarch, but she also had a pool, so even though most of the family had to drive up from Lumbee territory in Robeson County, North Carolina, for the weekend, it was worth it. The reunion was basically a three-day house party. Dozens of people slept all over every inch of floor space in her small ranch home (with more sleeping in the campers parked in the driveway). It was hard to walk through the house without tripping over napping bodies or running into one of her display cases full of Native memorabilia while trying to avoid tripping. There was a twenty-four-hour buffet on the kitchen table; every time one of the kids walked into the house my grandma or one of her sisters would say, "You want something to eat, honey?" or "You hungry, baby?" We spent hours and hours playing with our cousins from "down home" in the pool while the adults sat and chatted. Even though they were the ones traveling to the city in which I lived, I always felt like the one being offered hospitality. Not being from Robeson County, growing up away from the sights and sounds and ways of being that make the Lumbee who they are, always felt like a hurdle to my belonging among my kin. But as a child, it was never my Lumbee family who imposed that hurdle on me. I was welcomed with open arms each summer into their lives and their experiences.

The yearly family reunion is one of the deeply imprinted memories I have of my grandmother. We'd often go to her house after church on Sundays for lunch, and I remember reading the bumper sticker she had on her car every time we pulled into her driveway: "Native Americans are a living people—not mascots!" As children, my brother and I would go to her house to spend the night and I would beg her to tell us my favorite story—an American Indian folktale about a turtle who couldn't keep his mouth shut and ended up paying dearly for it. I remember attending the Metrolina Native American Association's annual powwow with her and my father. The sights, the smells, and especially the music of those powwows are embedded in me. I remember watching her interact with people at the powwow. Everybody loved "Ms. Earlene." She wasn't just my family's matriarch; she was a matriarch in the American Indian community in North Carolina. I found out later in life that she taught English at a segregated school for Indian children during the 1950s, and that she served for many years on the North Carolina Commission on Indian Affairs, the North Carolina Indian Housing Authority, and the Metrolina Native American Association. She was a fierce and persistent advocate for the Lumbee, and for Native people in general.

In *The Souls of Black Folk*, W. E. B. Du Bois articulates what has become one of the most enduring descriptions of the Black experience in the United States: "it is a peculiar sensation, this double-consciousness, this sense of always looking at one's self through the eyes of others, of measuring one's soul by the tape of a world that looks on in amused contempt and pity."[1] I have had a kind of "reverse double consciousness" my entire life. My father is an American Indian of the Lumbee tribe of North Carolina. My mother is White, descended from the British people who, for centuries, colonized and attempted to erase my father's people from the face of the earth. I grew up listening to the accents and the stories of my father's people, wondering why my skin was light and my cousins' skin was dark, intuiting that their lives and experiences were not my own. I have moved through the world with light skin and all its attendant privilege, while knowing that for half of my family the world is radically different.

I—like Du Bois and the freedom singing Black folk I discuss in this book—look at myself through the eyes of others. But instead of contempt, the gaze of others confers undeserved privilege on me. This reverse double consciousness has shaped my interactions and interests, including my research on freedom singing after 1968. The fact that a genetic dice roll made my skin light instead of dark like my cousins' (who also have a White mother) has heightened for me the arbitrary capriciousness of our society's system of racial hierarchy. My racial positionality has influenced the types of questions in which I am interested, and the critiques I bring to bear on the historiography and collective memory of the greatest social movement in U.S. history. I have been particularly interested in the reputation of freedom singing as a site of interracial coalition building, and the challenges that rise to the surface when you train a critical eye on that line of reasoning.

My own activism and participation in freedom singing have confirmed for me that many of the dynamics and tensions discussed in this book remain present in the act of freedom singing in the contemporary United States. I have led groups of predominantly White Protestants on freedom rides from Raleigh, North Carolina, down to civil rights sites in Alabama and out to the border in Arizona. On those trips we did a lot of freedom singing. We sang songs that were sung on the original freedom rides in 1961. We also sang songs that the Black Freedom Movement and the immigrant rights movement have generated since 1968, including several that are discussed in this book. There were many moments where my reverse double consciousness raised unique contradictions for me in that space. The questions that consistently came to my mind were: What meanings are being generated in the act of freedom singing by this specific group of mostly White people who are trying to educate themselves and understand more deeply how the history of the freedom struggle impacts people's lives today? What problematic memories or nostalgias are generated because the group is largely White? How can we, in the act of freedom singing, begin to overthrow faulty narratives of the Civil Rights Movement and attend to a more complex and fruitful history? What music are we leaving out of our singing that could aid us in our quest? It is also clear to me through my participation in immigrant rights movements that more research is needed into the freedom singing of the array of movements that have impacted U.S. culture after 1968.

In the end, I hope to do justice, with the small contribution this book makes, to the great organic intellectuals who have "brought us this far on the way." I think of this book as one part of my response to reverse double consciousness. It represents my intellectual grappling with the sounds of freedom movements in the United States, but I also hope it goes beyond mere intellectualizing into the realm of action. I hope it gives freedom fighters a better view of the terrain and another hammer to swing for justice.

Acknowledgments

I wrote this book with generations of freedom fighters and freedom singers in my heart; their stories lit a fire in me. I'm especially grateful for the witness of Martin Luther King Jr., whose real legacy is only just beginning to unfold, and Bernice Johnson Reagon, whose soaring voice and indomitable spirit were the soundtrack and inspiration for thc book.

Thank you to my editor Laurie Matheson and the rest of the team at the University of Illinois Press for believing in this book and for making it better at every stage.

Thank you to all of my colleagues at UNC Chapel Hill, who read earlier drafts of the research that would become this book, and whose feedback has been invaluable. I'm especially grateful for the mentorship of David Garcia, who has sharpened my thinking and buoyed me along the way. I am also incredibly grateful for the generosity of Tammy Kernodle, who has encouraged me and invested in me in ways I cannot repay.

Thank you to all my interlocutors for sharing their lives and stories with me, especially those people from Warren County, North Carolina, who gave generously of their time and helped me understand the intricacies of the movement there. Thanks as well to my friends at Greenwood Forest Baptist Church, who have shown me what it means to dream of freedom for everyone and who have been collaborators in my own experimentation with freedom singing.

Lastly, I'm grateful for my family. Without their support and patience, this book would not have materialized. Thank you especially to E, C, and S for inspiring me every day—I love you.

Notes

Introduction

Epigraph: Zepp and Palmer, eds., *Drum Major for a Dream*, 4.

1. The phrase "dynamite in the ghetto" comes from Stokely Carmichael and Charles Hamilton, *Black Power*, 1967, and "Dynamite," *The Atlantic* (October 1967).

2. "Mayor Kevin White with James Brown at The Boston Garden, 04/05/1968," WGBH Open Vault, https://www.youtube.com/watch?v=lfEpQb_H1Pk.

3. See https://www.youtube.com/watch?v=JkPjEKCTKME for a recording of the performance in question.

4. The title of King's final published book before his death asked the question, *Where Do We Go From Here: Chaos or Community?* This questioning posture was a new development in King's rhetorical strategy—a far cry from the certainty of titles such as *Stride Toward Freedom*, *Strength to Love*, and *Why We Can't Wait*.

5. For a definition of freedom song, see chapter 2.

6. See Southern, *The Music of Black Americans*, 475–78, and Jackson, *Blowin' the Blues Away*, 146.

7. I capitalize the adjectives "White" and "Black" when they refer to racial identities throughout the book. Following the lead of many Black writers and thinkers, I have long capitalized Black as an acknowledgment of the coherent, specific, and vital identity group that the word connotes. Until recently, I left White lowercase to emphasize the fact that most White people do not consider their whiteness to be distinctly constitutive of their identity in a coherent way, but consider aspects of their identities that are conditioned by race as normative. However, I have decided to capitalize White to call into question the often unmarked nature of whiteness and call attention to the ways in which White people do assume a raced identity, whether or not individual White people acknowledge this fact.

8. Author's transcription of Simone's mid-song monologue: "Uh, I heard—we've heard all kinds of stories—but I heard this was his favorite song, at least I think near the end of his life. Last year, a year ago maybe more, Lorraine Hansbury left us and she was a dear friend and [piano vamping begins] she had her favorite song. And then Langston Hughes left us, Coltrane left us, Otis Redding left us. Who can go on? Do you realize how many we have lost? Then it really gets down to reality doesn't it? No microphones and all that crap. But really something else! We've lost a lot of them in the last two years. But we have remaining Monk, Miles (from crowd: Nina!), Haha! I love you too. And of course, for those that we have left we are thankful, but we can't afford any more losses! Oh no! Oh my God! They're shooting us down one by one. Don't forget that. Cause they are. Killing us one by one. Well, all I have to say is that, those of us who know how to protect those of us we love, stand by them, and stay close to them. And I say if there had been a couple more a little closer to Dr. King he wouldn't have got it, you know? Really. Just a little closer to him, stay there, stay there. We can't afford any more losses."

9. Bernice Johnson Reagon, the most important scholar/practitioner of the music of the Civil Rights Movement (discussed in detail in chapter 3), defines "freedom song" as "a body of songs, sung in jails, meetings, rallies, on marches, and in informal settings, that utilized all forms of Black music from all segments of the Black community, and were linked by a common message: involvement in the Civil Rights Movement." I discuss at length the problem of defining freedom song in chapter 2 and propose a new definition decoupled from its current genre/canonical connotations.

10. Kernodle, "'I Wish I Knew How It Would Feel to Be Free,'" 295–317.

11. Ibid., 295–96.

12. Overwhelmingly, the standard ideological position supported self-defense and defense of one's family. Many Southern Black men kept weapons in their homes for defense against White violence and other threats. In fact, King himself had to get rid of the gun he kept in his home for the defense of his family and his armed bodyguards after he fully embraced nonviolence. See Garrow, *Bearing the Cross*.

13. See Rosenbloom, *Redemption*, 141 and following, and *King in the Wilderness*, directed by Peter Kunhardt.

14. See Carson, *In Struggle*, and Garrow, *Bearing the Cross*.

15. West, ed., *The Radical King*, x.

16. To see this narrative at its most obvious (and most insidious), see Boorstin and Kelly, *A History of the United States*, which is one of the five most popular secondary school history books from the 1990s. The construction and reinforcement of this narrative is discussed in significant detail in chapter 1.

17. Eyerman and Jamison, *Music and Social Movements*, 97.

18. Mary King, quoted in ibid., 45.

19. Reed, *The Art of Protest*, 29.

20. Malcolm X, "The Ballot or the Bullet," in *Malcolm X Speaks*, ed. Breitman, 35.

21. Ibid., 38.

22. Malcolm X, "The Black Revolution (April 8, 1964)," *ICIT Digital Library*, https://www.icit-digital.org/articles/malcolm-x-on-the-black-revolution-april-8-1964.

23. Malcolm X, "The Black Revolution," in *Malcolm X Speaks*, ed. Breitman, 50.

24. Ibid., 52.

25. See Turino, "Signs of Imagination, Identity, and Experience," 221–55.

26. Malcolm X, "The Ballot or the Bullet," in *Malcolm X Speaks*, ed. Breitman, 35.

27. Malcolm X, in *Malcolm X Speaks*, ed. Breitman, 107.

28. Tyson, "Robert Williams, 'Black Power,' and the Roots of the African American Freedom Struggle," 545–46.

29. Ling, "Gender and Generation," in Ling and Monteith, eds., *Gender and the Civil Rights Movement*, 112.

30. Reagon, "Let the Church Sing 'Freedom,'" 109.

31. Malcolm X and Haley, *The Autobiography of Malcolm X*, 306.

32. Julius Lester, "The Angry Children of Malcolm X," originally published in *Sing Out!* Oct./Nov. 1966, in *Black Protest Thought in the Twentieth Century*, ed. Meier, Rudwick, and Broderick, 469–85.

33. Spencer, "Freedom Songs of the Civil Rights Movement," 16.

34. Carawan, *Sing for Freedom*, xv.

35. Miller, "Remembering Freedom Songs," 51.

36. The idea of the "capaciousness" of Black musicking comes from conversation with Ambre Dromgoole after her talk at the 2022 joint meeting of the American Musicological Society, the Society for Ethnomusicology, and the Society for Music Theory entitled "'I'm Gonna Dedicate This One to Miss Franklin': Afro-Protestant Performance Pedagogies and Rethinking the Black Woman's Spiritual Voice." See Dromgoole, "'I'm Gonna Dedicate This One to Miss Franklin,'" 34/4.

37. Malcolm X, in *Malcolm X Speaks*, ed. Breitman, 105–6.

38. Spencer, "Freedom Songs of the Civil Rights Movement," 13.

39. See Goode, *Jürgen Habermas: Democracy and the Public Sphere*.

40. Lott, *Love and Theft*, 8.

41. For my purposes here, I am defining "contemporary" as the current milieu of the movement, which in my estimation includes the last ten-plus years since the inception of the Black Lives Matter movement.

42. Lipsitz, *Time Passages*, 214.

43. See the Afterword for more reflection on my subject position.

44. Harding, "Beyond Amnesia," 469.

45. Lipsitz, *Time Passages*, 214.

46. Abernathy, *And the Walls Came Tumblin' Down*, 440–42.

47. Harding, "Beyond Amnesia," 468–76.

48. Attali, *Noise: The Political Economy of Music*, 109.

49. Minrose, *Remembering Medgar Evers*, 1.

50. Garcia, *Listening for Africa*, 276. Baldwin said, "[T]he great force of history comes from the fact that we carry it within us, are unconsciously controlled by it in many ways, and history is literally *present* in all that we do." See Baldwin, "The White Man's Guilt," in *Collected Essays*, 722–27.

51. Harding, "Beyond Amnesia," 469.

Chapter 1. Memory, History, and Freedom Song

Epigraph: Schafer, *The Soundscape*, 180.

1. Derrick Bryson Taylor, "George Floyd Protests: A Timeline," *New York Times*, November 5, 2021, https://www.nytimes.com/article/george-floyd-protests-timeline.html.

2. Zaranyserak, "COMPLETE 'Lean on Me' Singalong from Washington, D. C. Protest June 3, 2020," YouTube video, 3:01, June 4, 2020, https://www.youtube.com/watch?v=cCsl_wij9Xs.

3. Darden, "The George Floyd Demonstrations Turned into a Movement When Protestors Began to Sing."

4. Jonathan Franklin and Emma Bowman, "What We Know about the Killing of Tyre Nichols," *NPR*, January 28, 2023, https://www.npr.org/2023/01/28/1151504967/tyre-nichols-memphis-police-bodycam-video.

5. Associated Press, "Funeral for Tyre Nichols at Mississippi Boulevard Christian Church in Memphis," YouTube video, 2:12:02, https://www.youtube.com/watch?v=Me2RmWIu-UE, accessed July 10, 2024.

6. See Nora, *Realms of Memory*; and Yerushalmi, *Zakhor*.

7. Olick and Robbins, "Social Memory Studies," 110.

8. Sturken, *Tangled Memories*, 5; see also Trouillot, *Silencing the Past*.

9. Romano and Raiford, eds., *The Civil Rights Movement in American Memory*, xiii.

10. See also David Blight, "Historians and 'Memory,'" *Commonplace* 2.3, http://commonplace.online/article/historians-and-memory/, accessed July 10, 2024, and Berlin, "American Slavery in History and Memory and the Search for Social Justice."

11. Halbwachs, *On Collective Memory*.

12. Irwin-Zarecka, *Frames of Remembrance*, 4.

13. Ibid., 9.

14. Blight, "Historians and 'Memory,'" *Commonplace* 2.3.

15. Sturken, *Tangled Memories*, 1.

16. Ibid., 3.

17. Romano and Raiford, *The Civil Rights Movement in American Memory*, xiv.

18. Thelen, ed., *Memory and American History*, xii. Emphasis added.

19. Foucault, *Language, Counter-Memory, Practice*; Olick and Robbins, "Social Memory Studies," 126.

20. Lipsitz, *Time Passages*, 213–14.

21. Ibid., 212.

22. See below for an explanation of contemporary vignettes.

23. The classical phase of the Civil Rights Movement is a concept defined by Bayard Rustin in his essay "From Protest to Politics: The Future of the Civil Rights Movement." See Rustin, "From Protest to Politics," in *Black Protest Thought in the Twentieth Century*, ed. Meier, Rudwick, and Broderick.

24. "Civil Rights Movement," https://en.wikipedia.org/wiki/African-American_Civil_Rights_Movement_(1954–1968); "Timeline of the Civil Rights Movement,"

https://en.wikipedia.org/wiki/Timeline_of_the_civil_rights_movement, both accessed July 10, 2024.

25. "Research: Wikipedia Editors Survey 2011 April," https://meta.wikimedia.org/wiki/Research:Wikipedia_Editors_Survey_2011_April, accessed July 10, 2024.

26. The survey contains data on nationality but not on race.

27. Jemielniak, *Common Knowledge? An Ethnography of Wikipedia*, 62.

28. Reagle Jr., *Good Faith Collaboration: The Culture of Wikipedia*, 98.

29. Among other works, Carson wrote the most influential history of the Student Nonviolent Coordinating Committee, *In Struggle: SNCC and the Black Awakening of the 1960s*.

30. Clayborne Carson, "American Civil Rights Movement," https://www.britannica.com/event/American-civil-rights-movement/From-black-power-to-the-assassination-of-Martin-Luther-King, accessed July 10, 2024.

31. Jenny Walker, "A Media Made Movement: Black Violence and Nonviolence in the Historiography of the Civil Rights Movement," in *Media, Culture, and the Modern African American Freedom Struggle*, ed. Ward, 47.

32. Ibid., 48.

33. Dowd Hall, "The Long Civil Rights Movement," 1236.

34. Walker, "A Media Made Movement," 47.

35. Loewen, *Lies My Teacher Told Me*.

36. Boorstin and Kelley, as quoted in Epstein, "Tales from Two Textbooks," 125.

37. Current et al., *American History: A Survey*, 869.

38. Tindall and Shi, *America: A Narrative History*.

39. Ibid., 1233 and 1252.

40. Ibid., 1252.

41. Ibid., 1263.

42. Owen Dwyer, "Interpreting the Civil Rights Movement," in Romano and Raiford, eds., *The Civil Rights Movement in American Memory*, 7.

43. "Civil Rights Memorial Celebrates 25th Anniversary," November 5, 2014, https://www.splcenter.org/news/2014/11/04/civil-rights-memorial-celebrates-25th-anniversary. Visitors to the memorial are also encouraged to envision how their names and accomplishments could be added to the space after 1968.

44. This is to be expected to some degree given that it was the first memorial to the Civil Rights Movement and its heroes designed and built in this country at a time when the consensus memory was being firmed up over and against more negative understandings of the movement and its accomplishments.

45. Dowd Hall, "The Long Civil Rights Movement," 1234.

46. Joseph, ed., *The Black Power Movement*, 3.

47. The most incisive and insightful critique of the Long Civil Rights Movement trend comes from Sundiata Keita ChaJua and Clarence Lang, "The 'Long Movement' as Vampire," 265–88.

48. One of the ways my contribution to the long movement thesis strengthens applications of Freedom Movement history to the present is through the 1968 lens concept discussed below.

49. Nora, *Realms of Memory*.

50. Redmond, *Anthem*, 264.

51. Noel King, "3 Generations in Memphis Reflect on Martin Luther King, Jr.'s Legacy," *NPR*, April 4, 2018, https://www.npr.org/2018/04/04/599361730/3-generations-in-memphis-on-martin-luther-king-jr-s-legacy; Cornel West, "Martin Luther King Was a Radical. We Must Not Sterilize His Legacy," *The Guardian*, April 4, 2018, https://www.theguardian.com/commentisfree/2018/apr/04/martin-luther-king-cornel-west-legacy; P. R. Lockhart, "The Sanctification-and Sanitization-of Martin Luther King, Jr.," *Vox*, April 4, 2018, https://www.vox.com/identities/2018/4/4/17193286/martin-luther-king-assassination-50th-anniversary-jeanne-theoharis; Danielle Belton, "#ReclaimMLK Seeks to Combat the Sanitizing of Martin Luther King Jr.'s Legacy," *The Root*, January 19, 2015, https://www.theroot.com/reclaimmlk-seeks-to-combat-the-sanitizing-of-martin-lu-1790858510.

52. Sturken, *Tangled Memories*, 7.

53. See Morrison, *Beloved*.

54. "Making remembering safe" is a phrase used by David Blight to describe the ways in which the United States transformed the memory of the Civil War in the century that followed it. See Blight, *Race and Reunion*, 9.

55. Baldwin, "The Fire Next Time," in *Baldwin: Collected Essays*, ed. Morrison, 321.

56. Dr. Cornel West claimed that Antifa protestors "saved his life" at the rally. See "Clergy in Charlottesville Were Trapped by Torch-Wielding Nazis," August 14, 2017, https://www.democracynow.org/2017/8/14/cornel_west_rev_toni_blackmon_clergy.

57. Michael D. Shear and Maggie Haberman, "Trump Defends Initial Remarks on Charlottesville; Again Blames 'Both Sides,'" *New York Times*, April 15, 2017, https://www.nytimes.com/2017/08/15/us/politics/trump-press-conference-charlottesville.html.

58. "Alveda King Responds to Charlottesville Violence," August 13, 2017, http://video.foxnews.com/v/5539940160001/#sp=show-clips.

59. David Kaiser, "What the 1960s Reveal about What's Next for American Protestors," *Time*, August 25, 2017, http://time.com/4915622/protest-cycle-1960s-charlottesville/.

60. Andrew Flanagan, "Spotify Removes Racist Music in Response to Charlottesville," *NPR*, August 17, 2017, https://www.npr.org/sections/thetwo-way/2017/08/17/544240096/spotify-removes-racist-music-in-response-to-charlottesville.

61. McBride et al., "Waiting for the Perfect Protest?"

62. Darden, "The George Floyd Demonstrations."

63. See the discussion in chapter 4 of productive and counterproductive nostalgias.

Chapter 2. From Freedom Song to Freedom Singing

Epigraph: Bernice Johnson Reagon, in *The Songs Are Free: Bernice Johnson Reagon and African-American Music*.

1. NBC News, "Congressional Leaders Sing 'We Shall Overcome,'" June 24, 2014, https://www.nbcnews.com/video/congressional-leaders-sing-we-shall-overcome-288080963592.

2. CNN, "Pelosi on Singing 'We Shall Overcome'-Loved It," YouTube video, July 21, 2016, https://www.youtube.com/watch?v=vEhL5zjUXIw.

3. Ally Mutnick, "Congress Marks 50th Anniversary of Civil Rights Act," *USA Today*, June 24, 2014, http://www.usatoday.com/story/news/nation/2014/06/24/civil-rights-act-anniversary/11332243/.

4. Elahe Izadi, "Medical Examiner Rules Eric Garner's Death a Homicide, Says Police Chokehold Killed Him," *Washington Post*, August 1, 2014, https://www.washingtonpost.com/news/post-nation/wp/2014/08/01/eric-garners-death-was-a-homicide-says-new-york-city-medical-examiner/?utm_term=.931590e97759.

5. Pantaleo was fired from the New York Police Department on August 19, 2019, almost five years after he killed Garner.

6. "The Peace Poets," https://ignatiansolidarity.net/iftj/speakers/the-peace-poets/, accessed July 11, 2024.

7. "Extended Bio," http://thepeacepoets.com/extended-bio/, accessed July 11, 2024.

8. *Chicago Sun Times*, "Janelle Monae Brings Her #BlackLivesMatter Activism to Chicago," YouTube video, August 17, 2015, https://www.youtube.com/watch?v=IPvYfPHrhMo; Cat April Watters, "STOP POLICE KILLING w Janelle Monae, WONDALAND, HELL YOU TALMBOUT," YouTube video, August 14, 2015, https://www.youtube.com/watch?v=C8h_LWlrmpQ.

9. BlackTechz, "BlackLivesMatter-We Gonna Be Alright DTLA Protest 7–7–2016," YouTube video, July 8, 2016, https://www.youtube.com/watch?v=c2hKKT7JWcA&pbjreload=10.

10. Details on use of the term "musicking" follow the description of Christopher Small's work below.

11. Reagon, *Songs of the Civil Rights Movement 1955–1965*.

12. See Reagon, "Let the Church Sing 'Freedom,'" 105–18, and *If You Don't Go, Don't Hinder Me*.

13. Reagon, "African Diaspora Women," 77–90.

14. See Dunson, *Freedom in the Air*; Sanger, *The Rhetoric of the Freedom Songs in the American Civil Rights Movement* and *"When the Spirit Says Sing!"*; Appleton, "Singing in the Streets of Raleigh," 243–52; Seeger and Reiser, *Everybody Says Freedom*; Carawan, *Ain't You Got a Right to the Tree of Life* and *Sing for Freedom*; Eyerman and Jamison, *Music and Social Movements*; Reed, *The Art of Protest*; Martin, *The Theater Is in the Street*; Bobetsky, ed., *We Shall Overcome*.

15. Kernodle, "I Wish I Knew How It Would Feel to Be Free," 295–317.

16. See Monson, *Freedom Sounds*; Saul, *Freedom Is, Freedom Ain't*; Ward, *Just My Soul Responding*; and Guralnik, *Sweet Soul Music*. A work that does not fit into this narrative is Charles Keil's *Urban Blues*, which prefigured this move toward a broader scope of inquiry by more than two decades. Keil challenged the disciplinary climate at the time by not only taking the music of people such as Ray Charles and B. B. King as a serious topic of study, but also by approaching that study with a sociocultural analysis that emphasized the political nature of these musicians and their roles as "culture heroes." See Keil, *Urban Blues*. For an assessment of how *Urban Blues* fit into the disciplinary and cultural climate of

1966, see Sakakeeny, "Disciplinary Movements, the Civil Rights Movement, and Charles Keil's *Urban Blues*," 143–68.

17. See Jerry Rodnitzky, "Protest Music," in *Oxford Dictionary of Music*, ed. Deane Root, https://doi.org/10.1093/gmo/9781561592630.article.A2252188. Oxford Dictionary of Music does have an excellent article on music of the Civil Rights Movement written by Tammy Kernodle, just no specific article on freedom song. See Kernodle, "Civil Rights Movement," ed. Deane Root, https://doi.org/10.1093/gmo/9781561592630.article.A2228003.

18. Reagon, "Songs of the Civil Rights Movement," 107.

19. See Turner, "Guy and Candie Carawan," and chapter 5 of this book.

20. See Eyerman and Jamison, Turino, and Noah Adams, "The Inspiring Force of We Shall Overcome," *NPR*, August 28, 2013, https://www.npr.org/2013/08/28/216482943/the-inspiring-force-of-we-shall-overcome.

21. See chapter 5 of this book for more detail.

22. Reagon, "Songs of the Civil Rights Movement," 25.

23. Denisoff, *Sing a Song of Social Significance*, and Turino, *Music as Social Life*.

24. Carawan, "The Living Folk Heritage of the Sea Islands," 31. See chapter 5 as well.

25. Eyerman and Jamison, *Music and Social Movements*, 102.

26. Small, *Musicking*, 2.

27. See chapter 5 for more discussion of this.

28. Small, *Musicking*, 138–39.

29. Ibid., 214.

30. Ibid., 115.

31. Again, see chapter 5.

32. Small, *Musicking*, 99.

33. Ibid., 100.

34. Andrew Dell'Antonio also points out that Small's musicking theory is not foreign to the ethnographic study of music. See Dell'Antonio, review of *Musicking*, 883.

35. This may be partially due to the disciplinary diversity of the scholars who have engaged with freedom song. Ethnomusicologists, who may be more inclined to discuss the act of musicmaking in more depth, form only a small portion of those who have written on freedom song, with historians, communications scholars, folklorists, literary scholars, and sociologists making significant contributions.

36. See also these helpful critiques of Small: Charles Keil, review of *Musicking: The Meanings of Performing and Listening* by Christopher Small, *Ethnomusicology* (January 2000) 161–63; Richard Rischar, review of *Musicking: The Meanings of Performing and Listening* by Christopher Small, *Music Theory Spectrum*, vol. 25/1 (March 2003), 161–65.

37. Ramsey, *Race Music*.

38. Tausig, "Sound and Movement," 25–45.

39. Ibid., 26.

40. Mark, "'Keepin' It Real,'" 122–34.

41. Ibid., 126.
42. Reagon, "Let the Church Sing 'Freedom,'" 108.
43. Reagon, "Music as an Agent of Social Change," 344.
44. Monson, *Saying Something*, 80.
45. Jamila Jones, quoted in Reagon, "Music as an Agent of Social Change," 346.
46. Fischlin, Heble, and Lipsitz, *The Fierce Urgency of Now*, 19.
47. Ibid.
48. Peter Townsend, "Musical Style and Liberationist Ethic, 1956–1965," in *Media, Culture, and the Modern African American Freedom Struggle*, ed. Ward, 153.
49. Ibid.
50. Ibid.
51. Davis, *Blues Legacies and Black Feminism*, 113.
52. Kanellopoulos, "Musical Improvisation as Action," 110–11.
53. Fischlin, Heble, and Lipsitz, *The Fierce Urgency of Now*, 15.
54. This phrase comes from a recently published collection of essays on "We Shall Overcome" that makes this very argument, subjecting the song to a narrative of universalization that makes moments like this one politically unintelligible. See Bobetsky, ed., *We Shall Overcome*.
55. See King, "Beyond Vietnam: A Time to Break Silence," in *The Radical King*, ed. Cornel West.
56. The Peace Poets, "Who We Are," https://thepeacepoetsblog.wordpress.com/who-we-are/, accessed July 11, 2024.
57. The Peace Poets, "Extended Bio," http://thepeacepoets.com/extended-bio/, accessed July 11, 2024.
58. Ibid.
59. If one searches the hashtag "#icantbreathechallenge," there are still dozens of videos on YouTube and Facebook of individuals performing the song. According to online reports, there were many more shares and uploaded versions of the song initially following Jackson's call. See Debbi Baker, "Samuel Jackson Wants 'Ice Bucket Challenge' Celebs to Sing Police Protest Song," https://www.sandiegouniontribune.com/opinion/the-conversation/sdut-samuel-jackson-cant-breathe-song-challenge-2014dec15-htmlstory.html, accessed July 11, 2024.

Chapter 3. Bernice Johnson Reagon, Freedom Singing, and Musical Coalition Politics

Portions of this chapter were originally published in Stephen Stacks, "Bernice Johnson Reagon's Musical Coalition Politics, 1966–1981," *Journal of the Society for American Music* 18, no. 1 (February 2024), 1–17. Reprinted with permission.

1. See "Beyoncé-Formation (Official Video)," https://www.youtube.com/watch?v=WDZJPJV__bQ, accessed July 11, 2024.
2. "Beyoncé-Formation (Super Bowl 2016)," February 12, 2016, https://www.youtube.com/watch?v=uqGwekWZeRI.
3. The outfit also resembled one of Michael Jackson's most well-known performing outfits.

4. Jon Caramanica, Wesley Morris, and Jenna Wortham, "Beyoncé in "Formation": Entertainer, Activist, Both?," *New York Times*, February 6, 2016, https://www.nytimes.com/2016/02/07/arts/music/beyonce-formation-super-bowl-video.html.

5. Chris Richards, "The Night Beyoncé Won the Super Bowl," *Washington Post*, February 7, 2016, https://www.washingtonpost.com/news/arts-and-entertainment/wp/2016/02/07/the-night-beyonce-won-the-super-bowl/.

6. Jesse Holland, "Beyoncé's Super Bowl Nod to Black Activism Is Praised, and Also Criticized," *Seattle Times*, February 8, 2016, https://www.seattletimes.com/nation-world/beyonces-super-bowl-show-bringing-both-praise-and-criticism/.

7. Dianca London, "Beyoncé's Capitalism Masquerading as Radical Change," *Death and Taxes*, February 10, 2016, https://www.deathandtaxesmag.com/280129/beyonce-capitalism-black-activism/.

8. bell hooks, "Moving Beyond Pain," May 9, 2016, https://bellhooksbooks.com/moving-beyond-pain/.

9. Ibid.

10. College Park Baptist Church, "Rhiannon Giddens & Friends Sing Against HB2 in NC," YouTube video, February 21, 2017, https://www.youtube.com/watch?v=i_8BjHkVqsQ.

11. Allison Hussey, "Rhiannon Giddens Discussed Her Decision Not to Cancel Greensboro, Asheville Shows," *Indy Week*, April 11, 2016, https://indyweek.com/music/archives-music/rhiannon-giddens-discusses-decision-cancel-greensboro-asheville-shows/.

12. Ibid.

13. Taylor, *Performance*, 25.

14. DeNora, "Music and Self-Identity," in *The Popular Music Studies Reader*, ed. Bennett, Shank, and Toynbee, 141.

15. Ibid.

16. Daphne A. Brooks, "Open Channels," 64.

17. This chapter participates in the work of scholars such as Ruth Feldstein, Tammy Kernodle, and Bernice Johnson Reagon herself who have elevated the roles Black women musicians have played in political and cultural conversations. See Feldstein, *How It Feels to Be Free*; Kernodle, *Soul on Soul: The Life and Music of Mary Lou Williams*, "Black Women Working Together: Jazz, Gender, and the Politics of Validation," in *Music in Black American Life, 1945–2020*, ed. Matheson, and "'I Wish I Knew How It Would Feel to Be Free'"; and Reagon, *If You Don't Go, Don't Hinder Me* and "African Diaspora Women."

18. Butler, *Gender Trouble*.

19. Lloyd, "Performativity, Parody, Politics," 210.

20. Fish, *Is There a Text in This Class?*

21. See Moyers, producer, *The Songs Are Free*.

22. Reagon, *We Who Believe in Freedom*, 48.

23. See Turino, *Music as Social Life*, 23–65.

24. See Ward, *Just My Soul Responding*; Neal, *What the Music Said*; Kernodle, forthcoming work on Black women and the Civil Rights Movement; Guralnik, *Sweet Soul Music*.

25. Reagon, "Coalition Politics," in *Home Girls: A Black Feminist Anthology*, ed. Smith.

26. See Alexander, *The New Jim Crow*; Mazzacco, *The Psychology of Racial Colorblindness*, 11–25; and Dowd Hall, "The Long Civil Rights Movement and the Political Uses of the Past," 1233–63.

27. Reagon, "Coalition Politics," 357.

28. Ibid., 358.

29. Rustin, "From Protest to Politics," in *Black Protest Thought in the Twentieth Century*, ed. Meier, Rudwick, and Broderick, 455–56.

30. King, Jr., *Where Do We Go from Here*, 50–53.

31. See Williams, *From the Bullet to the Ballot* and Lopez, "'We Know What the Pigs Don't Like.'"

32. Hill Collins, *Black Feminist Thought*, 245.

33. Yuval-Davis, *Gender and Nation*, 117.

34. bell hooks, *Feminist Theory from Margin to Center*, 43–45. Along with these foundational Black feminist thinkers, Reagon's brand of coalition politics places her in the company of contemporary abolitionists such as Ruth Wilson Gilmore and Mariame Kaba. See Gilmore, *Abolition Geography: Essays Towards Liberation* (London and Brooklyn: Verso, 2022) and Kaba, *We Do This 'Til We Free Us: Abolitionist Organizing and Transformative Justice* (Chicago: Haymarket Books, 2021).

35. Reagon, *We Who Believe in Freedom*, 163.

36. James Smethurst, "The Black Arts Movement in Atlanta," in *Neighborhood Rebels*, ed. Joseph, 177–78.

37. Ibid., 179.

38. Ibid., 180.

39. Bernice Johnson Reagon, January 24, 1968, fundraising letter to supporters of the Penny Festival, Southern Folk Cultural Revival Project Collection, Southern Folklife Collection, Wilson Library, University of North Carolina at Chapel Hill.

40. Ibid.

41. Ibid.

42. "The Right to Be" and "The Black Flame" programs, Southern Folk Cultural Revival Project Collection, Southern Folklife Collection, Wilson Library, University of North Carolina at Chapel Hill.

43. Jamila Jones interview with Joseph Mosnier, *Civil Rights History Project*, April 27, 2011, 19–20.

44. Bernice Johnson Reagon, "Harambee Singers," https://www.bernicejohnsonreagon.com/2014/11/30/harambee-singers/, accessed July 11, 2024.

45. Ibid.

46. The National Museum of African American History and Culture has recently digitized a ten-minute film with clips of the opening ceremony of Malcolm X Liberation University from a 1969 episode of National Educational Television's Black Journal Program (including a brief clip of the Harambee Singers performance, the only recording of the group I know about). See https://nmaahc.si.edu/object/nmaahc_2012.79.1.68.1abc.

47. For a full history of Malcolm X Liberation University, see Benson, "From Malcolm X to Malcolm X Liberation University."

48. Jamila Jones interview with Joseph Mosnier, *Civil Rights History Project*, April 27, 2011, 19–20.

49. "Occupation of Greenville Air Force Base," https://snccdigital.org/events/occupation-of-greenville-air-force-base/, accessed July 11, 2024.

50. See the Introduction for Malcolm's critique of nonviolence and "We Shall Overcome."

51. Anderson, "Black Liberation Week: Cultural Excellence," 2.

52. Neal, *What the Music Said*, 94–95.

53. Anderson, "Black Liberation Week: Cultural Excellence," 2.

54. Hill Collins, *Black Feminist Thought*, 246.

55. Ibid.

56. Reagon, *We Who Believe in Freedom*, 32.

57. Bernice Johnson Reagon, "Harambee Singers," https://www.bernicejohnsonreagon.com/2014/11/30/harambee-singers/, accessed July 11, 2024.

58. The "Talented Tenth" was a pedagogical argument advanced by W. E. B. Du Bois in debates about the most effective way to educate Black Americans following Emancipation and Reconstruction. Put simply, Washington advocated for technical and industrial schools, while Du Bois argued for liberal arts education in order to uncover the "talented tenth" of every race who have the endowment to excel academically. See W. E. B. Du Bois, "The Talented Tenth," in *The Negro Problem*, ed. Booker T. Washington. 1903. Reprint, Amherst, NY: Humanity Books, 2003.

59. Stewart, Shapiro, and Romaine, *Oh, What a Time*, 45; Southern Folklife Collection, Wilson Library, University of North Carolina at Chapel Hill.

60. Reagon, in *Oh, What a Time*, 1.

61. Yuval-Davis, *Gender and Nation*, 88.

62. Anne Romaine and Bernice Johnson Reagon, "Proposal for Southern Folk Cultural Revival Project," Southern Folk Cultural Revival Project Collection, Southern Folklife Collection, The Wilson Library, University of North Carolina at Chapel Hill.

63. Ibid.

64. "Reflections by Anne Romaine on the Southern Folk Cultural Revival Project," December 1982, in Southern Folk Cultural Revival Project Collection, Southern Folklife Collection, The Wilson Library, University of North Carolina at Chapel Hill.

65. Reagon letter to Romaine, September 24, 1974, in Southern Folk Cultural Revival Project Collection, Southern Folklife Collection, The Wilson Library, University of North Carolina at Chapel Hill.

66. Reagon letter to Romaine, October 11, 1974, in Southern Folk Cultural Revival Project Collection, Southern Folklife Collection, The Wilson Library, University of North Carolina at Chapel Hill.

67. Reagon interview with David Garcia, 2004. The same tension is still resurfacing in current discourse within antiracist circles surrounding White participation in the Black Lives Matter movement.

68. Reagon letter to Romaine, May 20, 1981, Southern Folk Cultural Revival Project Collection, Southern Folklife Collection, The Wilson Library, University of North Carolina at Chapel Hill.

69. You can hear Anne Romaine's performance of "On the Line" thanks to the digitization efforts of the UNC Chapel Hill Southern Folklife Collection here: https://dc.lib.unc.edu/cdm/singleitem/collection/sfc/id/90582/rec/1. Reagon's "Joan Little" can be heard on her 1975 album *Give Your Hands to the Struggle*, Paredon P-1028, 1975, vinyl. The album was reissued by Smithsonian Folkways in 1997 and is available on most streaming platforms.

70. Bernice Johnson Reagon, "Uncovered and Without Shelter, I Joined This Movement for Freedom," *Hands on the Freedom Plow*, eds. Holsaert et al., 119–27.

71. For a discussion of the civil rights subject in the televisual discourse of the 1970s and 80s, see Gray, *Watching Race*, and Bodroghkozy, *Equal Time*.

72. Greene, "'She Ain't No Rosa Parks,'" 428–47.

73. Reagon gives the collective entity of Sweet Honey in the Rock she/her pronouns in her writing; this book generally uses the pronoun "they" here.

74. Harrington, "Singing the Freedom Song."

75. Reagon, *We Who Believe in Freedom*, 20–24.

76. Bernice Johnson Reagon, *Raise Your Voice*, directed by Stanley Nelson (New York: Firelight Media, 2005), 1:11.

77. See *Fundi: The Story of Ella Baker*, directed by Joanne Grant (Brooklyn: Icarus Films, 1981); and "Ella's Song," *Breaths* (Nashville: Rounder Records, 1988).

78. Reagon, *We Who Believe in Freedom*, 20.

79. See this performance by Charon Hribar, Keisha Soleil, and other demonstrators at a Poor People's Campaign mass meeting in the summer of 2016: https://www.youtube.com/watch?v=JRlV-XA8ii8.

80. See Mikki Halpin, "Toshi Reagon: 'We Have to Put Women at the Center of the Universe,'" *Spin*, March 8, 2017, https://www.spin.com/2017/03/toshi-reagon-we-have-to-put-women-at-the-center-of-the-universe/ and https://www.youtube.com/watch?v=KRiveZNEqjs.

81. "Sweet Honey in the Rock at the Voices Festival," 1990, https://www.youtube.com/watch?v=U6Uus-gFrc.

82. Reagon, *We Who Believe in Freedom*, 38.

83. Ibid., 31.

84. *Raise Your Voice*, 6:46.

85. Ibid., 6:15.

86. Ibid., 2:45.

87. Horowitz was also the assistant and acting director of Smithsonian Folkways, among many other things.

88. Horowitz, in *We Who Believe in Freedom*, 187.

89. Ibid., 29.

90. Hayes, *Songs in Black and Lavender*, 67.
91. Reagon, *We Who Believe in Freedom*, 32.
92. Ibid., 33.
93. Ibid., 46.
94. *Raise Your Voice*, 13:40.
95. Ibid., 11:20.
96. Ibid., 15:00.
97. Horace Clarence Boyer, "About Sweet Honey in the Rock," http://www.pbs.org/wnet/americanmasters/sweet-honey-in-the-rock-about-sweet-honey-in-the-rock/716/, accessed July 11, 2024.
98. *Raise Your Voice*, 38:30.
99. Ibid., 39:48.
100. Sweet Honey in the Rock, "I Remember I Believe," *Sacred Ground,* EMI, 1996.
101. Bernice Johnson Reagon, "Old Ship of Zion," *Give Your Hands to the Struggle*, Smithsonian Folkways, 1975.
102. *Raise Your Voice*, 1:17:00.
103. Rhiannon Giddens, Facebook post on July 18, 2024.
104. In other words, because Giddens is more closely paralleling the sound of 1960s protest, she is in danger of landing outside of what Benjamin Tausig would call the "vernacular of sonic dissent" in the 2010s. See Tausig, "Sound and Movement."
105. See the Introduction for more discussion of Black nationalist critique of freedom singing.
106. hooks, *Killing Rage*, 81.
107. Brooks, "Open Channels," 64.
108. Along the same lines, the freedom singing framework is flexible enough to provide useful analyses of the ways other Black women musick in relation to the expanded Black Freedom Movement (e.g., Abbey Lincoln, avant garde jazz, etc.).
109. Corey Townsend, "Beyoncé's Homecoming on Netflix Is an Historically Black Experience," *The Root*, April 17, 2019, https://thegrapevine.theroot.com/beyonces-homecoming-on-netflix-is-an-historically-black-1834102760.

Chapter 4. Warren County, Environmental Justice, and Freedom Singing in Protest

1. "North Carolina Moral Monday 7–15 Arrest Video," May 22, 2014.
2. "Dr. King's Vision: The Poor People's Campaign of 1967–68," https://www.poorpeoplescampaign.org/history/, accessed July 12, 2024.
3. Cornel West, in Barber, II, *The Third Reconstruction*.
4. "William J. Barber II," https://www.macfound.org/fellows/1005/, accessed July 12, 2024.
5. Yara Allen and Charron Hribar, *We Rise: A Movement Songbook*, https://www.poorpeoplescampaign.org/arts-culture/we-rise-a-movement-songbook/, accessed July 12, 2024.

6. Deborah Ferruccio, quote from email communication with author, April 25, 2019.

7. Anonymous, "Dumping on the Poor," *Washington Post*, October 12, 1982, at A12.

8. The Flint water crisis, mentioned in chapter 3, is a well-known example of the type of environmental racism this movement seeks to combat.

9. McGurty, "From NIMBY to Civil Rights," 301.

10. Ibid., 306.

11. Edward Wilson, "Afterword," in Rachel Carson, *Silent Spring* (1962. Reprint, Boston: Houghton Mifflin Harcourt, 2002), 357.

12. Linda Lear, "Introduction," in Carson, *Silent Spring*, xvii.

13. Michael H. Brown, "Love Canal and the Poisoning of America," *The Atlantic*, December 1979, https://www.theatlantic.com/magazine/archive/1979/12/love-canal-and-the-poisoning-of-america/376297/.

14. McGurty, "From NIMBY to Civil Rights," 307.

15. Ibid.

16. Ibid. Before the waivers were processed by the EPA, the regulations were changed to drastically reduce the requirements so that North Carolina did not need the three waivers.

17. Ibid.

18. Deborah Ferruccio, "Timeline," *NC PCB Archives*, https://web.archive.org/web/20160319030117/http://www.ncpcbarchives.com/?page_id=8, accessed July 12, 2024.

19. Deborah Ferruccio, interviewed by Stephen Stacks in Durham, North Carolina, December 4, 2014, 6:50.

20. Ken Ferruccio, interviewed by Stephen Stacks in Wake Forest, North Carolina, November 13, 2015, 4:15.

21. Ibid., 4:30.

22. Ibid.

23. See Julian Bond, "The Media and the Movement: Looking Back from the Southern Front," in *Media, Culture, and the Modern African American Freedom Struggle*, ed. Ward, 16–40; Murphree, *The Selling of Civil Rights*; and Bodroghkozy, *Equal Time*.

24. Jenny Walker, "A Media-Made Movement? Black Violence and Nonviolence in the Historiography of the Civil Rights Movement," in *Media, Culture, and the Modern African American Freedom Struggle*, ed. Ward, 41–66.

25. Reagon, quoted in Harrington, "Singing the Freedom Song."

26. Deborah Ferruccio, "Timeline," *NC PCB Archives*, https://web.archive.org/web/20160319030117/http://www.ncpcbarchives.com/?page_id=8, accessed July 12, 2024.

27. Tensions were mounting in Wilmington over integration of the schools in 1969. In 1971, students decided to boycott the high schools after the school board abruptly and without feedback closed the Black high school and laid off all of the teachers, staff, and administrators. In February of 1971, a White-owned business

was firebombed; firefighters claimed they were shot at from the church across the street where Chavis and his colleagues were meeting. Riots broke out in the neighborhood, and the National Guard was called in to enter the church and apprehend those inside. Chavis and the rest of the Wilmington Ten were arrested and charged with the arson. The trial was full of questionable irregularities and reasonable doubt; however, the Ten were convicted of sentences ranging from fifteen years (for the White woman who was in the group) to thirty-four years (Chavis's sentence). In 1978 Governor Jim Hunt reduced the sentences of the Ten, and in 1980 the Fourth Circuit Court of Appeals overturned their convictions. They were not retried, but were not officially pardoned until 2012, when Governor Bev Perdue granted their petition for pardon. See Janken, *The Wilmington Ten.*

28. Chavis, "Toxic Wastes and Race in the United States."

29. Ibid., ix-x.

30. See also Bullard, *The Wrong Complexion for Protection* and *Dumping in Dixie*, and McGurty, "From NIMBY to Civil Rights."

31. See Bullard, *Dumping in Dixie*, 1–20.

32. See Finney, *Black Faces, White Spaces*; Gibson-Wood and Wakefield, "'Participation,' White Privilege and Environmental Justice," 641–62; McLean, "The Whiteness of Green," 354–62; and Bullard, *Dumping in Dixie*.

33. Finney, *Black Faces, White Spaces*, 2. The exception to this is Indigenous/American Indian people, who are stereotyped in the opposite direction as one with nature regardless of their actual affinity for the land. White wilderness culture is rife with appropriation of Native American symbolism, rituals, and knowledge with very little acknowledgment or representation.

34. Ibid., 3.

35. Rhodes, *Environmental Justice in America*, 31.

36. Ibid., 37.

37. Taylor, "Race, Class, Gender, and American Environmentalism," 1.

38. Titon, "The Nature of Ecomusicology," 8–18.

39. Deborah Ferruccio, interviewed by Stephen Stacks in Warrenton, North Carolina, October 23, 2015, 25:50.

40. Rehding, "Ecomusicology Between Apocalypse and Nostalgia," 409–14.

41. See Stimeling, "Music, Place, and Identity in the Central Appalachian Mountaintop Removal Mining Debate," 1–29; and Allen, "Prospects and Problems for Ecomusicology in Confronting a Crisis of Culture," 414.

42. Reagon, "Let the Church Sing 'Freedom,'" 113.

43. Although freedom singing at a participatory level is accessible, songleading and improvising takes considerable practice and skill, and powerful collective singing takes a cultural competence that is not as widespread as it was in the 1950s and 60s, especially among the White American population.

44. Martin, *The Theater Is in the Street*, 29.

45. See Brill, *Music of Latin America and the Caribbean.*

46. Ibid., 521.

47. Deborah Ferruccio, interviewed by Stephen Stacks in Durham, North Carolina, December 4, 2014, 3:24.

48. Ferruccio, interviewed by Stephen Stacks in Durham, North Carolina, December 4, 2014, 13:45. Again, this is with the exception of Native American spirituality, which is often appropriated within the context of environmentalism with little understanding for its contextual significance.

49. Reagon, *If You Don't Go, Don't Hinder Me*, 4.

50. See Reagon, "Let the Church Sing 'Freedom,'" 105–18, and Pratt, *Rhythm and Resistance*.

51. See Schafer, *The Soundscape*, 74–78; and Radano and Olaniyan, eds., *Audible Empire*.

52. Deborah Ferruccio, interviewed by Stephen Stacks in Durham, North Carolina, December 4, 2014, 12:31–13:30.

53. Noting the reference to "forty acres and a mule" helps to understand the politicized nature of this project and its location within the Freedom Movement.

54. Valeria Lee, interviewed by Stephen Stacks in Durham, North Carolina, April 21, 2016, 5:40–5:48.

55. Valeria Lee, interviewed by Joshua Davis for the Southern Oral History Project at the University of North Carolina, Chapel Hill, March 17, 2011, transcript p. 20.

56. Kelley, *Freedom Dreams*, 125.

57. Ibid.

58. This line of thought has very interesting resonances with the resistance strategy of Black capitalist musicians such as Beyoncé. See chapter 3 for more discussion on Beyoncé's commercialism and its intersection with the Black radical tradition.

59. "700 Protest Proposed North Carolina Chemical Dump," *New York Times*, January 6, 1979, at 6.

60. Deborah Ferruccio, interviewed by Stephen Stacks in Warrenton, North Carolina, October 23, 2015, 1:00–3:38.

61. See chapter 5 for further discussion of this.

62. Neal, *What the Music Said*, 126.

63. Omojola, "Identity, Politics, and Nostalgia in Nigerian Music," 250.

64. Ahad-Legardy, *Afro-Nostalgia*, 62. Alexander Rehding's concept of how music may offer an appropriate and helpful nostalgia for mobilizing efforts against ecological crises is relevant here as well. See Rehding, "Ecomusicology Between Apocalypse and Nostalgia."

65. DeNora, "Music and Self-Identity," in *The Popular Music Studies Reader*, ed. Bennett, Shank, and Toynbee, 143.

66. Ndaliko, *Necessary Noise*, 15.

67. Ahad-Legardy, *Afro-Nostalgia*, 61. This type of destructive White nostalgia is evident in Europe and the United States in the nostalgia-based politics of figures such as Donald Trump and Nigel Farage, and their respective catchphrases "Make America Great Again" and "We Want Our Country Back." There are many forms of nostalgia, not all of them destructive and racist as these are.

68. In both of these nostalgias there are echoes of the Southern Folk Cultural Revival Project's work, discussed in chapter 3. In the SFCRP, we saw Anne Romaine and Bernice Johnson Reagon working through the building of a musical coali-

tion in the wake of the Civil Rights Movement, and attempting to weaponize the power of a past that Black and White roots music reveals as deeply and inseparably interconnected. We continue to explore the development of this association with traditional freedom song in chapter 5 as well.

69. See Reagon, "Songs of the Civil Rights Movement 1955–1965," "Let the Church Sing 'Freedom,'" 105–18; Sanger, *The Rhetoric of the Freedom Songs in the American Civil Rights Movement*, *"When the Spirit Says Sing!"*; and Dunson, *Freedom in the Air*.

70. McFadden and Whitehead adopted the visual trends of the 1970s, including leisure suits with wide lapels and shirt collars tucked out rather than in. A picture of young people performing at a Concerned Citizens rally features similar fashion, tying the young people in Warren County visually to Black Consciousness in popular culture. The picture can be seen here: "Almena Mayes and friends sing at a fundraiser circa 1981," https://ourroadtowalk.com/gallery/. Photo taken by Mac Owen Shaffer.

71. See Ward, *Just My Soul Responding*; Monson, *Saying Something*; and Bentley, *Los Angeles Troubadours*.

72. Neal, *What the Music Said*, 123.

73. Ibid., 120.

74. Orejuaela and Shonekan, *Black Lives Matter and Music*, 23.

75. See Ward, *Just My Soul Responding*, and Guralnick, *Sweet Soul Music*.

76. Joshua Davis, "WVSP-Warrenton," March 10, 2013, https://mediaandthe movement.unc.edu/2013/03/10/wvsp-radio/#comment-6666.

77. Valeria Lee, interviewed by Stephen Stacks in Durham, North Carolina, April 21, 2016, 15:00. The breadth of their musical programming and the emphasis on folk music recalls the concept of the SFCRP's Southern Folk Festival from chapter 3.

78. Ibid., 14:50.

79. Ibid., 16:30–17:50.

80. Russakoff, "As in the 60s, Protestors Rally."

81. Deborah Ferruccio, interviewed by Stephen Stacks in Warrenton, North Carolina, October 23, 2015, 1:17:45. See also Dollie Burwell, "Remembering to Remember: The Birth of an Environmental Justice Movement, *Warren Record*, February 2, 2022, https://www.warrenrecord.com/news/article_c163420e-8431-11ec-9b02-033fce80b479.html.

82. Russakoff, "As in the 60s, Protestors Rally."

83. Reed, *The Art of Protest*, 299.

84. Eyerman and Jamison, *Social Movements*, 98.

85. Reagon, "Music as an Agent of Social Change," in *Issues in African American Music*, eds. Maultsby and Burnim, 344.

86. Brian Ward, "'People Get Ready': Music and the Civil Rights Movement of the 1950s and 1960s," *History Now* 8 (2006), https://archive.is/20060712033257/http://www.historynow.org/06_2006/historian2.html#selection-593.1–593.697.

87. Orejuaela and Shonekan, *Black Lives Matter and Music*, 32.

88. Turner, *Comunitas*.

89. Steven Connor, "Choralities," in *Twentieth-Century Music*, 3.

90. Chenjerai Kumanyika, "Dispatch from Charleston: The Cost of White Comfort," June 24, 2015, https://www.npr.org/sections/codeswitch/2015/06/24/417108714/dispatch-from-charleston-the-cost-of-white-comfort.

91. An article by Petter Dyndahl, Sidsel Karlsen, Odd Skårberg, and Siw Graabræk Nielsen that appeared in *Action, Criticism, and Theory for Music Education* in 2014 also used the term "musical gentrification." The usage is slightly earlier but less relevant to the current study.

92. Andrew Aprile, "The Missing Blue Note: Transmutation and Appropriation from the Gospel Lineage of 'We Shall Overcome,'" in *We Shall Overcome*, ed. Bobetsky, 51.

93. Cornel West, "On Afro-American Music: From Bebop to Rap," in *The Cornel West Reader*, 482.

94. Cornel West, "Prophetic Christian as Organic Intellectual," in *The Cornel West Reader*, 426.

95. Kwame Ture, formerly Stokely Carmichael, "The Myths of Coalition," in *Black Power*, 59–60.

96. See Rustin, "The Negro Needs White Allies," in *Time on Two Crosses*, eds. Carbado and Weise.

97. Reed, *The Art of Protest*, 4.

98. Ibid, 5.

99. See chapter 1 for discussion of the 1968 lens.

100. Ward, in *Media, Culture, and the Modern African American Freedom Struggle*, ed. Ward, 5.

101. Reagon, in Moyers, *The Songs Are Free*.

102. Julius Lester, "The Angry Children of Malcolm X," in *Black Protest Thought*, ed. Meier, Rudwick, and Broderick, 469.

103. Deborah Ferruccio, interviewed by Stephen Stacks in Durham, North Carolina, December 4, 2014, 23:35 and following. For Seeger's part, he corrected the assumption that he was the one who revived "Kumbaya" as a freedom song. Seeger maintained that a Black minister was responsible for bringing the song back from Liberia and integrating it into the Freedom Movement.

104. Aprile, "The Missing Blue Note," 51.

105. Ibid., 52.

106. See Stephen Winick, "Kumbaya: History of an Old Song," *Folklife Today: American Folklife Center and Veterans History Project*, February 6, 2018, https://blogs.loc.gov/folklife/2018/02/kumbaya-history-of-an-old-song/, for embedded recordings of the Wylie and Best versions of "Kumbaya."

107. Ibid.

108. This is knowledge I carry from my work as a leader of congregational singing in a White Protestant denomination and as a hymnologist.

109. See West, "On Afro-American Music."

110. Winick, "The World's First 'Kumbaya' Moment."

111. Deborah Ferruccio is aware of this dynamic. In an email to the author, she wrote, "The song may be satirized by today's comics, but there is nothing comical about needing God's hand in protecting our environment, and that truth was clear to Warren County citizens who called on God to stand with us." Personal email to author, December 7, 2014.

112. Barnwell, interview with Nishat Kurwa.

113. One need only look to the narrative constructed by Sam Rosenthal, which exaggerates Pete Seeger's role in the foundations of the freedom song tradition, or to Victor Bobetsky's tracing of the roots of "We Shall Overcome" to an Italian Catholic hymn to see the types of erasures that are commonly perpetuated. See Rosenthal and Bobetsky, in Bobetsky, ed., *We Shall Overcome*.

114. Deborah Ferruccio, interviewed by Stephen Stacks in Durham, North Carolina, December 4, 2014, 12:10–12:33.

115. Jones and Connelly, *Behind the Dream*.

116. McGurty, "From NIMBY to Civil Rights," 155.

117. This line of thinking is in keeping with the philosophy of colorblindness and forms the basis of critiques of affirmative action and many conservative rollbacks of Civil Rights Movement gains.

118. See Pavithra Vasudevan, *Memory and the Reinvention of Place: The Legacies of Environmental Justice in Warren County, North Carolina*, master's thesis, University of North Carolina at Chapel Hill, 2013.

119. See Poor People's Campaign, "Somebody's Hurting My Brother by Yara Allen," YouTube, August 18, 2018, https://www.youtube.com/watch?v=-QIhizB8wsU. See also "Introduction to Coal Ash in NC," https://www.deq.nc.gov/news/hot-topics/coal-ash-nc/introduction-coal-ash-nc, accessed July 12, 2024.

120. As an example of the positive construction of blackness extending back further than Black Power, "somebodiness" is a concept that came from King. See Martin Luther King Jr., "What Is Your Life's Blueprint," http://www.thekinglegacy.org/news/2015/05/what-is-your-lifes-blueprint.

121. Ken Ferruccio in 2014 letter to Gov. Pat McCrory, read to author in personal interview on October 23, 2015.

122. See Nixon, *Slow Violence and the Environmentalism of the Poor*.

123. Deborah Ferruccio, "Timeline," *NC PCB Archives*, https://web.archive.org/web/20160319030117/http://www.ncpcbarchives.com/?page_id=8, accessed July 12, 2024. This cleanup effort continues to be quite contentious in Warren County, and the tension has a racial component. See Vasudevan, *Memory and the Reinvention of Place*.

124. See Vasudevan, *Memory and the Reinvention of Place*, 1.

125. Leoneda Inge, "EPA Creates New Office to Advance Environmental Justice Initiatives," *NPR*, October 3, 2022, https://www.npr.org/2022/10/03/1126626956/epa-creates-new-office-to-advance-environmental-justice-initiatives.

126. Ibid.

127. Reagon, *Songs of the Civil Rights Movement*, 22–23.

128. Walker, *In Search of Our Mother's Gardens*, 120–21.

129. Rehding, "Ecomusicology Between Apocalypse and Nostalgia," 414.

Chapter 5. Documentary Media, Freedom Song, and the Construction of Sonic Blackness

1. *Soundtrack for a Revolution*, 1:08:50. The protestors at this march later learned that this sound was a car backfiring; however, because of the context, a gunshot was the most logical assumption.

2. Ibid., 1:09:05.

3. King frequently requested for the song to be sung, including asking Mahalia Jackson to sing it at his funeral and shouting down to saxophonist Ben Branch to play it at the meeting that night from the balcony of the Lorraine Motel in Memphis minutes before he was shot and killed. It is likely the conflation of these various stories that led to Ava DuVernay's depiction of King calling Jackson and asking her to sing him "Precious Lord" over the phone in *Selma*. See Ann Powers, "How One of Gospel's Essential Songs Gave 'Selma' Its Soul," *NPR*, January 15, 2015, https://www.npr.org/sections/therecord/2015/01/15/377427650/how-one-of-gospels-essential-songs-gave-selma-its-soul.

4. *Soundtrack*, 1:13:50.

5. Ibid., 1:19:08.

6. "American Experience: Soundtrack for a Revolution," May 6, 2011, https://www.kpbs.org/news/2011/may/06/american-experience-soundtrack-revolution/.

7. Keogh, "'Soundtrack for a Revolution.'"

8. I am indebted to Tammy Kernodle for bringing the term *sonic blackness* into the context of this chapter. She theorizes it in a forthcoming book on Black women musicians and their interactions with the Civil Rights Movement. This term is also related to Nina Eidsheim's theorizations of race and sound, as well as Mendi Obadike's work on "acoustematic blackness." See Eidsheim, *Listening, Timbre, and Vocality in African American Music* and Obadike, "Low Fidelity."

9. See Mulvey, "Visual Pleasure and Narrative Cinema," in *A Critical and Cultural Theory Reader*, ed. Easthope and McGowan, 167–76.

10. Stuart Hall, "The Whites of Their Eyes: Racist Ideologies and the Media," in *The Race and Media Reader*, ed. Rodman.

11. See Charbonneau, *Projecting Race*.

12. "White aurality" has been used in several contexts but has not been theorized in exactly the same way. For use of the term, see Thompson, "Whiteness and the Ontological Turn in Sound Studies," 266–82; and Black, "Little Dancing Indians" (forthcoming). Black's usage of "aurality of the White U. S. American spectator" and "racialized aurality" are more similar to what I am theorizing here.

13. Mark Slobin, "The Steiner Superculture," "The Superculture Beyond Steiner," and "Subcultural Filmways," in *Global Soundtracks*, ed. Slobin.

14. Bodroghkozy, *Equal Time*, 4.

15. Margot Adler, "Before Rosa Parks There Was Claudette Colvin," *NPR*, March 15, 2009, https://www.npr.org/2009/03/15/101719889/before-rosa-parks-there-was-claudette-colvin.

16. See Rasaki, "From SNCC to BLM," 31–38.

17. See Clifford, "On Ethnographic Allegory," in *Writing Culture*; Garcia, *Listening for Africa*; Hochman, *Savage Preservation*; Keil, *Urban Blues*; Lott, *Love and Theft*; Miller, *Segregating Sound*; Radano, "On Ownership and Value" and *Lying Up a Nation*; Radano and Bohlman, eds., *Music and the Racial Imagination*; and Stoever, *The Sonic Color Line*.

18. Hochman, *Savage Preservation*, xii.

19. Ibid., xiii.

20. Radano and Bohlman, *Music and the Racial Imagination*, 16.

21. Radano, *Lying Up a Nation*, xii.

22. Garcia, *Listening for Africa*, 9.

23. Stoever, *The Sonic Color Line*, 1.

24. Ibid., 7.

25. Ibid.

26. Taruskin, *Oxford History*, 850.

27. See Lott, *Love and Theft*.

28. Filene, "'Our Singing Country,'" 604.

29. Oforlea, "[Un]veiling the White Gaze," 290.

30. Gilroy, *The Black Atlantic*, 30–31.

31. Mullen, *The Man Who Adores the Negro*, 11.

32. Favor, *Authentic Blackness*, 4.

33. Homi Bhabha, "The 'Other' Question," 18.

34. The contributions of Candie Carawan are rarely explicated, as her work was mostly behind the scenes while Guy's was much more public. This book endeavors to be specific about attributing whether a certain aspect of their work is a joint effort, or whether something is attributed mostly to Guy or Candie. For instance, Guy was responsible for making the field recordings and was the trained folklorist, while Candie did most of the writing. They are often referred to as "the Carawans" to indicate that their approach to documenting freedom singing was largely a combined effort. For a more detailed discussion of Candie's contributions to their joint work, see Turner, "Guy and Candie Carawan."

35. Rose, *Black Noise*, 5.

36. Filene, "'Our Singing Country,'" 604.

37. Hirsch, "Modernity, Nostalgia, and Southern Folklore Studies," 193–94.

38. Mullen, *The Man Who Adores the Negro*, 81.

39. Carawan, "Remembrances of Alan Lomax."

40. Turner, "Guy and Candie Carawan," 14. This relatively small circle of influence also included Pete Seeger, Moses (Moe) Asch, and Ralph Rinzler.

41. See Jenny Walker, "A Media Made Movement: Black Violence and Nonviolence in the Historiography of the Civil Rights Movement," in *Media, Culture, and the Modern African American Freedom Struggle*, ed. Ward.

42. See below for a description of the preponderance of civil rights-related events in the 1980s.

43. Deborra Richardson, "Guide to the Bernice Johnson Reagon Collection," *Smithsonian Online Virtual Archives*, https://sova.si.edu//record/NMAH.AC.0653, accessed July 21, 2024.

44. Ella Jenkins, Review of *Sit-In Songs* and *Freedom in the Air*, *Community* 22, no. 11 (July 1963), Guy and Candie Carawan Collection, Southern Folklife Collection, University of North Carolina at Chapel Hill.

45. Eric Larrabee, "Jazz Notes: Protest," in *Harper's Magazine*, in Guy and Candie Carawan Collection, Southern Folklife Collection, University of North Carolina at Chapel Hill.

46. See discussion of Johns Island material below.

47. Field recordings that provided the material for the album are held in the Guy and Candie Carawan Collection, Southern Folklife Collection, University of North Carolina at Chapel Hill.

48. Reagon, "Let The Church Sing 'Freedom,'" 106.

49. Lomax in liner notes for *Freedom in the Air*, produced by Alan Lomax and Guy Carawan, Student Nonviolent Coordinating Committee, P. 1962, SNCC-627.

50. An interesting counterpoint to this is Mary Lou Williams's contention that jazz grows directly out of the African American spiritual tradition. See Tammy Kernodle, "You Can't Tell It Like I Can: Mary Lou Williams, Black Nationalism, and the Reframing of Jazz's History," lecture delivered on January 26, 2024, at the University of North Carolina at Chapel Hill and *Soul on Soul: The Life and Music of Mary Lou Williams*.

51. SFC Audio Open Reel 3721: Guy Carawan interview with Studs Terkel, WFMT Radio, Chicago: 18 January 1964: Reel 1 of 2: Side 1 in Guy and Candie Carawan Collection, Southern Folklife Collection, University of North Carolina at Chapel Hill.

52. Ibid.

53. Twining, "Field Notes on Reactions to 'Ain't You Got a Right to the Tree of Life' by Guy and Candie Carawan," 214.

54. Alan Lomax, "Folk Singing Is Rediscovered on Island," *News and Courier* (Charleston, S.C.) January 19, 1964.

55. Turner, "Guy and Candie Carawan," 46–59.

56. Ibid.

57. Ibid.

58. Carawan, *Sing for Freedom*, 103.

59. Ibid., 104.

60. Ibid., xv.

61. Miller, "Remembering Freedom Songs," 51.

62. Hall, "The Whites of Their Eyes," 44.

63. Carawan, *Sing for Freedom*, 104.

64. Ibid., xxii.

65. See Josh Dunson, "Slave Songs at the 'Sing for Freedom,'" *Broadside* 49 (May 30, 1964) and Turner, "Guy and Candie Carawan," 48–49.

66. Miller, *Segregating Sound*, 85–120.

67. See SFC Audio Open Reel 3721: Guy Carawan interview with Studs Terkel, WFMT Radio, Chicago: 18 January 1964: Reel 1 of 2: Side 1 in Guy and Candie Carawan Collection, Southern Folklife Collection, University of North Carolina at Chapel Hill.

68. See chapter 2 for more detail about Reagon's approach to freedom singing after 1968.

69. See Kernodle, "'I Wish I Knew How It Would Feel to Be Free,'" 295–317.

70. Hampton quoted in Else, *True South*, 60.

71. Else, *True South*, 28.

72. Ibid., 59.

73. See Alexander Pisciotta, "Race Riots," in *Encyclopedia of Race and Crime*, ed. Taylor Greene and Gabbidon, 687–89.

74. See chapter 4 for more detail on the Warren County environmental justice movement.

75. Else, *True South*, 91.

76. Charbonneau, *Projecting Race*.

77. Recording in Hampton Papers, Film and Media Archive, Washington University in St. Louis.

78. Letter from L. S. (Llewelyn Smith) to *Eyes* production team, Hampton Papers, Film and Media Archive, Washington University in St. Louis.

79. Else, *True South*, 60.

80. Keil, "Participatory Discrepancies and the Power of Music," 275–83.

81. See the 08/07/1989 letter from Sheila to Leah about the music selections for Episode 202 [Season 2, Episode 2], Hampton Papers, Film and Media Archive, University of Washington in St. Louis.

82. Sheila Curran Bernard in Hampton Papers, Film and Media Archive, Washington University in St. Louis.

83. Carawan in Hampton Papers, Film and Media Archive, Washington University in St. Louis.

84. *Eyes on the Prize*, Season 1, Episode 4, 16:00–18:30.

85. Reagon in liner notes for *Voices of the Civil Rights Movement*, produced by Bernice Johnson Reagon, Smithsonian Folkways (P. 1997) SF 40084.

86. Hill, *The Deacons for Defense*, 31–38.

87. See *Eyes on the Prize*, Season 2, Episode 3, 31:35.

88. Hampton Papers, Film and Media Archives, Washington University in St. Louis.

89. *Jet* (July 30, 1990), 56–59.

90. "Terri Lyne Carrington, Melba Moore's Lift Every Voice," https://www.youtube.com/watch?v=uvTnfDJyKPw, accessed July 21, 2024.

91. Redmond, *Anthem*, 265.

92. Ibid.

93. Carson et al., eds. *The Eyes on the Prize Civil Rights Reader*.

94. For an example of a documentary filmmaker who plays with the elision of time in a generative, nonproblematic way, see Arthur Jafa, especially his short film *Love Is the Message, the Message Is Death*.

95. Gilroy, *The Black Atlantic*, 32.

96. Ibid., 33.

97. Ibid., 32.

98. Ibid.

99. See Dowd Hall, "The Long Civil Rights Movement."

100. Mullen, *The Man Who Adores the Negro*, 177–78.

101. Ibid., 184.

102. See Turner, "Guy and Candie Carawan."

103. In fact, the impetus for Mullen's writing *The Man Who Adores the Negro* was Fanon's critique of White people who love and consume Black culture, which Mullen took to heart and used as encouragement to investigate why he himself was drawn to Black folk culture.

104. Favor, *Authentic Blackness*, 137–52. See also the discussion in chapter 3 of Judith Butler and performativity.

105. Ibid., 152. Also see chapter 2 of this book.

Conclusion

Epigraph: Walker, *In Search of Our Mother's Gardens*, 128–29.

1. Ture (formerly known as Stokely Carmichael) and Hamilton, *Black Power*.

2. The *Los Angeles Times* reports sixty-three deaths, while Lou Cannon's history of the riots says fifty-four. The *Times* number appears to include some deaths that may or may not be related to the rioting. See "Deaths During the LA Riots," April 25, 2012, https://latimesblogs.latimes.com/lanow/2012/04/los-angeles-riots-remember-the-63-people-who-died-.html; and Cannon, *Official Negligence*.

3. George H. W. Bush, "Address to the Nation on the Civil Disturbances in Los Angeles, California," May 1, 1992.

4. Lyndon Johnson, "Statement on Watts Riots," August 17, 1965.

5. King, "The Other America," in *The Radical King*, ed. West, 235–44.

6. Darda, "MLK at the LA Riots," 216.

7. See Rose, *Black Noise*, 99–145.

8. Ibid., 183.

9. Ice Cube, "The Predator," *The Predator*, produced by Ice Cube (Los Angeles: Lench Mob Records, 1992).

10. Stephen Betts, "See Garth Brooks Get Political with Unearthed 'We Shall Be Free' Video," March 7, 2017, https://www.rollingstone.com/music/music-country/see-garth-brooks-get-political-with-unearthed-we-shall-be-free-video-194518/.

11. Garth Brooks, "We Shall Be Free," *The Chase*, produced by Allen Reynolds (Nashville, Liberty Records, 1992).

12. See Spencer, "Freedom Songs of the Civil Rights Movement."

13. DeNora, "Music and Self-Identity," 146.

14. Darda, "MLK at the LA Riots," 216.

Afterword

1. Du Bois, *The Souls of Black Folk*, 9.

Bibliography

Books, Journal Articles, and Other Written Sources

Abbington, James, ed. *Readings in African American Church Music and Worship*. Chicago: GIA Publications, 2001.

Abernathy, Ralph. *And the Walls Came Tumblin' Down: An Autobiography*. Chicago: Lawrence Hill Books, 2010.

Ahad-Legardy, Badia. *Afro-Nostalgia: Feeling Good in Contemporary Black Culture*. Chicago: University of Illinois Press, 2021.

Alexander, Michelle. *The New Jim Crow: Mass Incarceration in the Age of Colorblindness*. New York: New Press, 2012.

Allen, Aaron. "Prospects and Problems for Ecomusicology in Confronting a Crisis of Culture." *Journal of the American Musicological Society* 64, no. 2 (Summer 2011): 414–24.

Allen, Aaron and Kevin Dawe, eds. *Current Directions in Ecomusicology: Music, Culture, Nature.* New York: Routledge, 2016.

Allen, Aaron, Jeff Todd Titon, and Denise Von Glahn. "Sustainability and Sound: Ecomusicology Inside and Outside the Academy." *Music and Politics* 8, no. 2 (Summer 2014): 1–26.

Anderson, Juanita. "Black Liberation Week: Cultural Excellence." *The Michigan Daily*, March 16, 1971.

Anderson, Paul Allen. *Deep River: Music and Memory in Harlem Renaissance Thought*. Durham: Duke University Press, 2001.

Appleton, Clyde R. "Singing in the Streets of Raleigh, 1963: Some Recollections." *The Black Perspective in Music* 3, no. 3 (Autumn 1975): 243–52.

Araiza, Lauren. *To March for Others: The Black Freedom Struggle and the United Farm Workers*. Philadelphia: University of Pennsylvania Press, 2014.

Arendt, Hannah. *On Revolution*. 1963. Reprint, London: Penguin Books, 2006.

Attali, Jacques. *Noise: The Political Economy of Music*. Minneapolis: University of Minnesota Press, 1985.

Axelrod, Alan. *Minority Rights in America*. Washington, D.C.: CQ Press, 2002.

Baldwin, James. *Baldwin: Collected Essays*, ed. Toni Morrison. New York: The Library of America, 1998.

Baker, Houston A. *Betrayal: How Black Intellectuals Have Abandoned the Ideals of the Civil Rights Era*. New York: Columbia University Press, 2008.

———. *Blues, Ideology, and Afro-American Literature: A Vernacular Theory*. Chicago: University of Chicago Press, 1987.

———. *Long Black Song: Essays in Black American Literature and Culture*. Charlottesville: University Press of Virginia, 1972.

———. Review of Tricia Rose's *Black Noise: Rap Music and Black Culture in Contemporary America*. *African American Review* 29, no. 4 (Winter 1995): 671–73.

Banner, Lois W. *Women in Modern America: A Brief History*. Belmont, CA: Thomson Wadsworth, 2005.

Baraka, Amiri. *Blues People: Negro Music in White America*. New York: William Morrow and Company, 1963.

———. *Black Music*. New York: William Morrow and Company, 1968.

Barber II, William J. *The Third Reconstruction: Moral Mondays, Fusion Politics, and the Rise of a New Justice Movement*. Boston: Beacon Press, 2016.

Barnwell, Ysaye. Interview with Nishat Kurwa. *Medium*. June 7, 2016. https://medium.com/@nishatjaan/sometimes-really-devastating-things-happen-so-that-better-things-can-come-into-your-life-7732fc6def98.

Bell, Derrick. *Gospel Choirs: Psalms of Survival for an Alien Land Called Home*. New York: Basic Books, 1996.

Benson, Richard D. "From Malcolm X to Malcolm X Liberation University: A Liberatory Philosophy of Education, Black Student Radicalism and Black Independent Educational Institution Building 1960–1973." PhD diss., University of Illinois at Urbana-Champaign, 2010.

Bentley, Christa. "Los Angeles Troubadours: The Politics of the Singer-Songwriter Movement, 1968–1975." PhD diss., University of North Carolina at Chapel Hill, 2016.

Berlin, Ira. "American Slavery in History and Memory and the Search for Social Justice." *The Journal of American History* 90, vol. 4 (2004): 1251–68.

Bhabha, Homi. "The 'Other' Question." *Screen* 24, no. 6 (1983).

Black, Amanda M. "Little Dancing Indians: Tradition and Utopian Listening in San Miguel de Allende, Mexico." *Journal of the Society for American Music* 13, Special Issue 4: "Music, Indigeneity, and Colonialism in the Americas" (November 2019): 436–60.

Blight, David. *Race and Reunion: The Civil War in American Memory*. Cambridge: Harvard University Press, 2002.

Bobetsky, Victor, ed., *We Shall Overcome: Essays on a Great America Song*. Lanham, MD: Rowman and Littlefield, 2015.

Bodroghkozy, Aniko. *Equal Time: Television and the Civil Rights Movement*. Urbana: University of Illinois Press, 2012.

Bonds, Mark Evan. *A History of Music in Western Culture, 4th Edition*. Upper Saddle River, NJ: Pearson Education, 2013.

Boorstin, Daniel and Brooks Mather Kelly. *A History of the United States*. Needham, MA: Prentice Hall, 1996.

Bourdieu, Pierre. "The Field of Cultural Production, or: The Economic World Reversed," in *The Field of Cultural Production*. Cambridge: Polity Press, 1993.

Branch, Taylor. *Parting the Waters: America in the King Years, 1954–1963*. New York: Simon and Schuster, 1989.

———. *Pillar of Fire: America in the King Years, 1963–1965*. New York: Simon and Schuster, 1998.

———. *At Canaan's Edge: America in the King Years, 1965–1968*. New York: Simon and Schuster, 2006.

Brill, Mark. *Music of Latin America and the Caribbean*. New York: Routledge, 2017.

Brooks, Daphne A. "Open Channels: Some Thoughts on Blackness, the Body, and Sound(ing) Women in the (Summer) Time of Trayvon." *Performance Research* 19, no. 3 (August 2014): 62–68.

Brooks, Maegan Parker. *A Voice That Could Stir an Army: Fannie Lou Hamer and the Rhetoric of the Black Freedom Movement*. Jackson: University Press of Mississippi, 2014.

Brooks, Tilford. *America's Black Musical Heritage*. Englewood Cliffs, NJ: Prentice Hall, 1984.

Brown, Robert McAfee. *Spirituality and Liberation: Overcoming the Great Fallacy*. Philadelphia: The Westminster Press, 1988.

Bullard, Robert. *The Wrong Complexion for Protection: How the Government Response to Disasters Endangers Minority Communities*. New York: New York University Press, 2016.

———. *Dumping in Dixie: Race, Class, and Environmental Quality*. London: Taylor and Francis, 2018.

Butler, Judith. *Bodies That Matter: On the Discursive Limits of "Sex."* New York: Routledge, 1993.

———. *Gender Trouble: Feminism and the Subversion of Identity*. New York: Routledge, 2006.

Cannon, Lou. *Official Negligence: How Rodney King and the Riots Changed Los Angeles and the LAPD.* Boulder: Westview, 1999.

Carawan, Guy and Candie Carawan. *Ain't You Got a Right to the Tree of Life?* New York: Simon and Schuster, 1966.

———. *Sing for Freedom: The Story of the Civil Rights Movement Through Its Songs*. Montgomery, AL: New South Books, 2007.

Carawan, Guy. "Remembrances of Alan Lomax, October 2002." http://www.culturalequity.org/alan-lomax/remembrance/gc, accessed July 12, 2024.

———. "The Living Folk Heritage of the Sea Islands." *Sing Out!* 14, no. 2 (April–May 1964): 29–32.

Carson, Clayborne. *In Struggle: SNCC and the Black Awakening of the 1960s*. Cambridge: Harvard University Press, 1995.

Carson, Clayborne, et al., eds. *The Eyes on the Prize Civil Rights Reader: Documents, Speeches, and Firsthand Accounts from the Black Freedom Struggle*. New York: Penguin Books, 1991.

Cash, W. J. *The Mind of the South*. New York: Alfred A. Knopf, 1941.

Chafe, William. *Civilities and Civil Rights: Greensboro, North Carolina and the Black Struggle for Freedom*. Oxford: Oxford University Press, 1981.

ChaJua, Sundiata Keita and Clarence Lang. "The 'Long Movement' as Vampire: Temporal and Spatial Fallacies in Recent Black Freedom Studies." *The Journal of African American History* 92, no. 2 (Spring 2007): 265–88.

Chappell, David L. "Religious Revivalism in the Civil Rights Movement." *African American Review* 36, no. 4 (Winter 2002): 581–95.

Charbonneau, Stephen. *Projecting Race: Postwar America, Civil Rights, and Documentary Film*. New York: Wallflower Press, 2016.

Chavis, Benjamin. "Toxic Wastes and Race in the United States: A National Report on the Racial and Socio-Economic Characteristics of Communities with Hazardous Waste Sites." *The United Church of Christ Commission for Racial Justice*, 1987.

Ciment, James, ed. *Postwar America: An Encyclopedia of Social, Political, Cultural, and Economic History*. Armonk, NY: M. E. Sharpe, 2007.

Clifford, James and George E. Marcus, eds. *Writing Culture: The Poetics and Politics of Ethnography*. Berkeley: University of California Press, 2010.

Cobb, James. *Away Down South: A History of Southern Identity*. New York: Oxford University Press, 2005.

Collier-Thomas, Bettye. *Sisters in Struggle: African-American Women of the Civil Rights-Black Power Movements*. New York: New York University Press, 2001.

Collins, Patricia Hill. *Black Feminist Thought: Knowledge, Consciousness, and the Politics of Empowerment*. New York: Routledge, 2000.

Cone, James H. *The Spirituals and the Blues: An Interpretation*. Maryknoll, NY: Orbis Books, 1992.

———. *Black Theology and Black Power*. Maryknoll, NY: Orbis Books, 1997.

———. *A Black Theology of Liberation*. Maryknoll, NY: Orbis Books, 1990.

———. *God of the Oppressed*. Maryknoll, NY: Orbis Books, 1997.

Connor, Steven. "Choralities." *Twentieth-Century Music* 13, no. 1 (March 2016): 3–23.

Crawford, Vicki, Jacqueline Rouse, and Barbara Woods, eds., *Black Women in the Civil Rights Movement: Trailblazers and Torchbearers*. Bloomington: Indiana University Press, 1993.

Current, Richard N., et al. *American History: A Survey*. New York: Alfred A. Knopf, 1987.

Curry, Constance, et al. *Deep in Our Hearts: Nine White Women in the Freedom Movement*. Athens: University of Georgia Press, 2000.

Darda, Joseph. "MLK at the LA Riots: Civil Rights, Memory, and Neoliberalism in Charles Johnson's *The Dreamer*." *Twentieth Century Literature* 60, no. 2 (Summer 2014): 197–222.

Darden, Robert F. "The George Floyd Demonstrations Turned into a Movement When the Protestors Began to Sing." *Dallas Morning News*. June 14, 2020. https://www.dallasnews.com/opinion/commentary/2020/06/14/the-george-floyd-demonstrations-turned-into-a-movement-when-the-protesters-began-to-sing/.

Darnovsky, Marcy, Barbara Epstein, and Richard Flacks, eds. *Cultural Politics and Social Movements*. Philadelphia: Temple University Press, 1995.

Davis, Angela Y. *The Meaning of Freedom*. San Francisco: City Light Books, 2012.

———. *Blues Legacies and Black Feminism: Gertrude "Ma" Rainey, Bessie Smith, and Billie Holiday*. New York: Pantheon Books, 1998.

Dell'Antonio, Andrew. Review of *Musicking*, *Notes* 55, no. 4 (June 1999): 883–86.

Denisoff, R. Serge. *Great Day Coming: Folk Music and the American Left*. Urbana: University of Illinois Press, 1971.

———. *Sing a Song of Social Significance*. Bowling Green, OH: Bowling Green University Popular Press, 1972.

Denisoff, R. Serge and Richard A. Peterson, eds. *The Sounds of Social Change*. Chicago: Rand McNally and Company, 1972.

DeNora, Tia. "Music and Self-Identity," in *The Popular Music Studies Reader*, ed. Andy Bennett, Barry Shank, and Jason Toynbee. London: Routledge, 2006.

Dowd Hall, Jacquelyn. "The Long Civil Rights Movement and the Political Uses of the Past." *The Journal of American History* 91, no. 4 (March 2005): 1233–63.

Dromgoole, Ambre. "'I'm Gonna Dedicate This One to Miss Franklin': Afro-Protestant Performance Pedagogies and Rethinking the Black Woman's Spiritual Voice." *Journal of Popular Music Studies* 34, no. 4 (December 2022): 19–38.

Drott, Eric. "Music and May 1968 in France: Practices, Roles, Representations," in Beate Kutschke and Barley Norton, eds. *Music and Protest in 1968*. Cambridge: Cambridge University Press, 2013.

Du Bois, W. E. B. *The Souls of Black Folk*. 1903. Reprint, Lexington: Tribeca Books, 2014.

Dunson, Josh. *Freedom in the Air: Song Movements of the Sixties*. Westport, CT: Greenwood Press, 1980.

Dyndahl, Petter, et al. "Cultural Omnivorousness and Musical Gentrification: An Outline of a Sociological Framework and Its Applications for Music Education Research." *Action, Criticism, and Theory for Music Education* 13, no. 1 (2014): 40–69.

Easthope, Anthony and Kate McGowan, eds. *A Critical and Cultural Theory Reader*. Toronto: University of Toronto Press, 2004.

Ehle, John. *The Free Men*. Lewisville, NC: Press 53, 2007.

Eidsheim, Nina Sun. *The Race of Sound: Listening, Timbre, and Vocality in African American Music*. Durham: Duke University Press, 2018.

Else, Jon. *True South: Henry Hampton and Eyes on the Prize, the Landmark Television Series that Reframed the Civil Rights Movement*. New York: Viking, 2017.

Epstein, Dena J. *Sinful Tunes and Spirituals: Black Folk Music to the Civil War*. Urbana: University of Illinois Press, 1977.

Epstein, Terrie L. "Tales from Two Textbooks: A Comparison of the Civil Rights Movement in Two Secondary History Textbooks." *Social Studies* 85, no. 3 (May 1994): 121–26.

Eskew, Glenn T. *But for Birmingham: The Local and National Movements in the Civil Rights Struggle*. Chapel Hill: University of North Carolina Press, 1997.

Eyerman, Ron and Andrew Jamison. *Social Movements: A Cognitive Approach*. University Park: Pennsylvania State University Press, 1991.

———. *Music and Social Movements: Mobilizing Traditions in the Twentieth Century*. Cambridge: Cambridge University Press, 1998.

Fanon, Frantz, tr. Richard Philcox. *The Wretched of the Earth*. New York: Grove Press, 2004.

———. *Black Skin, White Masks*. New York: Grove Press, 2008.

Favor, Martin. *Authentic Blackness: The Folk in the New Negro Renaissance*. Durham: Duke University Press, 1999.

Feld, Steven. "Sound Structure as Social Structure." *Ethnomusicology* 28, no. 3 (September 1984): 383–409.

Feldstein, Ruth. *How It Feels to Be Free: Black Women Entertainers and the Civil Rights Movement*. New York: Oxford University Press, 2013.

Ferris, William and Mary L. Hart, eds. *Folk Music and Modern Sound*. Jackson: University Press of Mississippi, 1982.

Filene, Benjamin. *Romancing the Folk: Public Memory and American Roots Music*. Chapel Hill: University of North Carolina Press, 2000.

———. "'Our Singing Country': John and Alan Lomax, Leadbelly, and the Construction of an American Past." *American Quarterly* 43, no. 4 (December 1991): 602–24.

Finney, Carolyn. *Black Faces, White Spaces: Reimagining the Relationship of African Americans to the Great Outdoors*. Chapel Hill: University of North Carolina Press, 2014.

Fischlin, Daniel, Ajay Heble, and George Lipsitz. *The Fierce Urgency of Now: Improvisation, Rights, and the Ethics of Cocreation*. Durham: Duke University Press, 2013.

Fish, Stanley. *Is There a Text in This Class? The Authority of Interpretive Communities*. Cambridge: Harvard University Press, 1980.

Floyd, Jr., Samuel A. *The Power of Black Music: Interpreting Its History from Africa to the United States*. New York: Oxford University Press, 1995.

Floyd, Jr., Samuel A., ed. *Black Music in the Harlem Renaissance: A Collection of Essays*. New York: Greenwood Press, 1990.

Foucault, Michel. *Language, Counter-Memory, Practice: Selected Essays and Interviews*. Ithaca: Cornell University Press, 1977.

Forman, Murray and Mark Anthony Neal, eds. *That's the Joint!: The Hip Hop Studies Reader*. New York: Routledge, 2013.

Franklin, V. P. *Black Self-Determination: A Cultural History of African-American Resistance*. Brooklyn: Lawrence Hill Books, 1992.

Friedman, Jonathan, ed. *The Routledge History of Social Protest in Popular Music*. New York: Routledge, 2013.

Garcia, David. *Listening for Africa: Freedom, Modernity, and the Logic of Black Music's African Origins*. Durham: Duke University Press, 2017.

Garrow, David. *Bearing the Cross: Martin Luther King, Jr. and the Southern Christian Leadership Conference*. New York: Morrow, 1986.

Gates, Jr., Henry Louis. *The Signifying Monkey: A Theory of African-American Literary Criticism*. New York: Oxford University Press, 1995.

Gibson-Wood, Hilary and Sarah Wakefield. "'Participation,' White Privilege and Environmental Justice: Understanding Environmentalism among Hispanics in Toronto." *Antipode* 45, no. 3 (2013): 641–62.

Gilroy, Paul. *The Black Atlantic: Modernity and Double Consciousness*. Cambridge: Harvard University Press, 1993.

Glass, Michael R. and Reuben Rose-Redwood, eds. *Performativity, Politics, and the Production of Social Space*. New York: Routledge, 2014.

Goldwater, Robert. *Primitivism in Modern Art*. Cambridge: 1938. Reprint, Belknap Press of Harvard University Press, 1986.

Goode, Luke. *Jürgen Habermas: Democracy and the Public Sphere*. London: Pluto Press, 2005.

Gramsci, Antonio. *The Gramsci Reader: Selected Writings, 1916–1935*. New York: New York University, 2000.

Gray, Herman. *Watching Race: Television and the Struggle for Blackness*. Minneapolis: University of Minnesota Press, 2004.

Greene, Christina. *Our Separate Ways: Women and the Black Freedom Movement in Durham, North Carolina*. Chapel Hill: University of North Carolina Press, 2005.

———. "'She Ain't No Rosa Parks': The Joan Little Rape-Murder Case and Jim Crow Justice in the Post-Civil Rights South." *The Journal of American History* 100 vol. 3 (Summer 2022): 428–47.

Greene, Helen Taylor and Shaun Gabbidon, eds. *The Encyclopedia of Race and Crime*. Thousand Oaks, CA: Sage Publications, 2009.

Greenway, John. *American Folksongs of Protest*. Philadelphia: University of Pennsylvania Press, 1953.

Guralnick, Peter. *Sweet Soul Music: Rhythm and Blues and the Southern Dream of Freedom*. New York: Back Bay Books, 1999.

Gwin, Minrose. *Remembering Medgar Evers: Writing the Long Civil Rights Movement*. Athens: University of Georgia Press, 2013.

Habermas, Jürgen. *The Structural Transformation of the Public Sphere: An Inquiry into a Category of Bourgeois Society*, tr. Thomas Burger with Frederick Lawrence. Cambridge: MIT Press, 1991.

Halbwachs, Maurice. *On Collective Memory*. 1925, reprint ed. and trans. Lewis Coser. Chicago: University of Chicago Press, 1992.

Hampton, Henry, and Steve Fayer with Sarah Flynn. *Voices of Freedom: An Oral History of the Civil Rights Movement from the 1950s through the 1980s*. New York: Bantam Books, 1990.

Harding, Vincent. "Beyond Amnesia: Martin Luther King and the Future of America." *The Journal of American History* 74, no. 2 (September 1987): 468–76.

Harrington, Richard. "Singing the Freedom Song." *Washington Post*. June 25, 1987. https://www.washingtonpost.com/archive/lifestyle/1987/06/25/singing-the-freedom-song/93cdb852–497f-48a9–9886–2221261474d7/?utm_term=.b2d5d7ddd674.

Hayes, Eileen M. *Songs in Black and Lavender: Race, Sexual Politics, and Women's Music*. Urbana: University of Illinois Press, 2010.

Herskovits, Melville. *The Myth of the Negro Past*. Boston: Beacon Press, 1958.

Hill, Lance. *The Deacons for Defense: Armed Resistance and the Civil Rights Movement*. Chapel Hill: University of North Carolina Press, 2004.

Hill, Sarah. "'This Is My Country': American Popular Music and Political Engagement in '1968,'" in Beate Kutschke and Barley Norton, eds. *Music and Protest in 1968*. Cambridge: Cambridge University Press, 2013.

Hirsch, Jerrold. "Modernity, Nostalgia, and Southern Folklore Studies: The Case of John Lomax." *The Journal of American Folklore* 105 (Spring 1992): 183–207.

Hochman, Brian. *Savage Preservation: The Ethnographic Origins of Modern Media Technology*. Minneapolis: University of Minnesota Press, 2014.

Holsaert, Faith S., et al., eds. *Hands on the Freedom Plow: Personal Accounts by Women in SNCC*. Urbana: University of Illinois Press, 2012.

Honey, Michael. *Black Workers Remember: An Oral History of Segregation, Unionism, and the Freedom Struggle*. Berkeley: University of California Press, 1999.

hooks, bell. *Feminist Theory: From Margin to Center*. New York: Abingdon, 2015.

———. "Moving Beyond Pain." May 9, 2016. http://www.bellhooksinstitute.com/blog/2016/5/9/moving-beyond-pain.

———. *Killing Rage. Ending Racism*. New York: Holt Publishing, 1995.

Irwin-Zarecka, Iwona. *Frames of Remembrance: The Dynamic of Collective Memory*. New Brunswick, NJ: Transaction Publishers, 1994.

Izadi, Elahe. "Medical Examiner Rules Eric Garner's Death a Homicide, Says Police Chokehold Killed Him." *Washington Post*. August 1, 2014. https://www.washingtonpost.com/news/post-nation/wp/2014/08/01/eric-garners-death-was-a-homicide-says-new-york-city-medical-examiner/?utm_term=.931590e97759.

Jackson, Travis. *Blowin' the Blues Away: Performance and Meaning on the New York Jazz Scene*. Berkeley: University of California Press, 2012.

Janken, Kenneth Robert. *The Wilmington Ten: Violence, Injustice, and the Rise of Black Politics in the 1970s*. Chapel Hill: University of North Carolina Press, 2016.

Jemielniak, Dariusz. *Common Knowledge? An Ethnography of Wikipedia*. Stanford: Stanford University Press, 2014.

Jones, Clarence B. and Stuart Connelly. *Behind the Dream: The Making of the Speech that Transformed a Nation*. New York: St. Martin's Griffin, 2012.

Joseph, Peniel E., ed. *The Black Power Movement: Rethinking the Civil Rights-Black Power Era*. New York: Routledge, 2006.

———. *Neighborhood Rebels: Black Power at the Local Level*. New York: Palgrave Macmillan, 2010.

Kanellopoulos, Panagiotis. "Musical Improvisation as Action: An Arendtian Perspective." *Action, Criticism, and Theory for Music Education* 6, no. 3 (2007): 97–127.

Keil, Charles. "Participatory Discrepancies and the Power of Music." *Cultural Anthropology* 2 (1987): 275–83.

———. *Urban Blues*. Chicago: University of Chicago Press, 1991.

Keil, Charles and Steven Feld. *Music Grooves: Essays and Dialogues*. Chicago: University of Chicago Press, 1994.

Kelley, Robin D. G. *Freedom Dreams: The Black Radical Imagination*. Boston: Beacon Press, 2002.

Keogh, Tom. "'Soundtrack for a Revolution': A Powerful Mix of Music, Civil Rights History." *Seattle Times*. April 29, 2010. https://www.seattletimes.com/entertainment/movies/soundtrack-for-a-revolution-a-powerful-mix-of-music-civil-rights-history/.

Kernodle, Tammy Lynn. "'I Wish I Knew How It Would Feel to Be Free': Nina Simone and the Redefining of the Freedom Song of the 1960s." *Journal of the Society for American Music* 2, no. 3 (2008): 295–317.

———. *Soul on Soul: The Life and Music of Mary Lou Williams*. Urbana: University of Illinois Press, 2020.

———. "Work the Works: The Role of African-American Women in the Development of Contemporary Gospel." *Black Music Research Journal* 26, no. 1 (Spring 2006): 89–109.

King, Jr., Martin Luther. *Stride Toward Freedom: The Montgomery Story*. 1958. Reprint, Boston: Beacon Press, 2010.

———. *In a Single Garment of Destiny: A Global Vision of Justice*. Ed. Lewis V. Baldwin. Boston: Beacon Press, 2012.

———. *Why We Can't Wait*. Boston: Beacon Press, 2010.

———. *Where Do We Go from Here: Chaos or Community?* 1968. Reprint, Boston: Beacon Press, 2010.

———. *All Labor Has Dignity*. Boston: Beacon Press, 2011.

Klein, Kerwin Lee. "On the Emergence of Memory in Historical Discourse." *Representations* 69 (Winter 2000): 127–50.

Lincoln, C. Eric and Lawrence H. Mamiya. *The Black Church in the African-American Experience*. Durham: Duke University Press, 1990.

Ling, Peter J. "Developing Freedom Songs: Guy Carawan and the African-American Traditions of the South Carolina Sea Islands." *History Workshop Journal* 44 (Autumn 1997): 198–213.

Ling, Peter J. and Sharon Monteith. *Gender in the Civil Rights Movement*. New York: Garland Publishing, 1999.

Lipsitz, Geroge. *Rainbow at Midnight: Labor and Culture in the 1940s*. Urban: University of Illinois Press, 1994.

———. *Time Passages: Collective Memory and American Popular Culture*. Minneapolis: University of Minnesota Press, 1990.

Lloyd, Moya. "Performativity, Parody, Politics." *Theory, Culture & Society* 16, no. 2 (1999): 195–213.

Locke, Alain, ed. *The New Negro: An Interpretation*. 1925. Reprint, New York: Johnson Reprint Corporation, 1968.

Loewen, James. *Lies My Teacher Told Me: Everything Your American History Book Got Wrong*. New York: The New Press, 2007.

Lomax, Alan. "Folk Singing Is Rediscovered on Island." *News and Courier* (Charleston, SC), January 19, 1964.

———. *The Land Where Blues Began*. New York: New Press, 2002.

Lopez, Antonio R. "'We Know What the Pigs Don't Like': The Formation and Solidarity of the Original Rainbow Coalition." *Journal of African American Studies* 23 (2019): 476–518.

Lott, Eric. *Love and Theft: Blackface Minstrelsy and the American Working Class*. New York: Oxford University Press, 2013.

Malone, Bill C. Review of "Sing for Freedom: The Story of the Civil Rights Movement Through Its Songs" by Guy Carawan and "Everybody Says Freedom" by Pete Seeger and Bob Reiser. *The Journal of Southern History* 59, no. 1 (February 1993): 175–76.

Manabe, Noriko. "Chants of the Resistance: Flow, Memory, and Inclusivity." *Music and Politics* 13, no. 1 (Winter 2019).

Marini, Stephen A. *Sacred Song in America: Religion, Music, and Public Culture*. Urbana: University of Illinois Press, 2003.

Mark, Andrew. "'Keepin' It Real': Musicking and Solidarity, the Hornby Island Vibe," in *Current Directions in Ecomusicology*, eds. Aaron Allen and Kevin Dawe. New York: Routledge, 2015.

Martin, Bradford D. *The Theater Is in the Street: Politics and Performance in Sixties America*. Amherst: University of Massachusetts Press, 2004.

Matheson, Laurie, ed. *Music in Black American Life, 1600–1945*. Urbana: University of Illinois Press, 2022.

———. *Music in Black American Life, 1945–2020*. Urbana: University of Illinois Press, 2022.

Mazzacco, Phillip. *The Psychology of Racial Colorblindness: A Critical Review*. New York: Palgrave Macmillan, 2017.

McAdam, Doug. *Freedom Summer*. New York, Oxford University Press, 1988.

———. *Political Process and the Development of Black Insurgency, 1930–1970*. Chicago: University of Chicago Press, 1982.

McAdam, Doug and David Snow, eds. *Social Movements: Readings on Their Emergence, Mobilization, and Dynamics*. Los Angeles: Roxbury Publishing, 1997.

McBride, Michael, et al. "Waiting for the Perfect Protest?" *New York Times*. September 1, 2017. https://www.nytimes.com/2017/09/01/opinion/civil-rights-protest-resistance.html.

McGurty, Eileen Maura. "From NIMBY to Civil Rights: The Origins of the Environmental Justice Movement." *Environmental History* 2, no. 3 (July 1997): 301.

———. *Transforming Environmentalism: Warren County, PCBs, and the Origins of Environmental Justice*. New Brunswick, NJ: Rutgers University Press, 2007.

McLean, Sheelah. "The Whiteness of Green: Racialization and Environmental Education." *The Canadian Geographer* 57, no. 3 (2013): 354–62.

Meier, August, Elliott Rudwick, and Francis L. Broderick, eds. *Black Protest Thought in the Twentieth Century*. Indianapolis: Bobbs-Merrill Educational Publishing, 1971.

Miller, Elizabeth Ellis. "Remembering Freedom Songs: Repurposing an Activist Genre." *College English* 81, no. 1 (September 2018): 50–72.

Miller, Karl Hagstrom. *Segregating Sound: Inventing Folk and Pop Music in the Age of Jim Crow*. Durham: Duke University Press, 2010.

Monson, Ingrid. *Freedom Sounds: Civil Rights Call Out to Jazz and Africa*. Oxford: Oxford University Press, 2007.

———. *The African Diaspora: A Musical Perspective*. New York: Garland Publishing, 2000.

———. *Saying Something: Jazz Improvisation and Interaction*. Chicago: University of Chicago Press, 1996.

Morris, Aldon. *The Origins of the Civil Rights Movement: Black Communities Organizing for Change*. New York: The Free Press, 1984.

Morrison, Toni. *Beloved*. New York: Columbia University Press, 1998.

Mullen, Patrick B. *The Man Who Adores the Negro: Race and American Folklore*. Urbana: University of Illinois Press, 2008.

Muller, Carol. "Spontaneity and Black Consciousness: South Africans Imagining Musical and Political Freedom in 1960s Europe," in Beate Kutschke and Barley Norton, eds. *Music and Protest in 1968*. Cambridge: Cambridge University Press, 2013.

Mulvey, Laura. "Visual Pleasure and Narrative Cinema," in *A Critical and Cultural Theory Reader*. Anthony Easthope and Kate McGowan, eds. Toronto: University of Toronto Press, 2004. 167–76.

Murphree, Vanessa. *The Selling of Civil Rights: The Student Nonviolent Coordinating Committee and the Use of Public Relations*. New York: Routledge, 2006.

Murray, Albert. *Stomping the Blues*. New York: McGraw-Hill, 1976.

Murray, Gail S., ed. *Throwing Off the Cloak of Privilege: White Southern Women Activists in the Civil Rights Era*. Gainesville: University Press of Florida, 2004.

Mutnick, Ally. "Congress Marks 50th Anniversary of Civil Rights Act." *USA Today*. June 24, 2014. http://www.usatoday.com/story/news/nation/2014/06/24/civil-rights-act-anniversary/11332243/.

Ndaliko, Chérie Rivers. *Necessary Noise: Music, Film, and Charitable Imperialism in the East of Congo*. New York: Oxford University Press, 2018.

Neal, Mark Anthony. *What the Music Said: Black Popular Music and Black Public Culture*. New York: Routledge, 1999.

Nixon, Rob. *Slow Violence and the Environmentalism of the Poor*. Cambridge: Harvard University Press, 2011.

Nora, Pierre. *Realms of Memory: Rethinking the French Past, Volume I: Conflicts and Divisions*. Translated by Arthur Goldhammer. Edited by Lawrence Kritzman. New York: Columbia University Press, 1996.

Obadike, Mendi. "Low Fidelity: Stereotyped Blackness in the Field of Sound." PhD diss., Duke University, 2005.

Oberschall, Anthony. *Social Movements: Ideologies, Interests, and Identities*. New Brunswick, NJ: Transaction Publishers, 1995.

Oforlea, Aaron, N. "[Un]veiling the White Gaze: Revealing Self and Other in the Land Where Blues Began." *The Western Journal of Black Studies* 36, no. 4 (2012): 289–300.

Olick, Jeffrey K. and Joyce Robbins, "Social Memory Studies: From 'Collective Memory' to the Historical Sociology of Mnemonic Practices." *Annual Review of Sociology* 24 (1998): 105–40.

Omojola, Bode. "Identity, Politics, and Nostalgia in Nigerian Music: A Study in Victor Olaiya's Highlife." *Ethnomusicology* 53, no. 2 (Spring/Summer 2009): 249–76.

Orejuaela, Fernando and Stephanie Shonekan, *Black Lives Matter and Music: Protest, Intervention, Reflection*. Bloomington: Indiana University Press, 2018.

Payne, Charles. *I've Got the Light of Freedom: The Organizing Tradition and the Mississippi Freedom Struggle*. Berkeley: University of California Press, 1995.

———. "Ella Baker and Models of Social Change." *Signs* 14 (1989): 885–99.

Peretti, Burton W. *Lift Every Voice: The History of African American Music*. Lanham, MD: Rowman and Littlefield Publishers, 2009.

Perry, Imani. *May We Forever Stand: A History of the Black National Anthem*. Chapel Hill: University of North Carolina Press, 2018.

Pratt, Ray. *Rhythm and Resistance: Explorations in the Political Uses of Popular Music*. New York: Praeger Publishers, 1990.

Rabaka, Reiland. *The Hip Hop Movement: From R&B and the Civil Rights Movement to Rap and the Hip Hop Generation*. Lanham, MD: Lexington Books, 2013.

Radano, Ronald. "On Ownership and Value." *Black Music Research Journal* 30, no. 2 (Fall 2010): 363–69.

Radano, Ronald Michael. *Lying Up a Nation: Race and Black Music*. Chicago: University of Chicago, 2003.

———. "Narrating Black Music's Past." *Radical History Review* 84, no. 1 (2002): 115–18.

Radano, Ronald and Philip Bohlman, eds. *Music and the Racial Imagination*. Chicago: University of Chicago Press, 2000.

Radano, Ronald and Tejumola Olaniyan, eds. *Audible Empire: Music, Global Politics, Critique*. Durham: Duke University Press, 2016.

Ramsey, Guthrie. *Race Music: Black Cultures from Bebop to Hip-Hop*. Berkeley: University of California Press, 2003.

Randall, Annie J., ed. *Music, Power, and Politics*. New York: Routledge, 2005.

Ransby, Barbara. *Ella Baker and the Black Freedom Movement: A Radical Democratic Vision*. Chapel Hill: University of North Carolina Press, 2003.

Rasaki, Titilayo. "From SNCC to BLM: Lessons in Radicalism, Structure, and Respectability Politics." *Harvard Journal of African American Public Policy* (2015–16): 31–38.

Reagle, Jr., Joseph Michael. *Good Faith Collaboration: The Culture of Wikipedia*. Cambridge: MIT Press, 2010.

Reagon, Bernice Johnson. "Let the Church Sing 'Freedom.'" *Black Music Journal* 7 (1987): 105–18.

———. "Songs of the Civil Rights Movement 1955–1965: A Study in Culture History." PhD diss., Howard University, 1975.

———. *If You Don't Go, Don't Hinder Me: The African American Sacred Song Tradition*. Lincoln: University of Nebraska Press, 2001.

———. "African Diaspora Women: The Making of Cultural Workers." *Feminist Studies* 12, no. 1 (Spring 1986): 77–90.

———. *We Who Believe in Freedom: Sweet Honey in the Rock . . . Still on the Journey*. New York: Anchor Books, 1993.

———. "Coalition Politics: Turning the Century," in *Home Girls: A Black Feminist Anthology*, ed. Barbara Smith. New Brunswick, NJ: Rutgers University Press, 2000.

———. "Music as an Agent of Social Change," in *Issues in African American Music: Power, Gender, Race Representation*, eds. Portia K. Maultsby and Mellonee V. Burnim. New York: Routledge, 2017.

Redmond, Shana L. *Anthem: Social Movements and the Sound of Solidarity in the African Diaspora*. New York: New York University Press, 2014.

———. *Everything Man: The Form and Function of Paul Robeson*. Durham: Duke University Press, 2020.

Reed, T. V. *The Art of Protest: Culture and Activism from the Civil Rights Movement to the Streets of Seattle*. Minneapolis: University of Minnesota Press, 2005.

Reger, Jo, Daniel J. Meyers, and Rachel L. Einwohner, eds. *Identity Work in Social Movements*. Minneapolis: University of Minnesota Press, 2008.

Rehding, Alexander. "Ecomusicology Between Apocalypse and Nostalgia." *Journal of the American Musicological Society* 64, no. 2 (Summer 2011): 409–14.

Rhodes, Edwardo Lao. *Environmental Justice in America*. Bloomington: Indiana University Press, 2003.

Rodman, Gilbert, ed. *The Race and Media Reader*. New York: Routledge, 2014.

Romano, Renee C. and Leigh Raiford, eds. *The Civil Rights Movement in American Memory*. Athens: University of Georgia Press, 2006.

Rose, Leslie Page. "The Freedom Singers of the Civil Rights Movement: Music Functioning for Freedom." *Update: Applications of Research in Music Education* (Spring–Summer 2007): 59–68.

Rose, Tricia. *Black Noise: Rap Music and Black Culture in Contemporary America*. Middletown, CT: Wesleyan University Press, 1994.

Rosenberg, Neil V., ed. *Transforming Tradition: Folk Music Revivals Examined*. Urbana: University of Illinois Press, 1993.

Rosenbloom, Joseph. *Redemption: Martin Luther King's Last 31 Hours*. Boston: Beacon Press, 2018.

Roy, William G. "How Social Movements Do Culture." *International Journal of Politics, Culture, and Society* 23, no. 2 (September 2010): 85–98.

Russakoff, Dale. "As in the 60s, Protestors Rally." *Washington Post*. October 11, 1982.

Rustin, Bayard. "From Politics to Protest: The Future of the Civil Rights Movement," in *Black Protest Thought in the Twentieth Century*, eds. August Meier, Elliott Rudwick, and Francis L. Broderick. Indianapolis: Bobbs-Merrill Educational Publishing, 1971.

———. *Time on Two Crosses: The Collected Writings of Bayard Rustin*, eds. Devon Carbado and Donald Weise. San Francisco: Cleis Press, 2003.

Sakakeeny, Matt. "Disciplinary Movements, the Civil Rights Movement, and Charles Keil's *Urban Blues*." *Current Musicology* 79 (2005): 143–68.

Sanger, Kerran L. *"When the Spirit Says Sing!": The Role of Freedom Songs in the Civil Rights Movement*. New York: Garland Publishing, 1995.

———. "The Rhetoric of the Freedom Songs in the American Civil Rights Movement." PhD diss., The Pennsylvania State University, 1991.

Saul, Scott. *Freedom Is, Freedom Ain't: Jazz and the Making of the Sixties*. Cambridge: President and Fellows of Harvard College, 2003.

Schafer, R. Murray. *The Soundscape: Our Sonic Environment and the Tuning of the World*. Rochester, VT: Destiny Books, 1977.

Schenbeck, Lawrence. *Racial Uplift and American Music: 1878–1943*. Jackson: University of Mississippi Press, 2012.

Seeger, Pete and Bob Reiser. *Everybody Says Freedom: A History of the Civil Rights Movement in Songs and Pictures*. New York: W. W. Norton and Company, 1989.

Silverstein, Shayna. "On Sirens and Lamp Posts: Sound, Space, and Affective Politics." *Music and Politics* 13, no. 1 (Winter 2019).

Sizer, Sandra. *Gospel Hymns and Social Religion: The Rhetoric of Nineteenth-Century Revivalism*. Philadelphia: Temple University Press, 1978.

Slobin, Mark, ed. *Global Soundtracks: Worlds of Film Music*. Middletown, CT: Wesleyan University Press, 2008.

Small, Christopher. *Musicking: The Meanings of Performing and Listening*. Middletown, CT: Wesleyan University Press, 1998.

Southern, Eileen. *The Music of Black Americans: A History*. New York: W. W. Norton and Company, 1997.

Spencer, Jon Michael. "Freedom Songs of the Civil Rights Movement." *The Journal of Black Sacred Music* 1, no. 1 (Spring 1987): 1–16.

———. *Protest and Praise: Sacred Music of Black Religion*. Minneapolis: Fortress Press, 1990.

———. *Black Hymnody: A Hymnological History of the African-American Church*. Knoxville: University of Tennessee Press, 1992.

———. *The New Negroes and Their Music: The Success of the Harlem Renaissance*. Knoxville: University of Tennessee Press, 1997.

———. "African American Religious Music from a Theomusicological Perspective," in Philip V. Bohlman, ed., *Music in American Religious Experience*. Oxford: Oxford University Press, 2005.

Stewart, Bruce, Linn Shapiro, and Anne Romaine. *Oh, What a Time: Southern Grassroots Music*. Nashville: Southern Folk Cultural Revival Project, 1982.

Stimeling, Travis. "Music, Place, and Identity in the Central Appalachian Mountaintop Removal Mining Debate." *American Music* 30, no. 1 (Spring 2012): 1–29.

Stoever, Jennifer Lynn. *The Sonic Color Line: Race and the Cultural Politics of Listening*. New York: New York University Press, 2016.

Sturken, Marita. *Tangled Memories: The Vietnam War, the AIDS Epidemic, and the Politics of Remembering*. Berkeley: University of California Press, 1997.

Szwed, John. *Crossovers: Essays on Race, Music, and American Culture*. Philadelphia: University of Pennsylvania Press, 2005.

Tarrow, Sydney. *Power in Movement: Social Movements, Collective Action and Politics*. Cambridge: Cambridge University Press, 1994.

Taruskin, Richard. *Oxford History of Western Music*. New York: Oxford University Press, 2013.

Tausig, Benjamin. "Sound and Movement: Vernaculars of Sonic Dissent." *Social Text 136* 36, no. 3 (September 2018): 25–45.

Taylor, Diana. *Performance*. Durham: Duke University Press, 2016.

Taylor, Dorceta. "Race, Class, Gender, and American Environmentalism." Gen. Tech. Rep. PNWGTR-534. Portland, OR: U.S. Department of Agriculture, Forest Service, Pacific Northwest Research Station, 2002.

Thelen, David, ed. *Memory and American History*. Bloomington: Indiana University Press, 1990.

Thompson, Marie. "Whiteness and the Ontological Turn in Sound Studies." *Parallax* 33, no. 3 (2017): 266–82.

Tindall, George Brown and David Emory Shi, *America: A Narrative History*. New York: W. W. Norton and Company, 2010.

Titon, Jeff Todd. "The Nature of Ecomusicology." *Música e Cultura* 8, no. 1 (2013): 8–18.

Trouillot, Michel-Rolph. *Silencing the Past: Power and the Production of History*. Boston: Beacon Press, 1995.

Ture, Kwame, formerly Stokely Carmichael, and Charles V. Hamilton. *Black Power: The Politics of Liberation*. 1967. Reprint, New York: Random House, 1992.

Turino, Thomas. *Music as Social Life: The Politics of Participation*. Chicago: University of Chicago Press, 2008.

———. "Signs of Imagination, Identity, and Experience: A Peircean Semiotic Theory for Music." *Ethnomusicology* 43, no. 2 (1999): 221–55.

———. "Peircean Thought as Core Theory for a Phenomenological Musicology." *Ethnomusicology* 58, no. 2 (Spring/Summer 2014): 185–221.

Turner, Edith. *Comunitas: The Anthropology of Collective Joy*. New York: Palgrave Macmillan, 2012.

Turner, Kristen Meyers. "Guy and Candie Carawan: Mediating the Music of the Civil Rights Movement." Master's thesis, University of North Carolina at Chapel Hill, 2011.

Twining, Mary Arnold. "Field Notes on Reactions to 'Ain't You Got a Right to the Tree of Life' by Guy and Candie Carawan." *Journal of the Folklore Institute* 10, no. 3 (December 1973): 213–16.

Tyson, Timothy. "Robert Williams, 'Black Power,' and the Roots of the African American Freedom Struggle." *Journal of American History* 85, no. 2 (September 1998): 540–70.

Walker, Alice. *In Search of Our Mother's Gardens: Womanist Prose*. San Diego: Harcourt Brace Jovanovich, 1983.

Walker, Wyatt Tee. *"Somebody's Calling My Name": Black Sacred Music and Social Change*. Valley Forge, PA: Judson Press, 1979.

Walzer, Michael. *Exodus and Revolution*. New York: Basic Books, 1985.

Ward, Brian. *Just My Soul Responding: Rhythm and Blues, Black Consciousness, and Race Relations*. Berkeley: University of California Press, 1998.

Ward, Brian, ed. *Media, Culture, and the Modern African American Freedom Struggle*. Gainesville: University Press of Florida, 2002.

Weissman, Dick. *Which Side Are You On? An Inside History of the Folk Music Revival in America*. New York: Continuum Publishing, 2005.

———. *Talkin' 'Bout a Revolution: Music and Social Change in America*. New York: Backbeat Books, 2010.

Werner, Craig. *A Change Is Gonna Come: Music, Race and the Soul of America*. Ann Arbor: University of Michigan Press, 2006.

West, Cornel. *Keeping Faith: Philosophy and Race in America*. New York: Routledge, 1993.

———. *Race Matters*. Boston: Beacon Press, 2001.

———. *Prophesy Deliverance!: An Afro-American Revolutionary Christianity*. Louisville: Westminster John Knox Press, 2002.

———. *The Cornel West Reader*. New York: Basic Civitas Books, 1999.

West, Cornel, ed. *The Radical King*. Boston: Beacon Press, 2015.

Westermeyer, Paul. *Let Justice Sing: Hymnody and Justice*. Collegeville, MN: The Liturgical Press, 1998.

Wiesel, Elie. *Messenger to All Humanity*. Notre Dame: University of Notre Dame Press, 1989.

Williams, Hettie V. *We Shall Overcome to We Shall Overrun: The Collapse of the Civil Rights Movement and the Black Power Revolt (1962–1968)*. Lanham, MD: University Press of America, 2008.

Williams, Jakobi. *From the Bullet to the Ballot: The Illinois Chapter of the Black Panther Party and Racial Coalition Politics in Chicago*. Chapel Hill: University of North Carolina Press, 2013.

Winick, Stephen. "The World's First 'Kumbaya' Moment: New Evidence about an Old Song," https://www.loc.gov/folklife/news/pdf/FCNews32_3-4_opt.pdf.

Woods, Randall Bennett. *Quest for Identity: America Since 1945*. Cambridge: Cambridge University Press, 2005.

X, Malcolm and Alex Haley. *The Autobiography of Malcolm X*. New York: Ballantine Books, 1999.

X, Malcolm. *Malcolm X Speaks*. ed. George Breitman. New York: Grove Press, 1965.

Yerushalmi, Yosef Hayim. *Zakhor: Jewish History and Jewish Memory*. Seattle: University of Washington Press, 1982.

Yuval-Davis, Nira. *Gender and Nation*. London: Sage Publications, 1997.

Zepp, Ira G. and Melvin D. Palmer, eds. *Drum Major for a Dream: Poetic Tributes for Martin Luther King, Jr.* Thompson, CT: Writer's Workshop, 1977.

Zinn, Howard. *SNCC: The New Abolitionists*. 1964. Reprint, Chicago: Haymarket Books, 2013.

Films and Sound Recordings

Been in the Storm So Long: A Collection of Spirituals, Folk Tales, and Children's Games from Johns Island, South Carolina. Recorded and edited by Guy Carawan. Folkways Records FS 3842, 1967, 33⅓ rpm.

Birmingham, Alabama, 1963 Mass Meeting. Recorded by Guy and Candie Carawan. Lest We Forget vol. 2. Folkways FD 5487, 1980, LP.

Eyes on the Prize: America's Civil Rights Years, 1954–1965. Created and produced by Henry Hampton and Blackside, Inc., and the Corporation for Public Broadcasting. Alexandria, VA: PBS Video, 1986–87.

Eyes on the Prize II: America at the Racial Crossroads, 1965–1985. Created and produced by Henry Hampton. Produced and directed by Judith Vecchione. Written by Steve Fayer. Alexandria, VA: PBS Video, 1989.

Freedom in the Air: A Documentary on Albany, Georgia, 1961–1962. Created and recorded by Guy Carawan. Produced by Guy Carawan and Alan Lomax. Student Nonviolent Coordinating Committee SNCC627, 1962, 33⅓ rpm.

King in the Wilderness. Directed by Peter Kunhardt. New York: HBO, 2018.

Movement Soul: Sounds of the Freedom Movement in the South, 1963–1964. Compiled by Moses Moon. Lest We Forget vol. 1. Folkways Records FD 5486, 1980, LP.

The Nashville Sit-in Story: Songs and Scenes of the Nashville Lunch Counter. Directed by Guy Carawan. Smithsonian Folkways Records 5658665, 1960, 33⅓ rpm.

Sea Island Folk Festival: Moving Star Hall Singers and Alan Lomax. Produced by Guy Carawan and Alan Lomax. Folkways Records, 1964, 33⅓ rpm.

Sing for Freedom: Workshop 1964 with the Freedom Singers, Birmingham Movement Choir, Georgia Sea Island Singers, Doc Reese, Phil Ochs, Len Chandler. Produced by Guy and Candie Carawan. Lest We Forget vol. 3. Folkways Records FD 5488, 1980, LP.

The Songs Are Free: Bernice Johnson Reagon and African-American Music. Hosted by Bill Moyers. Produced by Public Affairs Television. New York: Films Media Group, 1991.

Soundtrack for a Revolution. Written and directed by Bill Guttentag and Dan Sturman. Louverture Films, Freedom Song production, in association with Goldcrest Films International and Wild Bunch. Docurama Films: Distributed by New Video, 2010.

The Story of Greenwood, Mississippi. Produced by Guy Carawan. Folkways Records, 1965, 33⅓ rpm.

We Shall Overcome: Songs of the "Freedom Riders" and the "Sit-Ins." Folkways Records FH 5591, 1961, 33⅓ rpm.

Archival Collections

Anne Romaine Papers. Southern Historical Collection. Wilson Library. University of North Carolina at Chapel Hill.

Carawan Collection. Southern Historical Collection. Wilson Library. University of North Carolina at Chapel Hill.

Cleveland L. Sellers Jr. Papers. Avery Research Center. College of Charleston.

Henry Hampton Papers. Film and Media Archive. Washington University in St. Louis.

J. B. Matthews Papers. Rubenstein Library. Duke University.

North Carolina Fund Records. Wilson Library. University of North Carolina at Chapel Hill.

Southern Folk Cultural Revival Project Collection. Southern Historical Collection. Wilson Library. University of North Carolina at Chapel Hill.

Index

Stephen Stacks is an assistant professor of music at North Carolina Central University.

The University of Illinois Press
is a founding member of the
Association of University Presses.

Composed in 10.25/14 Chaparral Pro
with Univers LT Std display
by Lisa Connery
at the University of Illinois Press
Manufactured by Sheridan Books, Inc.

University of Illinois Press
1325 South Oak Street
Champaign, IL 61820-6903
www.press.uillinois.edu